Mount Olivet

The Rising

P. D. St. Claire

Cover art – Pat Leibowitz
Cover design – Peggy Carr

This book is a work of fiction. Any resemblance to actual events or persons, living or dead, is entirely coincidental.

"Mount Olivet – The Rising," by P.D. St. Claire. ISBN 978-1-62137-568-5 (Softcover) 978-1-62137-569-2 (eBook)

Library of Congress Control Number: 2014914146.

Published 2014 by Virtualbookworm.com Publishing Inc., P.O. Box 9949, College Station, TX 77842, US.

For all that's gone before, now,

and all's to come.

For each of us, now,

every one...

PROLOGUE

Bless me, Father, for I have sinned...
John Riley had confessed this sin before. And every time he had confessed it, it had come back. Every time. This time, though, it might be different. It was now a year and more since the war had ended. And this time, *this* time, the priest was Fr. Joseph Hara, his father's best friend.

They had grown up together, Joseph Hara and Paddy Riley. A chaplain in the European theater, Joseph Hara had ministered and comforted those who had done the killing and the dying there, those who had fought the *Great Crusade.* And it was in this that he had come to know about war and what it did to a person.

Paddy Riley had served as well, in the *Seabees* of the U. S. Navy, the name taken from the first two letters of *Construction Battalion* - CBs. Mostly volunteers too old for combat duty, the *Seabees* had followed the fighting across the Pacific, building harbors and roads and airfields on islands taken in the advance on Tokyo.

A veteran of the First War, Paddy Riley would not be denied his place in this one. Commissioned a Captain in the U. S. Navy Reserve, he had shipped out in 1943, bands playing and flags flying, only to return the year following, dead of a sniper's bullet on Tarawa atoll in the far Pacific.

Not yet eighteen the Saturday morning the telegram arrived, John Riley had enlisted in the U. S. Marine Corps. This thing, this killing of his father, this needed to get fixed, settled. So, where Joseph Hara had gone east to comfort and console the wounded and the fallen in Europe, John Riley had gone west, to the Pacific, to track down and to kill the man who had killed his father.

It has been two months since my last confession…

They were in Joseph Hara's rectory office at Blessed Sacrament parish in Chevy Chase, DC, a village of sorts in the Northwest quadrant of the city. The window shade drawn against an afternoon sun, they had settled into two oaken chairs set at an angle, each to the other, in front of Fr. Hara's desk. Joseph Hara's eyes were closed, his head bowed slightly against his left hand, shielding his eyes from John Riley. A thin stole of purple satin draped over his shoulders and down his front.

John Riley cleared his throat as he sat forward, his head down now as well, his arms resting on the arms of the chair, his hands joined before him, working slightly against each other, the words coming again, as before.

I killed a man, Father…

Memories of Iwo Jima rose in John Riley's mind, the maelstrom of the landing, head and neck scrunched down, working his legs through the surf, tracer bullets flashing by, one glancing off his helmet, another ripping through his shirt at the shoulder, burning, grazing his skin, he losing hold of his gun, then out of the water, legs weary, boots wet and dragging, sprinting up the beach, traction slipping in the sand, his right hand holding his helmet on, his left arm pumping, then half stumbling, half diving down into a shell hole, others of his unit there, cowering, one crying, the gunnery sergeant, Doyle from Chicago, now calling them up and forward, throwing him a Thompson submachine gun taken from a fallen comrade…

"You can all stay in this rat hole and die *for sure*," he shouted from a half stance above the roar of battle, "or you can follow me up to that ridge and have some chance of getting off this beach *alive!* Now on your feet! All of ya! And Hollister? You listening, Hollister? You pick up your weapon, Hollister, and stop crying or by Christ I'll shoot you my…"

Something tore through Doyle's left shoulder, ripping his arm and part of his side and most of his neck off, knocking what was left of him into the shell hole in a shower of blood and bits of his bones. Screaming as they squirmed away, those in the hole clustered, staring at Doyle's body as it jerked to a stillness, dead. John Riley remembered reaching for the Thompson and getting up in a crouch. 'Come on, you guys, come on. We gotta get outta here...'

"There was a lot of killing in the war, John." Fr. Joseph Hara spoke softly, evenly, his eyes closed. "A lot of killing. There was no other way..."

John Riley had heard this before, almost the exact words. 'War is hell,' another priest had said, his head nodding in the dark of the confessional box, seemingly dulled to a near sleep by the confessions of boys who had killed other boys on a beach or in a wood or on a sea or in the air...

The silence of the room surrounded John Riley as he tried to make this confession different, to explain the levels he had learned of killing, the purposes and the ways of it all, the roar of battle that falls to a silence in the heart and the mind, all gone, all life reduced to the reptile's lunge and snap, a tearing at the flesh, though not with scaled paws and bared teeth but the firing of a Thompson gun at 700 rounds per minute, bodies jerking and falling askew, then the sounds when done, the low cries and whimpers of the near dead and dying. That was the type of killing John Riley had done, and got a medal for it, too...

And as he told of these killings, he sensed that Joseph Hara understood them to be an opening, a way of getting to what John Riley had come to confess and with this hope he began.

"It was nearly done at Iwo. They said it'd be over in a couple of weeks, but they'd said that before, about

Peleliu, too…But Iwo was even worse, laced with caves, like some kind of bee hive. They'd pop up from anywhere and nowhere then disappear as quick, throwing grenades, bursts from their machine guns…" John Riley blinked his eyes, swallowed hard.

"It was the south end of the island, jagged cliffs and rocks and hot…Christ it was hot." He paused, licking his lips, swallowing hard, images in his mind of jungles rising to ridges and blinding white rocks against a crystal sky. His eyes fixed ahead.

"And they were *crazy*, Father, crazy…*lunatics*…" He looked at Joseph Hara for an instant, then quickly away. "When you'd get one in the open, no gun, defenseless? He'd run to some cliff…Jump rather than be taken prisoner." He fixed on Joseph Hara again, held his eyes. "They called it *bushido*, the code of the warrior…Death before dishonor, before surrender…"

Joseph Hara nodded. He knew.

John Riley closed his eyes, his head fixed ahead. "Four of us were on patrol, working our away along the south face of Suribachi. I was on point…so hot, rocks too hot to touch…" John Riley's hands came off the arms of his chair. "…Lost my footing, slipped down on my left hip, nearly going over a ledge, a shot whizzing by, just above me…" Another swallow taken, his eyes closing. "Caught Castellano square in the chest. *Pfft*… Right through him. Gone. Dead. Like that…" John Riley tried to snap his fingers but only motioned it, a voice now roaring from just behind him… "'Sniper!' Johnson shouted."

John Riley sat up a measure, startled by the shout of his own voice, then forward again, his breathing back. "We're all down now, me, Castellano, but he's dead, then Johnson and Miller, all pushing flat behind some rocks…Johnson getting his hand mirror out, scanning forward. 'Christ, there he is! I can see him. Maybe sixty, seventy yards out, a little up…' Another shot, ricocheting off the rocks where Johnson held the mirror. He jerked it back, moved lower, then put the mirror out again. 'Hey. What's this? He's out of his crouch. Looks like his gun's jammed...'

"Don't you believe it, Johnson!" Miller was laying flat against the rocks, his head down. "Could be a trap...a trap, sure thing...a trap..."

"Then Johnson said, 'No, don't think so. He's up, heading out. No gun...' I looked up." John Riley sat up straight in the chair, his eyes ahead, searching, focusing. "And there he was, working his way around some rocks, away from us, down low, crouching. Skinny, boney shoulders, khaki shorts, no shirt, no weapon... A sniper out of his hole, running for cover..."

John Riley shook his head, his eyes wide open. "Something in me snapped. 'Might be the son of a bitch...' I remember thinking, coming out of my crouch, Johnson calling me back down, 'Get down, Riley. Where you think you're going? You know better than...'

But I was up after him, the Jap...I could see him clear, crabbing his way along the lava rock, maybe seventy yards ahead. He slipped and fell down over a ledge, maybe five, six feet, got up limping, scratching over the rocks, blood at his left knee.

"The others were shouting me back, but them coming now, too. The Jap kept looking up, ahead. *He* knew where he was going." John Riley raised up a measure. "Sure, he knew...there was a cliff ahead, that's where he was headed. Didn't want him to jump, though, I didn't want him to kill Castallano and...and...maybe Dad and then get to choose how he died. He was *mine*, this Jap son of a bitch, he was mine, *he* was why I came, to kill this sniper son of a bitching Jap..."

John Riley shook off a bead of sweat that had formed on his right eyebrow.

"I could see him jumping from rock to ledge to rock, falling again and up, me closing on him as he limped, kept turning to see who's after him, then looking ahead to the cliff. I found a flat he'd missed, wide open, closed on him in a snap, just as he got to the cliff. He looked down, froze for a minute, then turned around, stared at me, up and down, then smiled…Son of a bitch's smiling at me! I'd left my Thompson where Castallano'd been hit.

"Jap went into a crouch, his arms low and out, looking to come at me, thinking I'm unarmed. He was wrong. Wore my .45 at my lower back, holstered out of the way. He couldn't see it, grinning at me…His mouth full of teeth, yellow and chipped…I pulled the .45 out now. He froze, stared at it, coming out of his crouch, backing to the cliff…"

John Riley was back in the rectory, sitting up, something coming to him as he turned to Fr. Hara. "All of a sudden, Father, I wanted him *alive*… I remember now. Yes. I wanted him to tell me if he was the Jap who killed Dad. It's crazy, I know, but maybe…And if he was, then he was…then he knew what Dad was doing when he was hit, if it was *this* Jap, then he was…was part of Dad in a way…don't you see..? Had the last living memory of him..?" John Riley turned away.

"I leveled my Colt at him, motioned him to put his hands behind his head, to sit down. He started into a crouch just as Johnson caught up, then Miller, too. This changed it all somehow. The Jap stood up, seven feet away, at attention. Saluted us, son of a bitch Jap, saluted us… then jumped. We ran to the edge as he fell…then shots, lots of shots and his body jerking as the bullets struck him before he careened off the base of the cliff, a blur of blood, his body breaking apart down into the sea…"

John Riley had never remembered it all so clearly before, every step, every shot, the body jerking as the bullets hit it, the blur of blood as it hit the rocks...

Joseph Hara shifted in his seat.

John Riley looked up at him, then away. "I went out there to kill the Jap who killed Dad. Ended up killing a lot of Japs. A lot of us killed a lot of Japs..." He turned quickly to Joseph Hara. "They'd come at us, you know, at a fortified position, and you'd just mow'em down, like tin ducks in a shooting gallery, like the movies, just like the movies..." He looked away.

"That's what they did, just like you see in the movies, came right at us. Nothing to us, though, like insects, just gnats and ants...nothing...robots doing what they were told to do and getting mowed down just like the people who sent them knew they would...But this Jap, this sniper...This was..." John Riley turned to Fr. Hara.

"If he *was* the Jap that killed Dad, if this was *that* Jap, then he wasn't just some gnat or bug. He was *that* Jap, don't you see? A distinct, separate person? A man who had done something I was going to kill him for doing...He had a name to me – *Dead Jap*, that was his name, that's what he was going to be – a dead Jap. And of all the Japs I killed out there, I don't even know how many, he's the only one, the *only* one, that won't go away..."

John Riley sat forward in his chair, his elbows on his knees, his hands joined, gripping to the white, his eyes closed and his body rocking forward, maybe for a full minute.

Joseph Hara cleared his throat.

John Riley didn't respond. He could hear Joseph Hara shift in his seat but stayed fixed forward, not responding, the pressure in his hands growing to painful as he tried to squeeze the sin away.

7

"John…" Fr. Hara shifted closer, not touching him. "John, can you hear me?"

John Riley nodded, sat up a measure, took a breath, sat up all the way, leaning back, a deeper breath taken, his arms resting on the oaken arms of the chair. He opened his eyes, looking ahead at first, then at Joseph Hara.

"Can I get you some water, John."

He shook his head 'no.'

"I'm sure you've already heard all the things we've been told to tell you about killing people in a just war, John. I'm not going to do any of that… What I am going to do is to give you the absolution of the sacrament of Penance." Fr. Hara made a sign of the cross as he spoke.

"'In the name of Jesus Christ, our risen Lord, I absolve you, John Riley.' This is from God the Father, John. You are absolved of this sin." Joseph Hara sat back, silent.

John Riley could feel his eyes on him and turned to him.

Joseph Hara leaned forward again, fixing on John Riley as he reached to take his forearm, gripping it firmly. "Now, John, I want to help you to absolve *yourself.* I want to help you come to a footing with this thing so you can live the good and Christian life you want to live and will live without this thing of war that holds you." He fixed on John Riley until John Riley looked to him. "Do you understand, John?"

John Riley nodded.

"I'm trying to picture you, John, on that cliff…you and Johnson and Miller, and the sniper, at what, seven feet away?"

John Riley nodded.

"Then he jumped, you said, and then you and Johnson and Miller went to the edge and shot at him as he fell?"

John Riley nodded, shivered as he sat forward again, his hands joined, his eyes closed.

"But you just said that you wanted him to surrender, that you pointed your gun at him and motioned him to sit down, to put his hands behind his head. Isn't that right?" John Riley nodded, his hands gripping more tightly.

"Look at me John. Open your eyes and look at me..." John Riley sat motionless, eyes closed, his head fixed ahead, stiff, unmoving.

"John, listen to me, now...look at me, John..." John Riley turned to Fr. Hara, opened his eyes.

"Now, John, I'm going to ask you a question and I want you to think carefully before you answer. Very carefully. Are you ready?"

John Riley nodded, his eyes fixed on the priest.

"What did you do with your gun, John, when it was all over?"

John Riley fixed more closely on Joseph Hara, not understating.

"What did you do with the gun?"

John Riley turned away, confused.

"It's a simple question, John - *What did you do with the gun, your gun?*"

John Riley turned back, his eyes unfocused, his head shaking slightly. "I don't...I don't know..."

"It must have been somewhere, John. Colt .45s just don't disappear, evaporate..."

John Riley looked away. "What difference does it make, for Chrissake, what happened to my gun, my weapon...it's what I did with it, that's why I'm here..." John Riley shook his head turning away, frustrated, angry...this was no help...

"Think back, John. You've told me everything, *every* detail. You left your Thompson with Johnson and Miller. You ran, you fell, you came to a flat the sniper hadn't seen and you closed on him. You have him trapped. He's at the edge, standing 'seven feet' away from you. Not ten feet, not four, but seven feet *exactly*...His teeth were chipped...You know all these things, John, all these details, why don't you know what happened to your gun?"

Joseph Hara moved closer, speaking firmly, his face close enough for John Riley to feel his breath as he spoke. "You're a Marine, goddamit! You're a highly trained, battle-tested, battle-hardened son of a bitching U. S Marine! You *kill* Japs for a living! Get medals for it, for Chrissakes! Where's your weapon, *Marine*? How you gonna kill any more Japs, *Marine*, if you don't have your goddam weapon, your *GUN*?"

John Riley sat bolt upright, staring at Fr. Hara, stammering. "But, but I, but I *don't* know…"

"DON'T KNOW? You don't *KNOW*? What do you mean '*Don't know*'? THINK, Marine! Where's your Colt? Where's your weapon?"

John Riley closed his eyes, his mind racing…the run, the cliff, the Jap's eyes, his face when he thought John Riley was unarmed, his fear when John Riley drew his .45, starting to sit until Johnson came up, then standing at attention, then jumping, the three of them stepping to the cliff, the Jap's arms flailing, trying to hold balance as he fell...

"You're on the cliff, Marine! Four hundred feet in the air, rocks and breakers below, the sniper, tumbling down and away from you...*for Chrissakes, Marine! Where's your GUN?!"*

John Riley lurched to his feet, staggering back, kicking his chair out from behind him, knocking it against a cabinet, leaning forward, crouching, looking down, over the cliff, breathing heavy, the Jap falling, arms flailing, bullets hitting him, then something passing him on the way down, John Riley's right arm and hand raising and coming down hard, "You Jap son of a *bitch*! You..." John Riley froze, his eyes fixed down, then rising to Fr. Hara.

"I-I *threw* it at him...*That's* what I did with my gun, I *threw* it at him..." John Riley rose full up, his eyes away, his mind racing. "I remember now, I do. I watched the gun pass him on the way down. I can still see it, hitting the rocks before he did...I *threw* my gun at him..."

"Then...?"

"...Then...then I *couldn't* have shot him..." John Riley became faint, his legs buckling as he fell forward, Fr. Hara rising to take his weight, holding him up as he leaned into him, sobbing. "I didn't shoot him, Father, I didn't kill him...That one I *didn't* kill..."

CHAPTER ONE
The Deal

September 1993

*I*t's your brother Michael. Come home.
Six words was all. His life changed? Another's maybe ending? Even gone by now?

John Riley folded the note again, putting it back in the breast pocket of his shirt as he looked out the window of the plane. They had been pulled out of a meeting on *The Deal*. That's what they had all come to calling it. It was close to the end, folks getting nervous with sets of six-inch-thick briefing books and everyone working really hard to keep straight all the parts and pieces of the thing, the numbers of it all by type asset and property.

For John Riley, there was an added factor: He didn't do real estate, not really.

An engineer by training and instinct, what John Riley *really* did was build things – office buildings mostly, whole parks of them and shopping malls and whatever else might need getting built. He had been President and CEO of Hennessey Construction since 1968, a company half-owned by him and his siblings - a married sister, Kay Rhinemann, and his brother, Michael. The remaining half of the company was owned by their mother, Mary Riley, all ninety-one years of her and looking to go for a hundred.

Hennessey Construction had been left to Paddy Riley, John's father, by Jack Hennessey in 1936. With it had come properties in Washington, DC that Jack Hennessey had been accumulating in the last quarter of his life, collecting really. 'Like baseball cards' one friend of his had put it. 'More by way of a hobby than anything else.' And he'd kept at it right to the end of his 88 years. Since then structured into an independent subsidiary, *The Hennessey Land Company*, the properties had been managed in a highly conservative manner, their value surging on the passing of each bust and boom in the real estate market.

By 1991, Hennessey Land Company's office properties, unimproved land, hotels and rental units, all located between Baltimore and Richmond, had a combined tax-assessed valuation of some $419 million. The market value was more than double that, even as they were just coming out of the 1989-91 bust. With Mary Riley at 91, John Riley, as chair of Hennessey Land Company, had decided that the lawyers could no longer be ignored.

As much as it seemed Mary Riley was going to live forever, clearly her expectation, she was going to go sometime. No one, not even Mary Riley, gets out alive. Settling the tax liability of her estate as Hennessey Land was now structured could force the sale of its assets into a market that looked to be moving sideways for another year or two, maybe more. Now, being an engineer, structuring things is what John Riley did best and for the last twelve months of his life, restructuring the assets of Hennessey Land Company was most of what he had been doing.

He had been helped in the decision to do this by Hennessey Land's President and CEO, Brigit Riley Winslow. At thirty-eight and his oldest child, it was Brigit Winslow who had sketched out their options. These ranged from selling off pieces one-by-one to arranging swaps of properties into real estate investment trusts whose shares could be sold on the market. Then there was breaking their holdings up into housing, office and retail subsidiaries and selling one of these off to cover the bulk of the anticipated tax liability of Hennessey Land's combined assets. What to do?

Get lucky, as it turned out, that's what to do. Get *lucky*. Near out of nowhere they had been approached by three suitors, Mid-America Holdings, Security National Life Insurance, and Great Basin Mutual Life, all three out of Chicago. Eyeing the Washington, DC real estate market, they each wanted the whole kit and caboodle, Hennessey Land Company, the lock, stock and barrel of it. 'Know your luck' was how Jack Hennessy always put it. 'Know your luck, and don't worry yourself about what the other fellow's getting out of it. Do your homework, take a fair price, and move on...'

But that was all on hold for now. Michael Francis Riley was in Georgetown University Hospital for open heart surgery, already under the knife. John Riley had spoken to Michael's wife, Margaret, from the car on the way to the airport in Chicago. He had gone in for a routine check-up that morning only to learn that three arteries in his heart were at imminent risk of closure, the radiologist wondering how he had even driven himself in that morning.

John Riley sat up a measure, stretching his legs beneath the seat before him looking about the cabin of the plane. Directly behind him sat Brigit Winslow and her assistant, Chelsea Reis. Across the aisle from them was Hardin Brooks, head Real Estate partner at Fox, Worthy, along with a junior partner from the firm. Beside him was Bryan Canny, a spread sheet displayed before him, his eyes tracking its columns and rows.

It was Bryan Canny who had been taken out of the room for Mary Riley's call and had given the note to John Riley. Born in Ireland, he had joined Hennessey Construction as an office assistant in September 1983. Rising to Special Assistant to the CEO, his particular gift was finding ways to be useful, most recently completing a graduate degree in Information Science just as Hennessey

Construction was undertaking an enterprise-wide upgrade of its IT system.

Catching John Riley's eye, Bryan Canny smiled a nod, rising and stepping into the aisle. "A coffee, now, John? A libation, perhaps?" Bryan Canny's six-foot-plus frame bent at the shoulders to accommodate the interior curve of the cabin.

"No, no thanks, Bryan. Nothing for now…"

Bryan Canny's eyes held John Riley for a moment. "How you doing, now, John? Good, are we?"

"Good enough…"

Bryan Canny stretched at the shoulders and arms, turning to his left and starting aft as a red light flashed in the forward bulkhead.

Looking up, John Riley reached for the seat belt and buckled himself in, leaning back as he looked again out the window at his left. He was on the port side of the plane, forward of the wing. His seat. They would be flying down the Potomac, to the southeast. This would put Georgetown Hospital to the left and almost directly below.

An afternoon sun brought out the full range of greens in the trees and foliage lining both sides of the C&O Canal that ran along the Potomac just below the hospital. John Riley had been to the hospital any number of times over the years, visiting the ill and dying as the generation preceding his own passed to their glory in the comfort and caring of the Jesuits. "They get you up to heaven and your reward, or to home and family for your comfort," he remembered his mother Mary once saying. "Guaranteed!"

Sitting up, looking down, he studied the building's wings and courtyards, trying to discern where the operating room might be from the main entrance, and where Michael Riley's life was being saved…or lost…

John Riley turned away from the window, his eyes closed, his mind on his brother. Michael Riley not being alive was unthinkable, ridiculous. *Unacceptable.* It made no sense at all. He was the healthiest human being John Riley had ever known. Energy just ran through the man, like electricity, like it might ignite his suits on a dry day. He just never stopped, Michael Riley didn't, always pushing something down the line. Hell, he'd played rugby well into his fifties and John Riley suspected he still snuck out for an old-boys game. And now he has a son, not yet a full year out...no sense at all, his dying. *Completely* unacceptable....

The Kennedy Center now caught John Riley's eye, huge and white, ringed with bronze coated columns, a behemoth of marble veneer at the Potomac's edge that for all its capacities and efficiencies had the critics howling at its grand opening.

Next, as the plane banked slightly to the right, staying along the river's line, was the Lincoln Memorial, seeming to fill the window of the plane. Looking beyond it, the full reach and expanse of the National Mall now displayed before him, stretching east in razor sharp lines of avenues and broad pebbled ways to the Capitol building, itself now bright and ever majestic as it caught the full light of the afternoon sun.

Anticipating the Tidal Basin and the Jefferson Memorial, John Riley sat up, finding Maine Avenue and the marinas and restaurants lining Washington Channel. This is where they had grown up, the Rileys, in the southwest quadrant of the Capital City.

Escaping thoughts and fears of his brother dying, John Riley took in the whole of the place, M Street now stretching out across South Capitol Street to the Anacostia River, the Southwest waterfront passing immediately below, the shadow of the plane racing across Water Street and its restaurants and bars and an easing coming to him now as he thought of his last time alone with Paddy Riley, just the two of them.

It was high summer of 1943, a late Saturday afternoon with Paddy off to war the following Tuesday. They lived near the corner of Fourth and N Streets, SW, two blocks from the Washington Channel and nearby the house where Jack Hennessey had lived for the last 40 years of his life. Jack had gifted the house to St. Dominick's Parish for an orphanage on his death and they had walked by it that afternoon in 1943 making their way along Water Street.

Not knowing what to say, John Riley had said nothing as they strode through the early revelry of a Saturday evening on Washington's waterfront. Fishing boats and crabbers' scows lined the docks and piers with watermen hawking their oysters and rockfish, some pounding their tables with cutting boards to get passersby's attention all amid the sound of honkytonk pianos and banjos wafting in the air as the music from one bar mixed and faded with that rising from the next.

At the west end of the waterfront was *The Salty Gael,* Paddy Riley's particular favorite. Mounting its front steps with the same purpose he brought to all things that he did, Paddy Riley led his son by the dining room and through an open double door to the outside bar on the far side of the building.

Stopping briefly to breathe in the shaded air under the canvas awning, a dark green, he took in the boats gliding by in the evening quiet before stepping to the bar. Here he turned to John Riley, nodding, his smile full and broad as he pulled out two bar stools, sitting himself down on the one and motioning his son to the other.

Taking his seat, John Riley looked farther to the west. The dome of the Jefferson Memorial rose above the willow trees marking the embankment at the closed end of the Channel and shading the benches and strolling paths that lined it. His arms resting forward on the edge of the bar, John Riley sat up abruptly when Paddy Riley signaled the barman and ordered two Harps, 'As cold as you have'em, please, Phillip, and chilled glasses as well.' Paddy Riley winked at his son and gave him a quick thumbs-up.

It being known that Paddy was soon off to war, the barman gave an extra hustle, a Harp and chilled glass in each hand held high as he worked down the bar. "Here ya go, now, Paddy, and Dennis said the first one's on the house..."

"Himself, then...?"

"Aye, *himself!* And who else?" A voice, thick and rough, roared out from behind them, John Riley ducking his head from the force of it. "And just *yours*, now, Paddy. Not the lad's, there!"

Paddy Riley turned, his head now up and back, his face breaking into a full smile as he fixed on a large man coming to his side.

"It's just a war, now, you know, Paddy. You'll be back soon enough." The man winked at John Riley as he nodded to the beers. "Sure, it's not like it's Christmas or any such..."

Paddy came off his stool, his hand out quickly, taking that offered by the man who stood almost to Paddy's six feet two. With a barman's apron tied high and tight across a full middle, the man's arms and hands were large even against Paddy's. Taking his hand, Paddy pulled him close before pushing him back, winking at John Riley.

"This here, son, is Dennis Aloysius Burke, owner and proprietor of this rat hole."

Dennis Burke shook John Riley's hand, squeezing hard with a wink of the eye, then back at Paddy Riley. "And where else, now, would I be finding the good company of the likes of yourself, then?" They laughed as Dennis Burke faked a jab at Paddy Riley before moving down the bar, smiling and nodding as he went.

Paddy Riley fixed on Dennis Burke, following him away, almost as if to avoid John Riley's eyes. Now looking quickly at John, Paddy Riley reached for his Harp, pouring his beer deliberately, maybe to show his son how it's done. His glass full, he raised it to John, the banter in his eyes now gone, his head down a measure. Finishing the pouring of his own beer, John Riley raised his glass, touching it with Paddy's, they each taking a pull.

"Well, son, here we are." Paddy Riley drew a deep breath as he fixed on John Riley, his eyes holding him. Breaking off, he gestured around the bar. "This is a good place, the Gael…as good as any," his eyes now back down on his son.

"When you're out for a night, you want to be where the people'll take care of you, you know, catch you when you fall, keep the riff raff from stepping on you and out of your pockets, too. That's important." He motioned down the bar. "Dennis, there, he's over from Killarney. Must be twenty years now. Put in his time and bought this place off a friend of Jack Hennessey's. A good man, Dennis."

John Riley nodded, sipping his beer, looking away as he savored its taste and effect.

Standing off from the bar, Paddy Riley gripped its edge, eyes fixed ahead for a moment before turning to John. "Look, son, you got to know that your mother's still pretty sore about me going off, volunteering and all. Hasn't left me alone about it all week." He shook his head, looked away then back. "But done's done." A breath taken and released, his eyes away again. "Didn't have a choice, really. Not to my thinking, anyway. Something I just had to do." He turned to John Riley, motioning about him. "Had to hold my place here."

John Riley nodded, looking about, uncertain what he meant.

"And not just here, son, at the Gael. No. I mean here, inside, too." Paddy Riley brought his fist to his chest.

"And yes, here, too," his arms out now and wide. "The country, America. Yeah, I learned that in the last one, in France." A pause, looking away. "Didn't really know what America was all about till I got away from it." Looking back at John Riley, a smile came to his face.

"We were all 'Yanks' to them, you see, *Over There* and all that. And let me tell you, *they* knew who we were, that's for sure. They'd pick us out before we even opened our mouths, even wearing civvies, no uniforms or nothing. Just us, just by the way we walked around...that's what they'd tell you, anyway.

"Yes, sir, going there, seeing other folks, Frenchies and all, meeting Yanks from all over – New York, Chicago, Dallas, wherever, all the same in some way...just this thing we all had...Never got a word for it, but the same. We all had it. Yeah, that's when I learned what being an American is all about, what we *are*." He paused, looking away for a moment, then back. "And for me, inside, any American able to serve, able to get an oar in, well, he's just *got* to do it."

John Riley, his eyes fixed on Paddy Riley, nodded, swallowing hard now.

"You're seventeen, son. You've another year at Gonzaga." Paddy Riley nodded for emphasis, to reassure. "You got to promise me, now, you're not going to do anything foolish before you finish your schooling, son. My going in is all this family has to put up until you finish high school, that's for sure." His eyes fixed harder now. "You understand, that now, son, don't you? Make sense to you?"

John Riley nodded.

"Then I have your hand on it?" Paddy Riley's hand went out.

John Riley's head went back, looking at his father's hand for moment, taking it now as he stood off the stool, feeling the full size and strength of it.

"Say it, now, son..."

"Say, it?"

"Yeah, you got to say it. I got to hear you say it…Say it…"

John Riley searched in his father's eyes, it all coming to him now what was going on, what was happening. All of a sudden it was Tuesday and they weren't just out for a beer. No. Paddy Riley was going to *war*. War wasn't something to come, war was here, *now*, at the outside bar of the *Salty Gael*. This was their time, *their good-bye.* John Riley felt his head nod as he formed the words, "Yes, I promise…"

"Promise what?"

"I promise that I'll stay on at Gonzaga, to graduate…"

Paddy Riley nodded, an unsure smile coming to his face. "Okay, then, that's done…done. And that's a promise I'll hold you to…"

Feeling his father's grip loosen, John Riley tightened his own, holding his father's hand fast, pulling them closer, looking up. "But you got to promise me something, too, Dad…"

Paddy Riley's head went up a measure, eyes back then looking down and deeply into his son's eyes. "Promise you...? Sure, son, sure…What's that?"

John Riley felt his father's grip waver, go soft a measure, unsure. Tightening his own grip even harder, he stepped closer. On his toes now, he spoke into Paddy Riley's right ear. "You got to promise me you're going to come home from that thing…"

Paddy Riley caught his breath, his eyes blank for a moment, gone inside himself, then looking away, his eyes now closing. "Yes, son…Yes, I do that. I promise. I promise I'll come back…get back." He turned to John Riley, his eyes clear, his head nodding to confirm. "I *will*…" Paddy gripped John Riley's hand back harder now, almost to hurting, almost it seemed to pull him close, to hug him, but he didn't.

Standing back instead, Paddy Riley's face went bright, his eyes as alive as John Riley had ever seen them, the blue of them sharp and brilliant, on him now. "Hell fire, boy, Japs ain't got a bullet hard enough to get through *this* thick Irish head." He rapped the side of his head with his right fist, laughing. "You'd think she'd know that by now, wouldn't you? Your mother? Wouldn't you? By now? Hell, what's she so worried about?"

They both laughed now, picking up their glasses, each taking a good pull of Harp, toasting each other, their thick pub glasses clanging and banging together with beer spilling on their hands and down their forearms in the thick August heat and then a full pull again each to empty. Paddy slammed his glass on the bar with a loud *thud*! "Phillip! Yes, you, there, Phillip Gallagher! A round all about, if you please! For all! And make it snappy!"

"Aye, Paddy, right you are! A round all about, it is…!"

The wheels of the *Gulfstream IV* came down hard on the runway, the plane bouncing several times more before settling on the tarmac.

John Riley was home now, and now to Michael…

CHAPTER TWO
The Waiting Room

J ohn Riley knew where the post-op waiting room was.
It had been two years ago, in the fall of 1991. Fr.
Joseph Hara, Paddy Riley's best friend and, later, Father
Confessor to the Riley clan, had had a second heart attack,
this one less than a week after the first. He never regained
consciousness, passing away in his sleep several days
later. 'Not this time,' John Riley spoke to himself as his
eyes found Mary Riley through the waiting room
windows, sitting alone, her eyes ahead and blank, a rosary
held idly in her right hand.

Pushing through the half-window door, reaching back
to hold it for Brigit, John Riley went directly to his
mother, sitting at her side, taking her left hand. "Mom,
we're here. Came as fast as we could." She didn't
respond.

He looked up and around. The room was empty
except for them, Brigit now pulling over a chair and
taking Mary Riley's other hand, squeezing and patting it,
fixing on her. "We're here, Nana. We're here…"

Mary Riley's eyes remained fixed ahead.

John Riley turned back to her, holding her hand
firmer, leaning closer, speaking directly into her left ear.
"What do we know, Mom? Where's Michael?" No
response. John Riley moved his hand in front of her eyes,
spoke louder. "Mom, can you hear me?" He snapped his
fingers.

Mary Riley's eyes blinked, her face now coming
alive, turning slightly to her son, recognizing him, now
leaning toward him.

"John, son…You're here, now, are you? So glad for
that…"

Brigit sat closer, raising Mary Riley's hand to her lips and kissing it. "Nana…"

Mary Riley turned to Brigit and cupped the back of her head in her hand as she looked to John Riley. "John…John, where's Michael, now? Where's my Michael…"

The door opened. John Riley rose, still holding his mother's hand, his other arm open. "Margaret…"

Margaret Riley came to his side and embraced him, kissing him quickly on the cheek before reaching for Brigit's hand and taking it.

Motioning to Brigit to remain seated with Mary, John took Margaret back by the door, his voice hushed. "What do we know, Margaret? Where is he? Is he still…"

Margaret Riley rose on her toes, looking past John Riley to check on Mary Riley before speaking in low voice. "He's in post-op, maybe right to the ICU, I'm not certain, can't remember exactly what they said…but he is out of the OR." She shook her head slightly, focusing on what to say before fixing on him. Looking quickly at Mary Riley again, she motioned back down the corridor. "It was worse than they thought going in, John. Had to do four, a quadruple…" She caught her breath, looked away.

John Riley took her by the elbow and walked her into the corridor, spied an alcove and led her to it. They sat down, he holding her hands. "When will they know…?"

"Don't know. Couple of days, maybe…I didn't ask, they didn't…"

"Is he conscious…can we see him? Have *you* seen him?"

She looked quickly away then back, shaking her head. "He's stable, they told me that…not sure when they'll let me see him. Maybe tonight, I think they said…"

Fr. Eugene Kennedy stepped into the alcove, sitting beside Margaret who turned to him. "Brigit said you were out here." He nodded to John Riley, turned back to Margaret. "I just spoke with the chaplain. He's going to get a place for you here. A spare day bed the interns use. It's just a couple of minutes from post-op and the ICU."

"Thank you, Gene. That's very thoughtful. Thank you very much."

Gene Kennedy looked at John Riley. "It's going to be a while, John. Some time, really, before any of you will be able to see him. Tomorrow morning, probably..." He looked down at Margaret, taking her hand to help her up. "Let's get you back to the waiting room, Margaret. See how Mary's doing..."

"Here you are..." Mary Riley stepped into the alcove, Brigit at her side. "Thought you'd gone missing." She was brighter now, almost smiling. "Ah, Fr. Kennedy. Yes, you were here before." Starting for the chair by Margaret, Mary Riley sat down. "So, Margaret, how's our Michael. They've done with him, then, have they?"

Margaret sat beside her. "For the moment, yes..."

"And..?"

Margaret took her hand, sat closer. "They had to do a quadruple bypass, Mary...a quadruple rather than the three they thought going in..."

Mary Riley sat up, a little back, fixing on her. "Triple, quadruple, sure 'tis all fadiddle to me. What does it all mean, now, what you're just telling me...?"

"It means he's got a fighting chance, Mom." John Riley sat on the other side of her. "We'll know more tomorrow." He sat up. "Been a long day, Mom. Let's get you home."

"And Michael?"

"Margaret will be here. Fr. Gene has arranged a place for her to stay."

Mary Riley looked up at Margaret and moved to stand, John helping her up. "Yes...Yes, he's your Michael, now, too, isn't he?" She smiled at Margaret then the others. "He's a tough one, that Michael of mine. Tough as they come. More trouble than he was worth some years of it." She reached for John's arm and started them all down the corridor. "But that was a time ago, now…aye, many years, indeed…" Mary Riley stopped, stood straight, looking about like a hen counting her chicks. "And Mary Kate, now?" She looked at John Riley. "Where's Mary Kate got to?"

"On a plane." Brigit took her other side and restarted them down the hall. "She was in California – Los Angeles. Her plane lands in an hour or so. I'll pick her up and get her right on out to East Irving."

"Aye, good girl, good girl, good as any. On top of it all, as usual. That's my Brigit…"

CHAPTER THREE
Matthew Malloy

J ohn Riley's earliest remembrance of Matthew Malloy
was after a day's fishing out of Deale, Maryland. It
was the Saturday before Jack Hennessey was to die and
Matt Malloy, Jack Hennessey's lawyer, Knight of Malta,
founding partner of Malloy, Henderson and Ryan, had
been put in charge of taking a picture of the fishing party.
Pointing here and nodding there, he had arranged
them all around John Riley who cradled across his chest a
38-pound rockfish he'd caught that afternoon. Of all the
pictures in John Riley's office, this had the place of
honor, framed well and hung on the wall behind his desk
for all to see.

Matt Malloy had run with the giants. Certainly, in the
field of labor law and the politics attending it, he had no
peer. Engaged by Jack Hennessey in 1936 to do the legal
work in transitioning Hennessey Construction from an
open-shop to a union-shop, he had built his practice in the
turmoil of the Great Depression as Roosevelt's New Deal
struggled on, looking to organized labor in turning the
economy around.

This had been Matt Malloy's start and he never
looked back, moving from private practice to government
and back, rising to Deputy Secretary of Labor under
Lyndon Johnson. And over the years, before and after the
Johnson Administration, he had served on the National
Labor Relations Board and on more task forces and
commissions than even he could remember.

Whatever the commission or task force, though, Matt
Malloy had made a practice of declining the
chairmanship. He didn't need the prestige of it and it kept

29

him safe from the press, a community to which he had developed a deep aversion.

While there was certainly the odd reporter who could be trusted, even one or two he called friend, his regard for reporters as a type had declined over the years. 'Hacks, most of them, their stock and trade the telling and talking about what *other* people did and do. The actual doing of a thing, starting something other than someone else's troubles? Well, that just never seems to occur to them.'

More purposefully, now, not being the chair of whatever the commission or task force allowed Matthew Malloy to do what he liked to do best – ask the questions others didn't see or lacked the care or courage to.

To Matthew Malloy, the questions were the most important part of the process. Since in his experience there had yet to be created a commission or task force whose purpose was other than to arrive at a conclusion already determined by the folks who had set it up in the first place, the only way to make the thing of any use at all was to climb aboard and make as much trouble as time and circumstance would allow.

Gifted by the Almighty with a photographic memory and the discipline to read all of what was provided to him, Matt Malloy made a practice of being the most informed, best prepared person at the table. And though a registered Democrat throughout his career, he never let that get in the way of the full and unfettered engagement of his own common sense. Now of this, common sense, Matthew Malloy had been given a full measure, one his mother had stropped to a razor's edge before turning him over to the Jesuits at Gonzaga College High School on North Capitol Street for further honing.

Before all else, though, Matt Malloy was a lawyer, and few were the decisions of importance to Hennessey Construction that John Riley made without his counsel. And of all the decisions for which he sought lawyer

Malloy's advice, none was more memorable to John Riley than Hennessey Construction Company's purchase of an open-shop construction company in Baltimore in 1975.

It was Hennessey Construction's opening shot at the national unions' control of the Greater Washington construction industry which, like the rest of the economy, was still shouldering through the aftershocks of OPEC's 1973 oil embargo. This had quadrupled the price of crude oil worldwide, putting millions out of work and making a fine mess of just about everything else in the non-Arab world.

They had lunched on a Tuesday noon in March, the second-floor dining room of the Metropolitan Club, one block north of the White House grounds and two west. Amid potted plants and linen table cloths, brilliantly white on an overcast day, Matt Malloy had said, 'It's time...' A breath taken, a nod offered. 'My union friends are fat and getting fatter and there's no one around with the stuff to stand up to them. They own the Democrats and now the *Republicans*, too, for Chrissake.' He had paused, fixing on John Riley with a sparkle in his eye.

'Now Nixon knew an opening when he saw one, linking up with Frankie Fitzgerald and the rest of *that* outfit. *Tricky Dick* and the Teamsters...There's a pair for you...Brothers to the bone.' Matthew Malloy had laughed out loud, turning more than a few heads in a dining room where a dropped fork could set off the burglar alarm.

'You just can't make stuff like that up. No, sir. Takes a true master to pull something like that off, that big, right in front of everyone, and on national TV to boot! And the Democratic National Committee? Stumbling around, bumping into each other, trying to find which barn door to close...yes, indeed...' Matt Malloy chuckled to himself, his eyes brightening again, fixing on John Riley, the devil in his eye now. 'And who could ever forget the '72 Convention...Miami?'

John Riley had smiled, nodding.

'Perfect, pitch perfect...' Matt Malloy had put down his napkin, head back for a minute, now forward and stifling a laugh. 'Should've been there, John. Maybe caught it on TV, went out coast-to-coast...Sammy Davis Jr., all 120 pounds and one eye of him, jumping up on stage with Richard Nixon himself at the Convention Center...Hugs and kisses all around. Good Christ in heaven..." His eyes looked away, then back at John Riley.

"John, the only question about any part of *that*, was who was first back to his hotel suite to shower off and incinerate whatever they were wearing, what the other *might* have *touched* – suit, shirt, tie, socks, shoes, cufflinks, all of it.' Another laugh, quieter now. 'No siree, Bob. Stuff like that cannot be made up. No, sir..."

Matt Malloy had then gone quiet, his eyes fixed on the table, somewhere else, maybe long ago, maybe just then but in a differing dimension. 'These are not good times...' He had turned to John Riley. 'We're not in a good place, John. Nixon gone in disgrace. Vietnam over and done...and badly so... New York City near broke. And *no* one knows where this economy's going, not anyone who's talking anyway." He had shaken his head.

"So many pieces, thousands of pieces to it all, millions, even...And no one really knows how they end, times like these..." He went quiet here, still for a moment, then sat up. "But they do, you know, they always have, anyway..." Another pause, looking away, then back, a smile.

"Mostly it's people who just get fed up with it all, tell the harpies from the press to go jump and stand up to the sonsobitches, whoever they are, whatever they're doing.' He had nodded at John Riley, fixing on him as never before, a quiet now between them. A challenge coming? 'It's time, John Riley, that's certain. The question is, Who's to do it? Who's to stand up?"

That had been 1975. And John Riley had bought the company in Baltimore with Hennessey Construction coming to prosper as never before.

"What's your end game, here, John? What do you want out of all this?"

They were in Mathew Malloy's apartment at The Westchester, a co-op complex in Northwest Washington, DC, just above Georgetown. Bryan Canny had dropped John Riley off there, taking Mary Riley and Brigit on up to East Irving Street.

The question had brought John Riley up, past the pleasantries and questions about Michael Riley's health with expressions of concern voiced and the promising of prayers to be said. "I'm not really sure any longer."

John Riley rose now, going to the window facing south, toward the hospital, a flashing memory of Michael Riley and their 'hunting trip' to Ireland in 1983, the voice mail from Hank Johnson of that morning. 'Important' was all it said, not a word the man used lightly. He turned back to Matt Malloy.

"When this all started, when Brigit had worked up the risk analysis of Mom passing with Hennessey Land structured as it is now, I just wanted to test the market for what we owned, get it in a stronger cash position than we were...that sort of thing." He sat down in an arm chair across from Matt Malloy, a glass of iced tea on the table in front of him. Sitting forward, his arms on his knees, his hands joined at the finger tips. "No idea how complex this would all be...none."

John Riley sat back, shook his head. "What's really catching up to me now, though, is what we've *got*. Just can't believe how much it's worth...never really focused on it..."

He looked up at Matt Malloy, fixing on him, nodding. "God's truth, Matt. All this land, the buildings, it was just something we owned through Hennessey

Construction, that's all. When Uncle Ed left…what? '84? We bought him out, promoted Bob Hathaway and brought Brigit down a year later. She was running circles around him before he even knew her extension." He shrugged, a hand wave off.

"Found a place for him with a group out in Tyson's Corner and gave Hennessey Land to her to run in '85. That was all she needed. Really shook the place up. Outsourced whatever made sense, got it down to a couple dozen staff. When the S&Ls went in the crapper? Well, we were flush with cash." He smiled, a hand waved.

"Then the Resolution Trust Corporation started calling up, every week it seemed. They'd come in with some of our paper wanting to cash out, a *dime* on the dollar, some of it. An easy 'Yes, thank you very much' on that." John Riley smiled at Matt Malloy, shrugging. "Hell, Matt, we hardly owe anything on any of it."

John Riley stood up, went to the window facing west, over the entry drive. Across was the restaurant in the complex, and behind it a small super market. Matt Malloy had told him once that, other than church for praying, an old man like himself could spend the rest of his life at The Westchester and never want for a thing truly needed.

He turned back, moving left to shade Matt Malloy's eyes from the sun behind him. "Roughly $900 million at market…" He watched as Matt Malloy's face reset, his hands falling into his lap. "That's right…Near a *billion* dollars, and in a real estate market that's on its back, exhausted…That's our 'in' in The Deal. Stupefying…"

Matt Malloy's head moved from side to side, seemingly incredulous. "Near a billion…? Yes, 'stupefying' is the word, impossible…"

"Well, you know what Jack Hennessey had when he died, what he left to Paddy? You did the will…"

"Yes, but I would have thought…"

"Mom wouldn't let us touch it till 1968. Incredible...the taxes nearly sank Hennessey Construction. That's when we brought Uncle Ed in and he got it all worked out, making sense."

Matt Malloy took a deep breath, exhaled, a slight shaking of the head as he settled in his chair, recrossing his legs. "Well, that's quite something, John. What does..."

"...Mom think?"

"Yes."

"Has no idea. How do you tell a 91-year old woman who's spent a life conflicted between her own success and a congenital distrust of wealth that she's worth near half a billion dollars? Could kill her!" They both laughed. "And we, her poor children, Mary Kate, Michael and me? Our share comes in at about $135 million...*each.*" John Riley went back to the chair and sat down.

"Jack Hennessey started Hennessey Construction in 1870, left it to Paddy in 1936. He ran it till '43, Mom until '68 and me since then. We're one of the most profitable construction outfits on the East Coast, have a two-plus year book of business in a recession and we *might* be worth $55-60 million, paper clips included. Maybe only seven percent of Hennessey *Land's* market value...Stupefying..."

"Yes, that remains the word." He fixed on John Riley, that smile again. "And your *problem*, John, is...?"

John Riley smiled back, shrugged, his hands out and open, now sitting back, his eyes on the ceiling above. He took a breath, held it, then spoke. "I've told you about Keith Pierson, from Chicago..."

"Yes...Out of Cleveland you said."

John Riley nodded, sat up, facing Matt Malloy.

"...And as you requested, John, I've asked my assistant to look into him..."

John Riley sat forward, fixed on Matt Malloy. "And?"

"He is the man I thought of when you first mentioned him." There was a shaking of the head. Matt Malloy had gone serious, an expression of fatherly concern on his face. "Keith Pierson, CEO of Mid-America Holdings and more companies than could be gotten on a sheet of legal paper. And that's just what he's got public, what we can trace. Mr. Keith Pierson of Chicago. I've met him, you know." Matt Malloy nodded at John Riley.

"Years ago. At the '76 convention. That's when Jimmy Carter smiled his way off some peanut farm in nowhere Georgia straight into America's politically exhausted heart." A breath taken and released. "Keith Pierson, a master by method and a giant by volume of the *double-down*."

"The double-down?"

"Yes. It's politics for 'sure thing'. This is a man, your Keith Pierson, who takes no chances, no prisoners. He sets an amount to play into the game and then cuts it in half – gives one half to the Ds and the other half to the Rs. 'Chicken feed' is how he once put it to an associate of mine. 'These guys,' he'd said, 'these politicians, they deal in billions every day, but they can be bought for peanuts, chicken feed. So why give one of them $100,000 and hope he's the one who gets elected when you can give each of them $50,000 and still have their staff falling all over themselves to take your call and do your bidding?'

Matt Malloy cleared his throat, sipped from the glass he lifted and returned to the table beside him.

"He keeps his name off the invitations, your Mr. Pierson. Stays under the radar, in the reeds. Picks his fights and pulls no punches, takes no prisoners. What he wants are his calls returned and his deeds done. Republican, Democrat, he couldn't care less."

John Riley was nodding, not that he knew each thing that Matthew Malloy had said but that none of it surprised him. "He's been the tough guy at the table, I'll tell you that. The hard-ass. He's the only other principal in The Deal. Just me and him. The rest are lawyers or executives from insurance and finance companies, trusts. Risk managers, really, most of them. He goads them and nods to me like he and I are some kind of special buddies or something, equals."

John Riley shook his head. "But it's a lie. He sees no man in the room as his equal. And if there was one there, a person he considered an equal? He'd leave it."

Matt Malloy nodded. "That's him, that's the type."

"Hosted us once at his place in Palm Beach." John Riley sat back. "Made a big point of telling everyone it was where Pamela Harriman started the Democratic Leadership Council in 1984…"

Matt Malloy sat up a measure, shaking his head, now nodding.

"That's so typical of the type, John, what you're telling me, that sort of thing. They buy the trappings of greatness and moment and then attach themselves to it …Want to *own* it. He's probably only a few years away from saying he was there when it happened!" Matt Malloy laughed, shaking his head as he cleared his throat, smiling a wink at John Riley.

"And by the way, John, the year was 1985, *after* the Mondale debacle in '84. That's why they set it up in the first place, the DLC." He nodded for emphasis. "Another thing, Pamela didn't *start* it. No, sir. Not at all. She just paid for the champagne and caviar, seated the tables and got that lovely face of hers in all the pictures." The smile again. "I know, you see…I *was* there, in the room."

CHAPTER FOUR
Karol Przystawski

'Brigits' and 'Norahs' is what they called them, 'they' being the Protestant folk of position and place, them who got there first and built the place out. And they came by the thousands upon thousands, the Brigits and the Norahs did, after the Great Hunger and well into the third part of the century, that being the nineteenth.

Unlike the others coming over at the time, though, they come alone, they did, without escort, without a man. And they didn't come so much to get one, now, neither, a man, though who's to turn a good one down? No, they came to get off a farm or out of the rain, for a house or place to live, somewhere safe from the wiles of fate, happy to be in the service of a good lady and her gentleman.

There were agencies for such things, either bringing them over or breaking them in once here. Seen by their betters as of a different race entirely, these Brigits and Norahs needed training and bringing along into a world that was prospering as no other in the memory of man. Great cities were abuilding and grand houses in them, too, all needing the service of others to tend to those in charge or where was the gain?

True, a girleen could lose her faith in such a place, even fall afoul of a dishonorable employer. True, all too true. But t'was far better in the eye of many a girl than anything on offer in Ireland where the land was titled in foreign hands and prospects of marriage to any better than a thatch roof over a dirt floor were grim indeed.

By the turn of the century, now, the path was beaten pretty well flat, with them coming after that time but a trickle against them that had come before. And it was amongst these latter that Dierdre Hannihan, at 23 years, had made her way, this being in 1926. Sure, now, the times were better in Ireland then, and everywhere else, too, but none so grand as in America where more money at the top – and great buckets of it, there was, too – meant more jobs at the bottom.

Cleveland was where, an aunt having a situation for her in Cleveland Heights. T'was the property of a captain of industry, Ward Overton, steel being his trade, tons and tons of it, too, the *Cuyahoga Iron and Steel Works* being its name. With $100 of 'pocket money' (whatever that might mean, she's thinking at the time, not knowing how many 'pockets' a person might have a need to buy in a lifetime), Dierdre Hannihan boarded in Cork like so many before, her passage full paid – by ship to New York, and by rail for the rest.

It was a September crossing for her, pleasant to start but an agony by its finishing. They'd come in behind a great storm, a 'hurricane' by some's calling, it leaving in their path towering seas racing across the horizon with green water breaking over the bows of the ship, itself pitching and rolling with every soul aboard sick beyond memory and any expectation.

'Tis the season' t'was said to her aboard ship. 'Aye,' says she, 'so why not be waiting, now? What's a month or two on firm ground to pay against such a misery at sea?' Sure, t'was as deep a fear of it all ending as she'd ever faced, and on both sides of it, now, too, her wanting to die from the roll of the ship and a hellish fear of it actually happening!

The train, now, was a world away from it all, a day and a night on the rails, rolling through farmland with rows of corn growing as far as the eye could see and at the end to be met by her Aunt Mary Alice and a driver named *Duesenberg*, sure a strange name she's thinking for a slip of lad from County Mayo.

Now there's no denying home had its pull on her, her missing the smells of the place, even the clouds and drizzle of a March afternoon, and sure her ma's cooking, too. But there was more than enough to distract a girl, now, in her new land. First there were her duties, which were many, then there being her own room, *her own room!* And food! Aye, now, food and in such quantities and variation as to spin her head and trouble her insides till used to.

And snow, great mountains of it there were, all for the groundskeeper and his lads to be tending, leaving to her the pleasure of watching it fall, making the place a wonderland till gone in the spring. And such a spring! Bright and green with flowers all about and in such colors and shapes, too, one after the other till high summer, leaving her to wonder in what particular way such a place was connected to Ireland even if ever at all!

And the people about…of every shape and calling, they were, starting at the top with Black Protestants, all being white, now, whiter than even the snow, no red in them at all, don't you know, not a hint or a tint of it. Then there was the rest, the Irish, for one, enough of them to cluster by home county. And others, too, latest being the Polacks which she took to mean the Polish, but hardly saw a one, these keeping to themselves and their own ways.

The churches, too, with the Protestants in theirs and happy for the Irish to have their own to keep, with schools for those to follow and with it a constant wondering how it all went so well and here with Dierdre Hannihan sitting dead center of it, sure and true!

And then came a night, *that night*. It was on her way back from a *ceilis* – Irish for an afternoon of dancing and merry making, generally done at a parish hall, this being her own, St Ann's. A fella taking a fancy to her, Billy Thompson being the name, had asked her to dinner after,

41

with her saying 'No, thank you, kind sir.' It was past eight and near dark, with him and his swagger not to her liking, anyway.

Not taking well to her refusal, now, young Billy Thompson and his mate trailed her a bit, at a distance at first, closing on her in Cumberland Park, then taking her there into some bushes to hand. She'd got a good slap on one of them and a scream that brought their hands to her mouth, she biting a thumb and its owner roaring in pain louder even than her scream, oaths taken and fists made ready and there now coming a rustling of the bushes and a full throated roar "WHAT'S IS THIS IS?"

"Foook off, ya dumb Pollack! Mind where you are…"

That was all the Billy Thompson got out, him on the ground, now, made quiet by a crushing blow to the jaw. His mate did little better, his head in a one-arm headlock of a great hulk of a fella, now punching on him with the full force of his free arm and yelling "Policja! Policja! Policja!"

And quick they were, too! Before she knows anything, Dierdre Hannihan is sitting on a hardwood bench in the Cleveland Heights police station with her attackers led away, down a corridor shouting oaths of their innocence and great threats of 'Uncle Mike Thompson' coming down in person to straighten them all out.

And as their voices faded, her attention turned to her rescuer. A large man with blond hair and handsome, too, he held his hat in both hands before him, working it hard as he struggled with his English to explain what had done.

She was rising to help the man when who should come strutting in but Mr. Overton himself, Aunt Mary Alice in behind him, his presence and manner quieting all in the room. It's to the desk sergeant he goes, asking to know what had happened to one of his 'girls' and the sergeant up to near standing before sitting and giving an account, nodding at the blond man and pointing down the corridor where Billy Thompson and his mate had been taken. Satisfied on knowing what's done, Mr. Overton turned to the blond-headed man and thanked him, shaking his hand before coming over to Dierdre.

"Are you alright, Dierdre? Were you harmed in any way?"

"No, sir." Her eyes were away at first, embarrassed by his attention. Looking up now, she smiled at him, a slight bow of the head and part of a curtsy, nodding toward the blond man. "He saved me, sir. Yes, him, it was. T'was him, there with his hat in his hands..." She smiled now at the blond-headed man, going to him to shake his hand, a slight curtsy again.

The blond man took her hand awkwardly, trying to say in English what he was thinking in Polish and not getting any of it out at all, at all.

Taking her arm at the elbow, Mr. Overton walked her to the desk sergeant. He was of Connecticut blood, Mr. Overton was, third generation, says Aunt Mary Alice. 'Used to own the whole lot of it, his people did,' says she, 'it being then part of Connecticut and them being from Hartford and coming out to settle it. *The Western Reserve* is what he and his missus talk about, and the times and trouble it took to make it all right and a place folks would be wanting to come to.'

Standing erect, Mr. Overton spoke clearly and with authority. "Thank you for your help on this, sergeant." He turned to Dierdre, motioning to her to thank him as well, which she did. Clearing his throat to regain the sergeant's attention, Mr. Overton raised his head, fixing down on the sergeant. "I will have Miss Hannihan down in the morning to sign a complaint against these men..." Mr. Overton fixed harder on the sergeant whose eyes had been avoiding his own.

"Is there something wrong, sergeant? This is the procedure, is it not? To file a complaint and have the brigands brought to justice?"

"The 'brigands,' now, is it? Aye, the brigands, indeed..." The desk sergeant looked at the only other person in the room, a patrolman standing to his left, him with a smirk on his face and rocking on his heels, his hands joined at the small of his back. Nodding slightly, the sergeant motioned the man to a far door with the end of his pen.

Tracking him out, the sergeant turned to Mr. Overton. "Yes, sir, it is, sir...the procedure, that is..." The sergeant looked side to side before leaning forward, his chest now against the desk with his arms gathered on it before him and him speaking in a raspy whisper. "But, you see, sir, one of these lads is the *nephew*, godson, perhaps, of Michael Thompson. You know, sir? *Big* Mike Thompson, sir?"

"Indeed? *Big* Mike Thompson, is it? Well, sergeant, I am very happy to hear that, for both Mr. Thompson and his nephew. But, frankly, I don't care if he's the nephew of President Coolidge himself. I will be here at eight o'clock tomorrow morning with Miss Hannihan to see justice is done."

"Yes, sir. As you say, sir..."

And that's how he came to be, Keith Pierson, that is, the very first inkling of him, this being. Born in 1929, he was the son and only child of Karol Przystawski and Dierdre Hannihan. A union organizer, Karol Przystawski was to die in a steel mill accident in 1932, falling off a gantry he could walk in his sleep. A killing it was, sure to every man in the mill, every man in the union. It was the depth of Great Depression with union organizers dying for their trouble every week it seemed, sometimes two and three at a time.

For Dierdre Hannihan, poor girl, the new life she had found in America would come to an end that night, and that quick, too. It all started, the ending of it, you see, when she signed the complaint against Billy Thompson and his mate, pointing them out the next morning in the police station. 'Them two on the left, is who.'

Mr. Overton would have his street safe from the riff raff of Newburg, telling Dierdre Hannihan sure that her situation would be lost if she refused to testify. But from her own, now, those from St. Ann's and about, there come another pull. 'Informer' is what they whispered, speaking against her own, is what... 'Aye, sure, nothing would have come of it, Dierdre darling, don't you know?', they'd be telling her. 'Just Billy Thompson and his mate having a bit of fun, is all.'

Well their 'little fun' got them each two years in Workhouse, a prison of sorts, all from a judge known well to Mr. Overton with Big Mike Thompson not taking kindly to any or all of it. Alderman to the poor and shield to the helpless, them that voted, that is, the Irish among them in particular, he was a brute to those he called enemy and sure to the owner of any steel mill about.

For his part, Mr. Overton was soon to discover that Big Mike Thompson was indeed big, and his Cuyahoga Steel and Iron Company soon finding itself in trouble with the city in ways and places that Mr. Overton had not until that time thought even possible.

And for Dierdre Hannihan, poor girl, sure, there was to come a shunning. An 'informer' in the service of a captain of industry is what she was, now unwelcome at *ceilis* and other places and times in the world she had come to know. With no one from her own for comfort and company, she welcomed the attention of Karol

Przystawski, there soon coming a caring between them and them marrying the summer following, in his church, St. Stanislaus, and to settle nearby. Aye, a new parish, it is, now, but more a new country is what, and it's all over again for poor Dierdre Hannihan, from Ireland to Cleveland and now to Warsaw. Ach! What's a poor girl to do?

Now being the widow of Karol Przystawski did have its comforts, she finding work when she needed it, at the union hall or wherever. And young Karol? Well he had as many 'uncles' as the union had members, growing to his father's size, six foot and thick from neck to toe, a gridiron player sure.

For all his size, though, he had to make do with a girl's first name in front of near a dozen consonants in a city still trying to digest its Irish. High school was bad enough, but after two years in the army taking guff from drill sergeants and flunkies, he'd had enough and changed his name to Keith Pierson at the same time he started night school for accounting.

There was grief to be had for it, from the Polish at the mill and neighbors from St. Stanislaus, too. The most hurt by it, though, was his mother. Stung to the core, she was, the name of the man she had come to love now rejected, refused. 'Who's to be your own, now then, son? Who's to be your own?'

Keith Pierson had brushed her away with a wave of the arm. 'It's 1951, Ma, and the Irish are shut in their hole and the Polish in theirs and I'm wanting none of it. Never did, never will. They can all go to hell with their parades and saints and May processions and whatever. It's every man for himself out there, Ma, that's how it is, and that's how I'm playing it…'

He'd got his degree and sat for his CPA, doing night work to build a practice while still at the mill. His clients were neighbors and small businesses and then lawyers as well, doing their practice accounts and later with their trade, wills and such.

It was the latter that he favored, auditing what's owned and what's owed, widows gone and their children unaccounted for and real estate to be settled, some as far away as 'The City,' this being Chicago. It had been this work, checking on plats and plots, that brought him to a truer knowing of the variances of 'book value,' 'tax value,' 'at market,' and then the worth of a place if mixed with pieces about it.

A world soon opened to Keith Pierson, one he had never before imagined. It was the world beyond hourly rates for his time and the piecework he had done. It was The Big Money, the world of participation and partnerships and knowing who wanted what and how to get it to them, of holding a thing till Chicago Transit got out to it and then putting in with others to do a shopping center and then the office buildings about it.

Before the decade had done, Karol Przystawski had become Keith Pierson of Mid-America Holdings, gone to Chicago, the sulfur and charcoal burns on his arms from the mills all hidden, now, under the silk sleeves of a dress shirt from Marshall Field or wherever else *Esquire* might say was better.

"His little brother runs a fever and his mama calls him home. Christ, what am I dealing with here?" Keith Pierson looked out over Grant Park from his corporate office on the twenty-first floor of the Blackstone Hotel on Michigan Avenue. "Another few hours, six on the outside, would have done it. Closed and done, with me on the ground and set in Washington." He looked across the Park to Lake Michigan and beyond, the sky a crystal blue in the midday sun. "We're getting close, though, that's for sure…"

"Perhaps." Richard Townsend rose from the conference table behind Keith Pierson, arranging the briefing books before him to be put away by Pierson's staff. Snapping his briefcase shut and reaching for his suit jacket before putting it on, he fixed across the table on Keith Pierson, in silhouette against the windows on the Lake. "He's up to something, Keith. I can feel it. Maybe gone a little off on this whole thing."

"What are you talking about?" Keith Pierson wheeled about, fixing back on Richard Townsend, a half step taken towards him, motioning him back down to his seat as he sat down across from him.

"What do you mean 'off this whole thing'?" Keith Pierson looked away then back, gripping the edge of the table, pulling himself closer. "I've got a lot at stake in this. A lot of money…and a lot more than that. So, Richard, at four hundred dollars an hour, tell me, please, what exactly are you telling me?"

Richard Townsend hesitated for a moment, then sat forward. "Vibes, that's all. Been getting bad vibes from him for the last couple of weeks. Don't know what it is really, just something there." He fixed on Keith Pierson. "You haven't noticed anything?"

"No, I haven't." Keith Pierson's head went back half a measure, his arms out. "And that's one of the things I do best." He sat forward, against the table. "What *vibes* are these? What do you *see*?"

"Well that's just it, Keith, now, isn't it? I can't *see* anything. Just feel it, that's all. That's what a *vibe* is, something you *feel*…" Richard Townsend sat back, fingering the edge of his briefcase, his eyes on Keith Pierson. "Yesterday, though, we picked up something…A major DC land company is looking for a lawyer here in town, a boutique firm with investment bank clients working real estate. All very hush-hush." He paused, smiled. "What's really special, though, is that it *has* to be a firm with no – as in *absolute zero* – connections with *Fox Worthy*, Hardin Brooks' firm. No former partners, no associates, no nothing…"

Keith Pierson sat back, looking away, then back at Richard Townsend. Rising, he returned to the window, looking out across the Lake. Cleveland was out there, 300 plus miles due east. Cleveland. "The *Mistake by the Lake*…" He turned back, motioning with his chin. "They found anyone yet?"

"Don't know."

"You're running it down?"

"Of course. Priority one…"

"I can have Stuka look into it, nose around…"

"No, thanks." Richard Townsend rose, standing at the edge of the conference table. "We should know something by tomorrow afternoon. I'll let you know…even if it's nothing." Richard Townsend opened his hands on the edge of table, cocking his head slightly as if to say 'Is that all?' As if to say 'Am I excused?'

Keith Pierson nodded, turning back to the window over the Lake as Richard Townsend reached for his briefcase and let himself out.

CHAPTER FIVE
then

M ary Catherine Riley Rhinemann, the only daughter of Mary Riley, had left Washington for New York City in the summer of 1954. Finding her way in advertising, by 1960 she had broken out with her own firm, *The Kay Riley Group*. Now 'Kay' to the fashion trade in New York, she remained 'Mary Kate' to family and friends in Washington.

She had read once that a person's deepest memories were of an olfactory order, the smell of a place or a thing. And as she stood at the arrival curb of National Airport amid the fumes of jet planes roaring above and about her, there was in the early evening air the scent of summer's close, if only a hint of it.

Yes, she was back in the air of her first breathing, hard by the Potomac and of a sudden needing to be in a car riding on the George Washington Parkway, by the river, looking across it to the Southwest waterfront, to where she had been born and raised...

"Kay!"

Turning, Mary Kate saw Brigit Winslow stepping out of the station wagon, coming around front to embrace her. She held Brigit for a moment, grateful for the feel of arms about her, then pulled back. They were birds of feather, Mary Kate and Brigit, each in her own time, each breaking out of the nest, each building a life apart from the place that had birthed her. "Thanks, thanks for coming out..."

"Don't even think about it. Great to see you. You deserve better than some hired car after six hours against the clock." Brigit smiled, turning to the rear door of the station wagon and lifting the window. Mary Kate lowered the gate and hefted her bag inside, fixing on Brigit. "What do we have? What do we know?"

Brigit avoided her eyes, closing the rear window of the station wagon and starting for the driver's door, speaking over her shoulder. "A little worse than they were thinking..." She stopped at the driver's door, turning to Mary Kate, speaking across the top of the car. "He needed four by passes, not the three they were expecting..."

Mary Kate bit her lip, nodding as she pulled the passenger door open, getting in the front seat, pausing before she clicked herself in with the seat beat.

Brigit got in on her side, quickly drawing the seat belt across her chest and lap. Slipping the car into gear, she checked for traffic, pulling into the airport exit lane. "So how was the flight?"

"Long, lonely..." Mary Kate drew a deep breath, holding it for a moment as she watched Brigit clear the arrival area, accelerating now into the traffic on the George Washington Parkway. "Then he's out of surgery?"

"Yes, just before we got here – about four."

"And Margaret?" Mary Kate fixed ahead, unsure, scared.

"Doing pretty well, really...for all of it..." Brigit shook her head, a quick glance at Mary Kate then ahead. "Think about it. She gets up, feeds the baby, fixes her husband breakfast, kisses him good-bye and four hours later she's holding his hand walking alongside his gurney as they wheel him in for open heart surgery...saying good-bye again, this time maybe *forever*..." Mary Kate reached for Brigit's forearm, squeezing it, holding it, needing something to touch.

'Irish Twins' is what they called them, Mary Kate and Michael, born the same calendar year, 1932, she in January and he in November. And they might just as well have been twins of the womb, as well, so close had they become. John Riley was six years her senior, with a boy named Dennis having come and died between them. Then there was Kevin, dearest Kevin. He was born four years after Michael, the baby of the family. He had died tragically trying to rescue a boy unknown to him in a wayside highway accident. That was 25 years ago, St. Patrick's Day weekend of 1968. It had become the *then* of their lives, the Rileys, a miracle of sorts, even if a horribly bitter-sweet one.

For Mary Kate Riley, *then* was to become the hinge point of her life, joining the two parts of it in years lived. But it more separated them, really, than anything else, resetting her life from what it had been to where it would go, what it would become – hers, and hers alone. For all of it, though, Kevin dying and all to follow, what most had defined her as a person was the forging wars of childhood.

The closeness of Michael's birth to her own had steeled them together against their strong-willed, older brother, John, even as they worked to separate themselves from Kevin, the 'trailer.' They were a team of sorts within the family, Mary Kate and Michael, a pair unto themselves. And now, for the first time in her life, she faced the reality, the certainty, that one of them would die before the other, forcing on her the possibility of being alone in a way of which she had no experience and, until now, had no real expectation. None at all.

Breaking her gaze ahead, Mary Kate turned right toward the Potomac, an early evening glow now coming to the whiteness of the Washington Monument and the Lincoln Memorial. Breathing in deeply, she held the air, the fumes of jet fuel now gone to the mixed bouquet of fresh cut grass along the parkway and the first hint of trees turning, the scent of the river, the water of it.

Looking right, across the river, she could see the Southwest waterfront, redone since the years she had lived there, now marked by large restaurants with townhouses and apartment buildings beyond, grown out of the land she had grown up on. They called it urban renewal and it cleared the poor blacks away from the shadow of the Capitol building. But it hadn't changed the ground, the dirt, only what was on it. The river and Washington Channel, they were the same, too, and they were what defined the place. She turned to Brigit. "Are we going to the hospital?"

"If you'd like…There's no hope of seeing Michael, though, speaking to him anyway. He's in the ICU." Brigit checked the rearview mirror. "Margaret's there overnight. Fr. Kennedy worked out a place for her to sleep…I'm sure she'd love to see you." She turned to Mary Kate then quickly back ahead. "But Nana's the one who needs you most right now…I can run you back down to Georgetown later…"

Mary Kate nodded. "Yes, Nana…Mom…"

They were crossing Memorial Bridge and would soon be in the summer lushness of Rock Creek Park, a forested wilderness through the middle of the city, ending at the Potomac just below Georgetown. On a summer evening, in the quiet of the Park's bottom, its streams and rivulets, it could be ten degrees cooler than in the city above and about it.

And as they made their way through the bends and turns of it, she felt the coming of Peirce Mill, at Park and Beach. To many, this was the dead center of it all. The creek had been dammed there and a mill pond formed whose water turned a wheel that ground wheat into flour and Mary Kate Riley closed her eyes and thought of Kevin.

It had been *then,* the Friday of it. Kevin had met her at Union Station. As they had made their way up through the Park that day, now twenty-five years past, Mary Kate had asked Kevin to stop in the parking lot of the mill. Getting out of the car, she had walked to the edge of the pond, fixing on the mill as she remembered her last time alone with Paddy Riley.

He had wanted his daughter to understand how a mill worked, what it did, how the water made the wheel turn the stone that ground the wheat into flour. As Brigit now drove across Park Road and north on Beach Drive, Mary Kate turned to the mill and the parking lot, fixing on the tree she had leaned against that day, now reliving it again, memories of her last day with Paddy Riley and...

She was supposed to marry Charlie Olmstead, Mary Kate Riley was. Everyone knew that, everyone who saw them together knew that. Wherever they went, wherever they were, they made it brighter, more alive. He handsome and she beautiful, both intelligent with the world and time stretching out before them, all just waiting to be lived. A person would have to have been blind not to see this, how meant for each other they were... in all things but one...

Born of the Olmsteads of Chevy Chase, Maryland, Charlie Olmstead's blood ran as far as back anyone could see and every drop of it, every dollar of it, blue...and most assuredly Protestant. A blue blood, is what, as blue as the deepest sea and nary a hint of green to be found, not in any part or corpuscle of him. It was 1954 and these things still mattered between and among the peoples of polite society, quiet murmurings of this or that, the *tsk, tsk* of it all betraying a prejudice under the cover of false compassion.

There were tolerances, though, understandings offered with some finding safe harbor in different quarters, even that of the Olmstead clan. Certainly not their choice, of course, she being born Irish and Catholic and out of the building trades in the bargain, but she *is* nice, a *lovely* girl, Charlie, *such* a *pleasure* to be with...

In the heart and mind of Mary Riley, though, there was to be no quarter given and none asked. She'd been born in Ireland, Mary had, and come over at six years in '08 with memories of it all burnt deep inside her. Aye, no land to be held by Catholics and, worse still, an uncle, Dennis being his name, hung in the rain for a traitor, his neck not breaking from the drop and his legs kicking an awful storm before they come still, his body limp and turning on the rope. Her godfather, he was, and favorite till he'd been done and never to leave her memory.

Mary Riley had refused Charlie Olmstead on a summer's evening in August of 1954, Mary Kate leaving that night for New York, building a life there in the shadow of what might have been. Torn in more ways than she understood, she was unable to break clear of the forces that bound her to her mother's will, yet had so driven them apart...until *then*...

Brigit turned left onto Broad Branch. "You always think of Paddy down here, don't you?"

Closing her eyes for a moment, Mary Kate turned to Brigit. She had no idea when their relationship had changed from aunt and niece to friends, but it surely had. Being the oldest of the grandchildren, Brigit knew of *then* more than any of the others. And it was about *then* that they had first become close.

Smiling at Brigit, Mary Kate turned ahead. "Yes, the Park, Peirce Mill. It's sacred ground to me, you know, my last time with Paddy, alone, just the two of us, then stopping here with Kevin *then*..."

Yes, thought Brigit, *then*...

Born in 1955, Brigit was 13 at the time and Kevin, a social worker in Appalachia, was her favorite. Brigit remembered asking once, when Kevin was twenty-four years old and she six, if Kevin was a 'grown-up'. Certainly, he could not have been more different from her father, John Riley. Where John Riley was driven, Kevin Riley was easy. Where John Riley dealt in answers that he knew to be right and correct *every* time, Kevin dealt in questions. Where John spoke, even barked at times, Kevin listened, his eyes on you, watching, caring, listening, searching.

Brigit had not seen Kevin *then*, though the others had, her father, her mother, Eileen, and then Mary Kate and Michael and Nana. Even Fr. Hara. They spoke softly in the days after he had died, of their last time with him, his last words.

But it made no sense to Brigit, none at all. There was an unspoken craziness to it, a sense of the deepest sorrow yet, still, a soaring wonder, a 'miracle' Nana had said, and then *pfft*, in a month, maybe two, hardly spoken of again, Kevin gone and they on with their lives.

Most troubling, though, was the article in the Washington Post – *Local Hero Dies in Truck Fire*. According to the article, Kevin Riley had been killed in an explosion on the *Thursday* night of *then*. She was certain of that. But this would have been *before* any of their remembrances when they spoke about their last time with him – Friday and Saturday and Sunday. When she asked her father about it, he had turned away, no answer given, no words said.

For all the horror of it, though, Kevin being killed and all, the part of *then* that most affected Brigit's life was how her father had changed after it. In the months prior to *then*, her parents were in a constant, wrenching battle over their youngest child and only son, Patrick.

Her mother would cry, plead for help as young Patrick stared blankly about at one moment and in the next be banging his head against a wall, her picking him up, his body wriggling, fitful in her arms, she trying to control him, to protect him from himself with John Riley saying again and again 'There is nothing wrong...he'll grow out of it' and then the word, the curse, *autism*, it driving deep, ever deeper into their lives... and into Brigit's mind and memory.

He had changed how he lived after *then*, John Riley had. He brought on a Chief Operating Officer to help at the company, never leaving the house before 8:30, and back for lunch most days. He was almost always home by five. Specialists were sought and seen, every resource brought to bear. 'There had to be a way,' he'd said, and it would be found.

But it never was. In the more than one full year that followed *then*, the Riley family lived the search for a cure, a way out, but none was ever found. Of the gradations of this thing, this *autism,* Patrick had the worst of it and there was nothing on God's good earth that was going to change this.

"He's dead to us," John Riley had said at the table after dinner. It was a Tuesday night in the early fall of 1969. "We are certainly not alive *to him...* no one is. There's just no one inside, nothing. The Patrick we knew at one year, or thought we knew, is gone, but he is not. He's still in our house and we are upside down with it."

A quiet had come to the table as Brigit Riley's father spoke these words, a stopping, a knowing that it was over and all the hoping and the loving and the praying had not worked, and would not work. Patrick Riley was gone, lost to them forever. What remained of him, a three-year old boy's body with a helmet affixed to his head so he would not hurt himself, his eyes blank and his mouth silent, would be going to another place...and out of their lives...

As Brigit's mind had reeled at the thought, she steadied herself against the table's edge, her breathing lost, then found, her mind racing at a million miles an hour, unable to form words, nor count the hours, the endless hours she had spent with him, with Patrick, trying to get a reaction – a smile, an anger, anything at all that would say that he was there, inside.

The things not done, the trips not taken, the dances not danced...Brigit's eyes had turned to her sisters that night, Annie and Katherine. Blank, their eyes were blank, forward, then down, avoiding her own. Nothing. Then to her mother, Eileen Riley. Would she permit this? Was not

Patrick part of their lives, their living? Is Patrick not *your son*, not somehow *part* of us, each of us, *all* of us, the *Rileys*? Is he not *alive*, upstairs, there, *in his room*, now as we all sit here numb, speechless?

Eileen Riley had not moved, her eyes down at the table, her arms limp, folded across her chest. It was over. Patrick was over, living, yes, but among the dead to those on East Irving Street, left by the wayside of their lives as they each and together went on, and his mother had not stirred, had not said a word.

CHAPTER SIX
Hank Johnson

O f all the Marines John Riley had served with in the Pacific, Hank Johnson was the only one to become a true friend. They had bonded, Hank and John, on guns and hunting, Hank telling of quail and water fowl in the fields and lakes north and east of Pittsburgh. The Chesapeake was what John Riley had told of, out before dawn with Paddy Riley and Jack Hennessey, tales of skies darkened by flocks of geese and of the whisper quiet of a duck blind just before the gunning started.

Two years older than John Riley, Hank Johnson had been born in 1923. His father had lost his shop in 1935, stringing odd jobs for more than three years before hiring on full time as the lathe foreman at a metal shop in Gary, Indiana.

But the shop's bank soon failed, taking the shop with it and the Johnsons as well, broke again and down, only now three hundred miles from home, in a place where nobody knew or wanted them. Hank was sixteen at the time but being early to a full beard, his father was able to pass him off for eighteen at the Civilian Conservation Corps office. One less mouth to feed.

He was to spend two years in the CCC, mostly in Oklahoma, coming to learn more about the bad in people than the good, hard knuckle fights over half a dollar 'cause that might be all that was left of a month of hard labor and sending some money home. He'd learned other things, though, useful things - that tree lines can break the wind over a plain and that the difference between a good crop and hardpan was water, plain ol' water, and getting it to where it was needed was what he and the rest did with the pipe they laid.

And there was time in the work to think, alone on a line with forty others, the rhythm of the work song, breaking ground with pickaxes and shovels under a skin-scorching sun, Hank Johnson thinking hard, trying to figure it all out. Exactly how in hell does a person get from digging a ditch to living a life? To owning stuff, his own place, having a family?

Now to most folks that December of nineteen and forty-one, Pearl Harbor may well have been a *Day of Infamy*. For Hank Johnson, though, with more than two years living in tents and bunkhouses across more states and counties than he cared to count, Pearl Harbor was a red, white and blue, all-American, board-certified, hand-delivered *miracle*, and not one ounce less. *Yes, sir!*

On enlistment in the Marine Corps, he had gotten orders to Camp Pendleton in California, arriving there in the morning of New Year's Day, 1942. A new year and a new life. It was the uniform in the poster that had first caught his attention, the white hat and the dark blue of the tunic with its brass buttons and red piping. And that belt! Couldn't stop looking at himself when he finally got one of his own. More clothes than Hank Johnson had ever owned in his entire life and he had it all on at the same time! Just craved the chance to wear it. Would've slept in it if they'd let him.

But that was after boot camp, thirteen weeks of fear, misery, exhaustion, loneliness, despair - but most of all *discovery*. The Marine Corps was a whole new America to Hank Johnson, the east, west, north and south of it. And it made of him a whole new type of person, an *American* person. From day one to day ninety, it never stopped. And the tougher they made it, the more he got it.

The surest way to get his company to do something was to tell them it couldn't be done and they'd find a way to do it – together, the unit, his unit. The world had divided into two types for Hank Johnson – there were Marines and there were those who were not Marines. That's all. That was it.

His first action was Guadalcanal. The spring of 1942 and Henderson Field and mosquitoes and swamps and snakes and the life of Hank Johnson came to a whole new birthing and place. It began as he watched the fleet that landed them retreat back over the horizon with no one knowing for sure when it was coming back, or even if it was coming back. It was a time when even the really smart ones, the super-smart, just had no idea at all what was going to happen.

Now Hank Johnson did a lot of thinking on Guadalcanal, too, mostly about how he was going to stay alive in a place crawling with Japs whose sole purpose in life was to end his own. They wanted him dead, even dreamt about it. Not captured, now. Dead. And he soon came to learn that the way to stay alive in a war on an island, locked in mortal combat with people who would commit suicide before surrendering, is to kill as many of the sons-a-bitches as you could find or might come your way. And while he never came to any sort of pleasure in it, like anything else, the more Japs he killed, the better at it he got.

From Guadalcanal, it was up to Peleliu and other islands, bombed and strafed and left scrubbed of Japs, wasting in a Pacific sun and the wakes of their transports as Iwo Jima was landed and taken and finally Okinawa for a front row seat on Hiroshima and Nagasaki. Before it was all over, Hank Johnson had made Gunnery Sergeant, volunteering for occupation duty in Japan.

As peace settled in, though, and the force levels dialed down, he faced the choice of leaving the Corps or taking a demotion to Lance Corporal. No decision at all, really, not for Hank Johnson, not for a true *Marine*.

Would have been like leaving home because he'd have had to bunk in with a brother. And they liked that in a fella, the Marines did. It just meant they got to keep the really good ones.

He'd drawn sea duty in the late 1940s, an aircraft carrier in the Caribbean, to be reassigned to Okinawa just in time for Korea. This put him in command of a point squad in the landings at Inchon. Here he was decorated for bravery and rewarded with Officer Candidate School. Now this was something they *really* liked, a jarhead gyrene off Henderson Field at 19 years old moving on up to the officer corps. A *mustang* is what they called them, an officer up from the ranks. Yeah, they liked this.

After OCS, Hank Johnson spent two tours at Quantico in Virginia before pulling ship duty again, this time in the Mediterranean and taking a company ashore in Lebanon in 1958. Operation Blue Bat is what they called it, the first try at the Eisenhower Doctrine, protecting regimes threatened by international communism.

The fighting though, was minimal with his company being assigned to security duty at the American Embassy in Beirut. It was here that he struck up a friendship with the Deputy Chief of Mission who later recommended him for assignment to the Marine Security Guard Battalion responsible for U. S. embassy security world-wide.

Retiring five years later as a Captain, Mr. Hank Johnson joined Pfizer International with responsibility for plant and office security in the United Kingdom and the Republic of Ireland. It was a whole new future opening wide to him – business, American business. The joke then was that the 'capital' of the United States was in Europe, every dollar of it.

A new world was abuilding and corporate America was out front, in Europe and Latin America, soon to be reaching out to Asia. And every office and factory of it would be needing people to keep it safe and secure. After three years at Pfizer, Hank Johnson was recruited by Atlantic Security Corporation to be Vice President for Western Europe. Here he spent another five years in Europe before transferring back to corporate headquarters in Arlington, Virginia.

"Great to see you, Hank. Thanks for coming over." John Riley stepped off the curb at the main entrance to The Westchester, shaking Hank Johnson's offered hand as he got into his four door Mercedes 500 SEL. "Real good to see you. Real good…"

"Happy to be of service." Hank Johnson slipped the transmission into gear, turning to the right out of The Westchester compound for Wisconsin Avenue, heading north toward Chevy Chase.

"New car?" John Riley fastened his shoulder belt.

"Yes, indeed, sir. Finest kind and brand new." Hank Johnson stretched back in his seat. "And you know me, Johnny Boy, all the frills and follies, the bells and whistles." He picked up the handset on the armrest between them. "Here, dial 0-011. Give them a number and you're connected, anywhere in the world. Anywhere! Here, try it…"

"Thanks. I believe you, but no thanks. Who'd I call? Everyone I want to talk to is pretty much around here." He smiled at Hank Johnson and found himself relaxing, the first time he was at ease since they'd been taken out of the meeting in Chicago. Settling in the leather seat, he put his head back for a moment, closed his eyes…

"Well *excuse* me…?" Hank Johnson's eyes were on him, quick and bright, jostling without touching. "You call me over from Virginia in rush hour to give you a lift to Maryland and you go to sleep? Hell, you can sleep in a taxi, for Chrissake. You're riding in *my* car? *Me* driving? No nappy time here, mister?"

John Riley sat up sharply, a quick salute, his hand and arm turning quickly to an 'up yours, pal.' They both laughed as they passed the National Cathedral to the right. John Riley cleared his throat. "So, your message said you had something 'important'?"

"Yeah. Couple of things, actually." Hank Johnson looked left and right, then quickly over his shoulder. John Riley knew he was checking the traffic, but it was more than that. Hank Johnson just needed to know how far away the people and things around him were. Fighting Japs in the jungle at midnight can do that to a fella. The traffic opened up and the car accelerated north, moving to the right for the turning lane.

"About Chicago…We've got two firms, two senior partners. Both small to middling outfits, like you wanted. Eighteen partners in one, fifteen in the other. Both Chicago. As far as we can tell, there are no links to Fox Worthy. None, full stop."

"The names?"

"The names?" Hank Johnson shook his head "Christ, Johnny Boy, it's after hours…let me think, Green, Oldfield or something and someone else, and Hastings Kline, yeah Hastings Kline. Lehman Brothers has used both of them at one time or another. Goldman, too." Hank Johnson turned right on to an access road toward Nebraska Avenue. "They've also handled real estate work for Prudential and Equitable. All large, complex, long-term income-producing properties."

Though John Riley nodded, he was uncomfortable with all this. Fox Worthy had been outside counsel to Hennessey Land Company for years and had served them well. While Hardin Brooks is not a person John Riley was ever likely to see as a friend, they each had come to a deep respect for one another in the last twelve months. Looking for another lawyer now, at this point, would not sit well. But John Riley had come to a turn in The Deal, a deeper understanding of what they were doing and what he wanted from it, what they were all to get from it.

He had not discussed this with anyone, not even Brigit. He doubted any of them - Mary Kate, Michael, or his mother, least of all Brigit - would understand. And he wasn't even really certain himself, not yet anyway. "You have a particular partner yet?"

"No, not yet. A few more things to get, to go through. We should be there by COB tomorrow. You get your pick."

John Riley nodded as he leaned with the turn of the car north off Nebraska onto Connecticut. Fixing on Hank Johnson as the road opened up and the Mercedes accelerated to make a light, he thought back on their times working together.

Hennessey Construction had advertised for security services and Hank Johnson, then senior vice president at Atlantic Security, was selling. It was all done in a morning with two lives, two tracks, reunited. Atlantic Security was at every Hennessey construction site, providing employee background investigation and other services.

Though retiring two years previously at 68, Hank Johnson still took on work such as John Riley had needed in locating a lawyer in Chicago, 'Just to keep the juices flowing,' he'd said. He had been married once, years ago, while he was still in the Corps. 'She never got it,' he had explained to John Riley once. 'Never understood that whatever I was doing was always going to be bigger than me, bigger than 'us,' that I needed to be part of something going on - a war, something, the Corps, whatever. She said that was just the problem, that I wasn't married to her, that I was married to the Corps. Said once *she* wasn't the wife in the deal, *she* was the mistress, the diversion, the part that got fit in when there was time or some passing need to fill. Turned out she was right...I guess. Who knows? Too bad, really. Wasn't a bad person, not at all. Good looking, too. A blond for most of it.' He had chuckled at this. 'Just wanted a life I couldn't give her."

John Riley pushed back in his seat, tensing his arms and legs. It had been a long day and he was happy to be nearing home. Then there was Michael in the ICU...He turned to Hank Johnson. "What else you got?"

"Keith Pierson..."

"Yes, Mr. Keith no-middle-name Pierson..." He turned ahead, stifled a yawn. "And?"

"The saga continues." Hank Johnson turned quickly to John Riley, shaking his head as he rolled his eyes, then back to the road. "How long you had me working on him?"

"I don't know. Six, seven months, maybe eight...check your invoices..."

Hank Johnson shook his head. "Christ, it's always the same with you folks. Check the invoices, all there can be of truth can be found in the invoices, the money, always the money..." They both laughed.

"We'll call it seven months, then. Whatever." Hank Johnson checked the rearview mirror. "Anyway..." he cleared his throat. "John, this man is a *prick*, and one of inter-galactic proportions. Does not appear to have a good friend. Never married, but is never without a companion. And he's of the fear-first school of management, perhaps a founding father. Pays people top dollar so he can terrorize them with the threat of being fired, then fires them anyway whenever he thinks they have enough money banked to cross him. This is how this man *thinks*, how he *lives*."

The car had come to a stop at Military Road. A long light. Hank Johnson put it in neutral and shifted in his seat, looking at John Riley. "John, Keith Pierson makes 'Chain Saw Al' look like Mother Teresa. How'd a nice fella like yourself ever get mixed with a son-of-a-bitch like this?"

John Riley half smiled, shrugging as he nodded at the light which had just changed to green. "What was the other thing?"

Hank Johnson turned ahead, accelerating north on Connecticut. "Other thing?"

"You said there were 'a couple of things'…"

"Oh, yeah." He moved into the right lane. "How's Michael?"

"My brother, Michael?"

"Yeah, that one, 'that Michael'." Hank Johnson shifted in his seat. "Christ, Johnny Boy, who else *we* got in common, know *really* well together named 'Michael'?…Gone through what we all did together? Our 'hunting trip'?"

John Riley laughed, shook his head. "Oh, yeah, that one, *that* Michael…" He paused, turning forward. "Well, as a matter of fact, he's in the ICU right now. Just had a quadruple bypass…"

"Whoa…" Hank Johnson's head and shoulders drew back, a quick glance at John Riley and then back ahead, on the traffic, slowing the car. "That's a load, now…Christ…How's he doing? Gonna ma…?"

"They think so…" John Riley didn't want to think about Michael in the ICU and whether or not he was 'gonna make it.' He turned to Hank Johnson as they entered Chevy Chase Circle. "So, the other thing?"

Hank Johnson got them through the circle and headed north on Connecticut, staying in the right lane. "Well, the 'other thing' is about Michael…And our time 'over there'…"

John Riley sat up, turned quickly to his left, fixing on Hank Johnson as the car turned right on to East Irving Street, coming to a stop opposite John Riley's home, the fourth house in from Connecticut Avenue. "What do you mean?''

Brigit Winslow had been sitting in a white wicker arm chair on the front porch, rising on seeing Hank Johnson at the wheel of his black, four-door Mercedes. Coming down the porch steps, she started across the front lawn to the sidewalk in front of the house. Stopping maybe twenty feet off, her eyes ran left and right to take in the full presence of the car. "Well, Mr. Johnson, howdy *do-do*?" Her arms were out, her head gesturing at the car. "I must say, Mr. Johnson, that is one fine looking automobile you have there…is it new?"

"I should hope so, figuring the price of the thing…"

Brigit Winslow laughed, her eyes on him, eyelashes batting. "Do I get a ride?"

John Riley opened the front passenger door, stepping out of his side of the car as he motioned with his left hand that Hank Johnson should say 'no.'

Hank Johnson rested his left arm in the open window of the driver's side. "No, Brigit, darling. Not tonight. Got to get back to Virginia. My side of the river, you'll understand…" He smiled, looking at Brigit's five-foot-six-inch frame, well turned out in a white blouse and crisply creased khaki slacks. "I must say, though, we are looking smart this evening…"

Brigit curtsied as might a school girl. "Why thank you, Mr. Johnson." She smiled, her eyes bright as John Riley stepped around to the driver's side, his hand resting in the open window of the car by Hank Johnson's shoulder, head down and speaking quietly. "Is it important, about 'over there'?"

"Could be to Michael, especially now." Hank Johnson paused, nodded again at Brigit then looked back up to John Riley. "You too…maybe all of you…"

"Okay." John Riley forced a smile, stood erect. "Call me in the morning…You good for lunch?"

Hank Johnson nodded a 'yes.'

"Set it up with Grace in the morning."

"Sure thing." Hank Johnson smiled, his chin up. "Hey, by the way, you're welcome for the ride home."

John Riley stood to his full height, his head back. "Yeah. Sure. You bet. Thanks for the lift." He smiled, waving him off as he turned toward Brigit, taking her arm as he started back across the lawn.

Turning ahead, Hank Johnson checked the rearview mirror and eased his Mercedes forward, moving quietly over the asphalt surface of East Irving and back around toward Chevy Chase Circle…and on home to Virginia.

CHAPTER SEVEN
East Irving

I t would be spaghetti and meat sauce at the Rileys' this night. And for all the fright of the day, Michael's operation and he in the ICU, there was a warming as well, a coming together with each finding a rhythm in what they were doing, Eileen at the stove with Mary Kate and Brigit getting on with the warming of the bread and the mixing of the salad.

Annie Warren was there, too, Eileen's youngest daughter with her girls of six and four, Shannon and Deirdre, sitting by Mary Riley at the kitchen table. Taking in her every word, they heard of the time her Michael had split his head open on a counter top. "Aye, there, now, by your mother, that one." She pointed to a corner by the stove top, her finger then going to her right forehead. "Five stitches it took, closing him up, and not a peep from him, neither. A tough one, my Michael, and all of that."

Mary Riley had come to live with them, John and Eileen, after Ed Kane had passed. 'Captain Kane' to Mary, Ed Kane had been chief of police in Chevy Chase from just after the War until the late 1970s. They had married, Captain Kane and Mary Riley, in the spring of 1969, Joe Hara doing the honors.

For their honeymoon, they went to Ireland, Mary Riley's first trip back since coming over in '08. 'A month and no more,' she'd said to Eileen, this stretching to the full summer, though, she enjoying it so and the memories of it all calling them back every June, the end of it coming with Ed Kane's passing in 1984.

They had lived in his bungalow on Turner Lane, Mary Riley and Captain Kane had. Given him by the village on his twentieth-fifth year as Chief of Police,

Mary was proud to share it with him. Though she had loved her Paddy with an intensity that held over the years, in Ed Kane she had a companion, a comfort, a person who brought to her days of meaning and pleasure she came to treasure, finding a depth of happiness of which she had no anticipation.

Mary Riley's only worry through it all, the marrying of Captain Kane, was the house on East Irving. In marrying a man such as he, a retired Master Sergeant of the U. S. Army and a veteran of Stillwell's 'walk out' in Burma, you went to his house because that's where he was, that's where he lived. Mary had told Eileen once that they never actually spoke about it, where they were to live, that there was never an agreement. 'Just worked out that way, don't you know, all being part of the same thing.'

It was in the early fall after Kevin had died that Mary Riley and Captain Kane began keeping company. Now there had been a time of sorts earlier for them. This was in the years after she had moved her family from the District of Columbia to Chevy Chase, that being 1947, all this to be nearby Joe Hara, then the assistant pastor at Blessed Sacrament.

They would find themselves sitting together at parish events, she and Captain Kane, or being the only single man and woman at a Sunday cookout. Then there would be the occasional coffee at the Olympia Grill on Brookville Road, in the village of the place – a market nearby to a drug store and a real estate office, with a barber shop and someone selling insurance on a second floor overlooking a one-pump gas station.

She had understood then that he wanted the relationship to go further. But there were children whose raising needed finishing and Hennessey Construction to run and Mary Riley's life, though perhaps the envy of some, was not so much her own to live. It had tugged on her then, times when she was alone and lonely, these coming in greater frequency over the years.

Then came *then*. *Then* had changed everything. In the course of two days she had stepped down as chair of Hennessey Construction and come to a new life with her Mary Kate, things past forgiven and forgotten. And her son Michael? He had his law and his rugby and his trips to Ireland, living the life of the Irish bachelor, and doing quite well at it, too. Then there was Kevin, too, her youngest, taken from her that same weekend, tearing a hole in her life she could see no way of filling or closing.

And so, it came that on a September afternoon in Brookeville Market - she at the meat counter sorting among the steaks with Captain Kane coming along, pushing his cart.

"Afternoon, Mrs. Riley…" Ed Kane's hand went to the visor of his cap, a quick nod of the head. "And how are we this fine afternoon?"

Catching him out of the corner of her eye, she turned full to him, happy for the sound of his voice, his eyes now of a blue unexpected and on her in a way not felt in near a lifetime. Her own eyes now welling at the warmth of his smile, she caught her breath at the wonder of the moment, near in a swoon as she went a bit weak at the knees.

Seeing this, Captain Kane stepped quickly closer, one hand out to steady her, the other to support. "Here, Mary, let me find a chair…"

"No, now, Captain Kane, don't be troubling yourself…" She steadied herself, taking a breath, her eyes on him now and of a sudden freeing her right hand and reaching for his left, covering it, marveling at its touch and strength, holding it closer, a half step nearer now taken.

They finished shopping together, she putting her things and her purse in his cart, the two of them collecting the parts of a dinner – steaks and potatoes and greens and what to drink - then walking the block to his place at the end of Turner Lane. It was set, his place, overlooking the northwest corner of Sheppard Park, an open field with soccer goals and a baseball cage all ringed by great poplars towering above alder trees and red oaks.

Captain Kane showed her the living room and dining area with the kitchen at the back, it opening to a small deck above a freshly cut yard marked by a short, trimmed hedge and they having dinner and he telling her of the war and his early years in Brooklyn and the life of a soldier and then she of the times in Southwest and the coming of the children and the passing of the parents and then Paddy's going off to war and they nodding off all together on a warm September's evening with him taking her home and saying he'd like to do this again and they did until it made no sense for her to go home at all because she already was...

Yet for all the joy and wonder of it, her life with Captain Kane, it came at the hardest of times - John and Eileen coming to know that their Patrick had to be put out from their home. Once done, Eileen had found herself unable to sleep in her house, every room of it a memory and her little Patrick gone now some place away from her attention and care, sleepless nights with her wondering how he was getting on.

So, there was Mary's house on East Irving, her not living in it but no one of them wanting it sold, so much having done there. It was Joe Hara who said the obvious. 'Why don't you and Eileen take it, John?' this being offered on the stone patio at the back of East Irving with all there, Mary Kate and Michael Rhinemann down for a weekend with Michael Riley in and out and it was all done and settled the week following.

"Table's done, Mom." Annie Warren came through the door from the dining room. A social worker married to a teacher in the DC school system, Annie lived in Adams Morgan, down and east of Connecticut Avenue, maybe fifteen minutes without traffic. Eileen had asked them to come to dinner, thinking the girls would be a comfort for Mary from the weight of the day, certainly a distraction.

"Is Katherine coming?" Annie stepped close by Eileen, taking a wooden spatula hung from under a cabinet and stirring the spaghetti as the water came to a boil.

"No. We spoke. George is on the road and she has a parent-teacher to do." Eileen looked away, stopped stirring the sauce, her eyes blank for a moment then at Annie. "It's always something with them. Never seems to stop, not since his promotion, anyway…" She reached for a serving spoon to her right and dipped a half measure for the sauce, cupping her other hand under it as she stepped to Mary. "How's that?"

Mary dipped a finger in it, the girls doing the same. Bringing it to her mouth, Mary savored the sauce and smiled, her eyes up at Eileen. "Not bad, now. Eileen. You're getting it…"

A smile came between them and Eileen was back to the stove, tasting it herself before sprinkling in a couple of turns of cracked pepper. They had become close, Eileen and Mary Riley. Giving up Patrick was the most difficult thing Eileen Riley had ever had to do and Mary was with her every step of the way. Eileen hadn't expected this, Mary being so forceful a person until then.

It was settling with Ed Kane, Eileen had come to think, that had changed Mary so, all the matriarch in her just seeming to melt away. There wasn't a large house to keep or Hennessey Construction to run or, somehow, a family to be the head of any longer. Just her family about her, as many children and grandchildren as she had any need, just to help along as best she could. And as painful as the leaving of Patrick must have been for her, Mary's first thoughts seemed always to be of what it was doing to Eileen and John.

Mary Kate came into the kitchen from the front hall, just finished a call, her rust red hair tied back. There was an energy about her that, over the years, Eileen had come to accept. Out of her business suit and wearing white linen slacks and a beige turtleneck, Mary Kate went to the kitchen table. Kissing Mary on the cheek and stroking Dierdre and Shannon, she smiled at Eileen before fixing on the pots on the stove and checking her watch. "What's to eat?"

"Spaghetti!" the girls called in unison, giggling, going silent as they heard the front door open and close with the sound of voices coming from the hall. They looked at each other, "Pop Pop!" Squealing the name again, they ran toward the hall, jumping into John Riley's out stretched arms as he came into the kitchen with Brigit following.

It was past nine before it had all done – Mary Kate and Brigit hurrying their meal and out quickly to get down to the hospital. Mary had fallen asleep on the couch in her apartment as she read to the girls, the girls knowing to slip out quietly and tell their mother. Roused by their leaving, Mary came out for a bit to say good night, kissing each girl and to the others, speaking with Eileen and John of Michael Riley, stiffening against a tear as she spoke of Margaret and their newborn son.

John Riley had helped his mother back to her room, closing the door and nodding to Mary as he made his way to the den. It was not until this time that Eileen sensed a sadness in him, and maybe a fear as well.

He was a hard man to feel sympathy for, John Riley. Not that he wasn't a caring man, for surely he was. *Then* had fixed that. It was just that he always seemed so much in control of what was about him, knew what might be coming and what could be done about it. There were few surprises in his life. But here was a surprise, Michael, his only brother and if John Riley truly had a best friend, that too, now laying in a hospital bed, perhaps only one poorly tied suture away from bleeding to death that night.

"Penny for your thoughts..." Eileen stepped into the den from the kitchen, sitting in her arm chair, it at an angle to his before the TV screen.

He looked over, forcing a smile, shrugging, saying nothing before turning back to the TV. Raising his arms above the arms of the chair, he brought them down, not in a rush or a slam, just down, gripping the end of the chair arms, his knuckles gone white for a moment.

"I feel so helpless...useless, even, just plain useless..." He looked at her, then back at the TV. "I'm an engineer. I build things, fix them, too. Big things...hard things...I don't do small things, especially soft, small things like hearts, and keeping brothers alive..."

Sensing that he was about to tear, she rose and went to him, sitting on the arm of his chair and holding him, feeling him tense at her touch and then relax, easing against her.

Breathing full in and holding it for a count before exhaling, he turned slowly toward her, his eyes blank, as if in a daze. "You just never know, I guess. Everything's going along so well, so fine - work's good, the kids are all healthy then *Kapow!* Brings you up short, I'll tell you that...tells you to watch out..." He closed his eyes for a moment then opened them on her.

"On the way home, on the plane? I thought of him dying, Michael. How awful that would be. Then tonight, just now, before you came in, I thought of *you* not being here...how...I don't think you could ever know how much you mean to me, Eileen. And not just now, but always, every day...how completely empty my life would be without you."

She nodded, smiling as she took his head in both her hands and kissed him on the forehead before rising and returning to her chair. "So, apart from racing home with the *brudder* gone to hospital, how was your day, John Riley?"

John Riley laughed now, a good and deep laugh. Looking across at her, their eyes fixed for a moment, he now sitting forward. "This is some kind of deal we got going here, let me tell you that. Judas Priest... makes putting up a ten-story office building look like an afternoon with an erector set." He put his hands out flat, one above the other, about six inches apart. "That's how thick the books are on this thing. And you know what?"

"What?"

"Your daughter Brigit, our little Brigit?" He extended his hand flat over the floor, waist high above it, smiling, gesturing with this other hand at the height of it. "Remember her? Little Brigit? Well she knows every page of them, every page of every book. She's one smart cookie, I'll tell that, and tough, too. You can't BS her and you can't scare her, neither, no sir. No way. You raised a champ there, Mrs. Riley..."

Eileen Riley smiled, holding it, hoping he didn't notice. He didn't seem to have. "So, it's close to done, then?"

John Riley sat back, he now seeming to hold a smile of his own. "Yeah, yes, very close. Matter of fact, closer than I'd really like right now...not so sure about it...the whole thing...some parts I didn't see at first." He looked up, his smile back, almost laughing.

"You might even say, my dear, that if Michael Francis Riley had to have an emergency-operation-absolutely-right-now-or-he-gonna-die-quadruple-bypass-surgery, he couldn't have picked a better minute than today at 12:35 pm Chicago time to get it done..."

He looked across at her, the smile on his face now fading, he thinking some thought, running some calculation...

Eileen Riley knew the look. Not that she knew what he was thinking, never that. Only that he was thinking, and for the moment away, out of the house, on the job...

Seeming to have sensed this, John Riley sat up, his eyes on her, bright. "Great to see Annie and the girls. Good idea to have them over. Did the trick with Mom. Did you call Katherine?"

Now Eileen sat up a measure. "Yes. Couldn't come...all George seems to do is travel...has got to be wearing on them, certainly her...Little George and William, too..."

John Riley looked back at the TV. "Yeah, has to...but that's his game. It's what he does. For him, there's no other way."

Eileen nodded, her thoughts running to Brigit and the hours she had worked over the last year on the Deal. She had a condominium on Connecticut Avenue, over-looking Rock Creek Park. She spent her weeks in it and weekends with Bertie in their brownstone off Washington Square in New York City. They'd do trips to far-off places as it struck them and when there was time to spend.

But this wasn't the life Eileen had wanted for her first born. Not at all. And it was this about the Deal that most bothered Eileen, this and the time it took John Riley away from her, as well.

"So, when do you think?"

"So, when do I think *what*?"

She could tell he knew what she was asking about, his eyes turned to the TV, on the screen of the thing. Fixing on his profile, she pressed on. "So, when does the Deal get done? How much longer?"

He didn't answer, his eyes staying on the TV.

"They haven't done one of their trips in over a year. I have no idea when they've had more than even a Saturday night together..."

He turned to her, his eyes uncertain of what she was speaking.

"Brigit and Bertie...they never have any time together, alone, a life together...like this." She gestured with her arms out to the room about them. "Just the two of them, together..."

He looked away, shaking his head, puffing a breath. "Yeah, I know what you mean..."

"Do you? Really?"

He looked back, turning in his chair, leaning toward her. "I don't know, maybe next week, now. There's no way to be sure in these things....so many parts and pieces."

"And what for her after it's done? For Brigit? What changes in her life when the Deal is done?"

John Riley looked past Eileen for a moment then back at her. "Not much, really. Maybe one or two new properties to manage, mostly it will be money, investing it, that sort of thing."

"More travel then?"

"Maybe, at first...yes, probably...it's hard to say."

She turned from him, fixing her eyes on the television set, fiercely now, not hearing his words after 'Maybe...'

It was now Eileen Riley who gripped the arms of her chair, her knuckles going to white...

CHAPTER EIGHT
The Visit

I t was eight by the time they got to the hospital. Finding their way to the ICU, Brigit nodded Mary Kate toward the waiting room area and started for the nurse's duty station. Mary Kate held her arm, stepping in front of her to the desk, reading the nurse's name tag. "Excuse me, Nurse Welling?"

The nurse looked up from her work, then quickly down. "Yes...how can I help you?"

"We're relatives of Michael Riley. Would you know where his wife Margaret might be?"

"Yes." The duty nurse completed an entry in what seemed to be a log book and looked up again, now smiling. "She's just gone to the cafeteria. Said she'll be right back. A coffee I think." She glanced at Brigit then back. "It's not far. If you..."

"Yes, thank you." Mary Kate looked in the direction of where the nurse was pointing, then back, stepping closer to the desk, waiting for her eyes. "I know we can't speak with him, my brother. But it would mean a great deal to me if I could just *see* him...that's all. I just need to see him. We're very close...and I've just come in from California."

The nurse sat back, fixed on Mary Kate, her eyes quickly to Brigit then back, a nod of the head. "Of course." Rising from behind her desk, she caught the attention of another nurse at a filing desk, putting her hand to her ear as if holding a phone. The other nurse nodded and Nurse Welling stood out from behind her desk, motioning to Mary Kate to follow. "Only a look, now, you understand...just a look..."

Mary Kate nodded, making way for Nurse Welling, staying just off her shoulder, her eyes fixed ahead, Brigit

Winslow trailing. As they approached a sealed emergency exit door at the far end of the corridor, the nurse stopped, an open hand motioning them to the room at the right. Mary Kate looked in, and caught her breath, her hand coming to her lips. Brigit stepped closer, but Mary Kate stood erect. "I'm fine," she said softly, her eyes fixed on Michael Riley, motionless, gaunt, his head in profile, an oxygen tube beneath his nose with other tubes affixed to his arms and a wire patched to his right temple.

"I'm sorry." Nurse Welling stepped closer, nodding back down the corridor. "But that's all we can do now." She took Mary Kate's elbow and started her back toward the duty station. "He's doing well. All signs are normal."

Mary Kate was comforted by the words and the ease of the nurse's grip on her elbow. At the desk, the nurse smiled and nodded to her right. "You can have a seat in the waiting room or, perhaps, you might want the cafeteria?"

Mary Kate looked in the direction of the waiting room. "We'll wait, thank you." Smiling at the nurse, she bowed slightly. "You have been extremely kind, more than you can realize." Gripping the nurse's upper arm, she stood close then stepped away, an arm out for Brigit to take. Once in the waiting room, she held Brigit's hand on her arm, bringing her to the chair beside hers as she sat down, her eyes closed, her breathing uneasy.

"Are you alright, Kay? Should I get a doctor?"

"No...No...I'm fine. It will pass. It was just when I saw him, Michael, just now, so pale... and the angle maybe...something, I don't know...just thought I was looking at *Kevin*..." She looked at Brigit, her eyes bearing in. "He looked more like Kevin to me than Michael...it just caught me, that's all..." She looked away, took several deep breaths, resting her arms on the arms of the chair, closing her eyes for a moment, then open, now back at Brigit. "Well, he's okay, then, that's what she said, isn't it?"

"Yes, normal, 'All signs normal,' that's what she said."

Mary Kate took a few breaths more, now breathing easier. She could feel the blood return to her hands which she flexed as she gave her head and shoulders a quick shiver. "Haven't been able to get Kevin out of my mind, keeps popping up. Just never thought of his profile being so much like Michael's. Their eyes are the same, deep set…and blue, like Dad's…his were the bluest, Dad's." Mary Kate turned to Brigit. "'Riley blue' is what Daddy Riley called them, and they were some kind of blue…"

Brigit sat off a bit, her shoulders more square to Mary Kate, as if she were about to speak, then away, her eye caught by a patient being wheeled past the open doorway. The gurney was attended by two nurses, one holding up an IV solution with its tube affixed to the man's left arm, and the other pushing and guiding them along.

"What is it, Brigit? What were you going to say?"

Brigit's eyes remained fixed at the now empty corridor.

"Brigit?" Mary Kate turned in her chair, gripping Brigit's forearm, squeezing it to get her attention. "What is it?"

Brigit cleared her throat, looking down and toward Mary Kate's lap. "You never speak about Kevin, you know." She looked up a measure. "You talk about all of them…the gone, the dead…Daddy Riley and Mom's father and mother, and Paddy, always about Paddy, and Jack Hennessey and Fr. Hara, now that he's gone…"

She fixed directly on Mary Kate. "Even Dennis. He died at two years, before you were even born. You all talk about them all, aunts and uncles, too. People I never met…but never Kevin, none of you, not even Nana…"

Mary Kate Rhinemann looked away, blankly for a moment then fixing on the table lamp on the far side of the room, her mind roaming back to *then*, St. Patrick's Day of 1968…the dining room at East Irving, she and her mother closing the gap of some fourteen years time, of forgiveness and love and then flying back to New York to be with Michael Rhinemann whose uncle, his only living blood, had just died and then the call that Kevin was gone, dead, killed trying to save another's life and then the bouquets of flowers and the silent murmurings of those in the line at DeVol's Funeral Home, the mass at Blessed Sacrament and Fr. Hara challenged beyond even his ability to see the good in a thing and the March cold and the wind of Mt. Olivet as the youngest of her siblings was the first to die. She turned to Brigit. "No, you're right, we never do…that's what we all seemed to have come to."

Mary Kate let go of Brigit's arm and rose, motioning her to remain seated. Stepping to the water cooler, she drew a small paper cup full, emptying it in a single swallow, crumpling the empty cup and letting it drop into the wastebasket beside the cooler, watching as it found its place among the refuse of the day. "John told me that you asked him once…about the dates not being right…"

Brigit sat up, re-crossing her legs, nodding and mouthing the word 'yes.'

Mary Kate turned to Brigit. "…The newspaper article you saw saying Kevin had died on the *Thursday* night and us all talking about times with him on Friday or Saturday, even Sunday…"

Brigit nodded again, sitting forward. "Yes, and I asked you about it once, too. It was in New York, after I moved up there…but something happened to the connection, I forget…"

Mary Kate returned to her seat, sitting on its edge, fixing on Brigit as she took her niece's arm. "There was no explanation that made any sense. Captain Kane had gone up on the Saturday morning to identify the body. They had to use dental records, he was that burnt up." Mary Kate bit her lip, looked up toward the corridor to Michael Riley's room.

"He came back Sunday morning to tell Joe Hara. Well, Joe Hara had seen Kevin on Thursday night, had breakfast with him the next morning and played basketball with him Saturday. Kevin *drove* me home from Union Station midday Friday. Your father and mother each saw him, separate times…they saw and spoke to him. And Mom, dear Lord, Mom saw him, fixed him breakfast…sat in church with him."

Mary Kate rose and began to pace the room. "It was all craziness. How was this possible?" She stopped, fixed on Brigit. "Well, of course, your father, being the head of the family, he being the oldest and in charge, good ol' practical John, he was going find out what was going on. Going to get to the bottom of…"

She stopped, looked at Brigit, thought of her words. "I said that the wrong way, Brigit. I'm sorry. Your father was struck as deeply as any of us." She looked away. "Maybe the most affected…" She turned back. "Yes, definitely, the most affected, the most changed, certainly. Anyway, he had Hank Johnson look into it all, the full Megillah." Mary Kate sat down, now across from Brigit.

"And, as we all know, Hank Johnson does good work, knows his job. He found the *taxi driver* who drove me from the station to East Irving on Friday. A positive, dead sure ID of my photo and the time and destination in his log.

"Then there's the portrait of Msgr. Ryan, something that everyone agreed they saw Kevin bring in on Saturday morning? Well it never left Ryan's house because Kevin had never picked it up. And the *maitre d'* at Trader Vic's, where Michael believes to this day that he'd had lunch with Kevin on Friday noon? Well the *maitre d'* specifically remembered that Michael had eaten alone on Friday and had the lunch chit to prove it."

Mary Kate began to pace again. "We got all this in the living room at East Irving. Everyone in the room, everyone except Hank Johnson, had seen Kevin that weekend *after* he died." She stopped, brought her hands together, shook her head and continued. "Well, John thanked Hank for his time and effort, walked him to the door then came back into the living room and sat down next to your mother, Eileen. I remember him taking her hand, and her sitting closer to him. No one knew what to say so no one said anything."

Mary Kate shrugged, sat down beside Brigit, smiling easy. "Now, of course, as far as I was concerned, Kevin had picked me up at the Station and had driven me home...I'm not crazy, right?"

Brigit smiled, shaking her head 'no.'

"But he didn't, did he? Couldn't have because he was dead, right?"

A nod from Brigit, "Yes."

"Whatever...in the silence, our heads and eyes began to turn to Joe Hara." She looked at Brigit and shrugged. "Who else at a time like *that*? The dead walking and talking amongst us? You look at the priest, right?"

Brigit smiled back, her head nodding, her eyes now bright. Yes, who else, indeed!

"Well, Joe Hara could feel us all looking at him, certainly seemed that way, anyway. He was sitting next to Nana, holding her hand as Hank went through it all, you know, basically telling us that we'd all had some sort of group hallucination, and one that ran off and on for the better part of three days." Another shrug. "Well, he let go of Nana's hand then fixed on your mother, of all people."

Brigit sat up. "Mom? *My* mother, *Eileen Riley?*"

"Yes, your mother...as if he expected her to *say* something." Mary Kate let a quiet laugh. "Well, of course, your mother *never* says *anything*! Certainly not back then. Anyway, just then, Nana stood up and crossed the room to where Captain Kane was sitting and sat next to him on the couch." Mary Kate gave a 'How about them cookies?' look at Brigit with a knowing wink of the eye. "He was there because he had seen Kevin, too. Hadn't spoken with him, now, but he did see him."

Mary Kate stopped and fixed on Brigit. "Mrs. Jackson, the cook/housekeeper at the rectory, she was there, too. She'd seen Kevin two or three times, and the boy…" She stopped herself, waved away. "No, don't worry about that. We don't have to go there. What's important is that everyone we knew who had 'seen' Kevin after he'd been killed was there."

Mary Kate shook her head, refocused. "Where was I?"

"Nana stood up and sat next to Captain Kane."

"Yes, yes. Well, she sat next to Captain Kane, resting her hand on his forearm, looking at all those around her before settling on your mother, Eileen, and speaking directly to her.

"'Banshees is what we called 'em in Ireland,' Nana started. 'It's why they'd wait three days to bury the dead, out of respect. Now my mother, Nora Coughlin, she knew all the tales and myths and believed a lot of them, too, she did. Spirits of the dead, the banshees are, and they'd be up and about, talking to this fella and that, some making trouble, it was said, others helping where they might. Some, says she, just going about saying good bye…the good ones, that is.'

"Now Eileen's eyes were closed for most of this, even though Nana had been looking right at her. Then she looked up, your mother, and turned to Joe Hara, smiling, then nodding."

Mary Kate now sat down next to Brigit, taking her arm and leaning close. "Looking right at Nana, Eileen says 'I saw my mother the day after she died. It was in church, at Blessed Sacrament. I had sat back from the kneeler and there she was, just there, sitting next to me. It was so quiet, not a sound anywhere, not even in my ears.'

Eileen paused for a moment, taking a deep breath, continuing, her eyes fixed directly ahead.

"She sat there, her head toward the altar, then turned to me. I cannot tell you she was smiling, but I can tell you that her eyes seemed to glow...so alive, so deeply loving. Then she spoke, I guess, I'm not really sure, you see. It doesn't seem I remember any specific words, but somehow, somehow she told me that 'the best years of my life were the last three, the years spent in your home, with your family, with your girls...' Eileen then looked up, first at John and then around the room. 'It is impossible for me to tell you how happy I was at that moment, how completely fulfilled. And it is that one moment that I will always have with me, the knowing that my life, our lives, gave her such happiness...'"

Mary Kate stopped now, the emotions of that night coming back, rising in her. She sat up, stiffened, determined to get this out now and done under control. No tears allowed.

"She sat there, your mother did, for a moment, then rose and went to Nana, taking both her hands, kneeling beside her. 'I cannot imagine your pain, Mary,' she said. 'I know that. But I can tell you this, that Kevin loved you with his entire being and that his times with you were his greatest happiness. You will have him with you, we will all have him with us, for the rest of our lives and beyond...He will *always* be among us...'"

Mary Kate closed her eyes. She had got it said, what had happened that night, what had happened *then*. It was the cruelest of miracles, but a miracle nonetheless, a knowing of the beyond, a knowing that there was an 'other'...but at such cost.

She looked at Brigit, then away, nodding. "It was how he lived, you know, Kevin...fearless for the good, for the right. Others would hem and haw, worry about what others might think, look around before saying anything. Not Kevin. Never Kevin." She looked at Brigit now, smiling. "Kevin could just see the truth in a thing, or the lie, and he'd call it for what it was, no matter whose nose got out of joint. Just see it and say it…"

She shook her head from side to side as she felt a smile come to her face, a warming. "I remember Michael once saying that people like Kevin, people of courage, they always die young. 'Their courage takes them to fearful places,' he said. 'To Appalachia, and to a young boy he'd never met, trapped in a car by a burning truck.'"

Mary Kate paused, looked in the direction of Michael's room, her eyes now closing, a slight nodding of the head. Breathing in, she sat up and turned to Brigit. "So, we had him for a while, Kevin, with us, and now, because of *then*, we have him with us forever…here." She brought her hand to her bosom. "Maybe that's why we never talk about him like the others. In some wondrous way, none of us who saw him *then*, who spoke with him, can think of him as gone…"

CHAPTER NINE
The ICU

"Michael Riley, is it, now?"

The voice came as from a chamber, deep, not quite an echo, far away in time and place, distant but known, all this amid lights about him and beeping sounds, his arms wrapped, bound down.

Something in him wanted to move, to stretch, something else telling him not to, then his own voice as he remembered the call. "Yes…" he had said, catching his breath at the voice. There was an edge to it, the voice, but more than that, a threat, Michael Riley's shoulders back a measure at the sound of it, some primordial signal firing off. "Yes…This is Michael Riley. And who…"

"Maira asked that I ring you up when I've come. Maira Canny, that is…"

Michael Riley's head was agog, stuck halfway between the hospital room he was coming to realize he was in and a dream-like remembrance of a call of long ago and far, far away. He had sat down at the dinette in his apartment kitchen, his mind spinning, flashing back to a pub in Dublin, a flat in Cardiff, her face, her smile, her energy, the force of her, the force in her…

"You know her then?"

"Yes…yes, I know her…it was some years ago…"

"Aye, it was that, now, 'some years ago' indeed. She's gone now, you know, that being some years ago, too…"

"I didn't know…I'm sorry to learn that." And now, as the blurred vision of a nurse approached, reaching for something above his right shoulder, his mind wandered back to their parting and the weeks before it, a crashing of sound and light, the shouting. His coat thrown at him, she at the door, it coming open with a yank of her arm, the light from the alley, the boy, Sean, at her far side, his face buried in the pleats of her skirt, crying. Then her last words to him, a shriek, metal on metal. *'Traitor! Traitor you are, and traitor you'll be, to your name and your race! Out now, with you, and be gone!'*

"Are you there, then?" The voice was calm, expectant, knowing.

"Yes." Michael Riley's eyes were closed, the phone pressed hard against his ear, his head down, breath short. "Is this...is this Sean?"

"Aye, you remember, now, do you? Good on you, lad!" There was a shifting about over the phone, a clearing of the throat. "No, not Sean, now. 'Tis about him though, sure enough. We'll need to be meeting, you and I."

Michael Riley's head came up sharply, his eyes open wide. 'Meet?' He stood up, looked around the kitchen, fixing on the window out on to Connecticut Avenue, alert to sounds and sights that might show where this voice was from. A quick look to the door, now, and quicker still to it, setting the chain lock. "'Meet?' Who are you? *Where* are you? *What's this all about?*"

"Aye, we have your attention, then? We'll be needing that, sure. I'll be back to you this evening, half seven, if you've time..." A click and then gone. Silence...

A hand covered his right hand, gripping it. "Mr. Riley? Can you hear me, Mr. Riley?"

He looked to his right, a nurse now clear in his vision, a sterile cap over her hair, her mouth and nose covered by a gauze mask. Starting to speak, he was unable to...something in his mouth, down his throat. He nodded 'yes,' motioning with his mouth and chin that he wanted to speak, squeezing her hand for emphasis.

"You want to speak?"

He nodded, comforted that she understood.

"It'll be a minute or two. Try to relax, work at it. You've been through a lot. You're doing quite well, but your body has been through a lot and there are things we have to take care of."

He closed his eyes, felt a slight swoon, gripping her hand for balance. Looking at her, he could see she was smiling at him, nodding to reassure as others' hands were on him, moving quickly, removing tape from his left arm and at his ankles and calves...the sound of tape coming off his skin.

The first nurse lifted his head gently and surely from behind. "Open wide, now, Mr. Riley" and the tube from his mouth was gone. Coughing, he brought up some phlegm which she took with a tissue and then adjusted the oxygen feed under his nose and rested his head back.

"I need to speak with my wife...it's very important. Do you understand?" His throat was dry, scratchy, his voice raspy.

"Yes, I do. She's just down the hall. We've told her you're awake. A few things more and we'll be bringing her in."

Michael Riley felt his body now relax as he worked the dryness out of his mouth.

"Would you like some water?"

He nodded as she reached for a cup with an angled straw and brought it to his lips. Nodding a thank you when done, he caught a look of his wife Margaret just outside the door, her hands joined at her bosom, her face aglow, her eyes tearing.

She looked at the nurse beside her who nodded a 'yes' and she came into the room, hesitant at first, then closer, reaching for his outstretched hand, holding it for a moment, then bringing it to her lips to kiss before holding it against her, her grip warm and sure.

"Margaret, we have to talk, I must tell you something. It's very important..." Michael Riley moved in the bed, resetting his shoulders as he gave his head a slight shake. He was about to speak but stopped, turning to the nurse at his right. She smiled and moved off, drawing the others in the room with her, to just outside the door. Michael Riley turned back to his wife. "Margaret, I have to tell you about Sean, my son, about Maira, and the years in Dublin, about…"

Margaret Riley put her fingers to his lips, stopping him. "You already have, Michael. Years ago…you've told me…you don't remember?"

"No…You're certain, Margaret?" He raised up, fixing on her eyes, seeing that she was telling the truth. "I have then…" He looked away. "Just had a dream about it…First time I've even thought about it…them…in years…" He closed his eyes, the voice now again in his head, the edge of it, his name said. He looked left as if expecting to see someone, then back at Margaret. "You're sure it's alright, that we're okay? You and me? You're sure?"

"Yes, dear. Like before when you told me, it's before, all before…"

The nurse's hand reached toward their joined hands, holding them. Her voice. "He's fine, Mrs. Riley. Just the anesthesia wearing off. That's all. He'll be drifting in and out. Twilight is what we call it." She placed Michael Riley's hand on the edge of the bed and took Margaret's arm, leading her out of the room. "Don't you worry, now, he'll be…"

The voices trailed off as Michael Riley's mind wandered back to the call and the call back. 'Half seven' he'd said and half seven it was. To the minute. Matt Kane's was where they were to meet, 'At nine, now,' the voice had said. 'Come alone. We'll know if you're not.' There'd been a pause here, then '…I'll know you when I see you. And why not be wearing that fine walking hat you got for yourself at Garfinkel's? Spring Valley, if I'm right. Saturday last, you and the missus and that lad of yours. I'll be wearing one me self, that and dark glasses, with a full face of hair, too… nine, now, and alone.'

And so it was in the upper room at Matt Kane's, the Guinness a-flowing and songs a-singing and barely enough light to strike a match for a smoke in some parts of it. It was 1983, twenty years plus since Michael Riley had last seen Maira and their son, Sean. They'd met, Michael and Maira, in 1955, he on a rugby tour with Old Blue. They were Columbia University alums - doctors and lawyers and architects and investment bankers and brokers – all chasing rugby balls and the colleens who fancied the game and the lads who played it.

"I need to get your name before we start." Michael Riley leaned across the table, talking above the music, a tin whistle and guitar. He was close enough to the man to see his own face reflected on the lenses of the man's sunglasses, large and wrapping around the corners of his upper face.

"Indeed?" The man leaned over from his side of the table, a quick drag of his cigarette. "Just so we're clear from the start, now, Mr. Michael Francis Riley, *I'm* the one saying what you'll be needing and what you'll be getting." Another pull on his smoke, a thick, filter less cigarette, its smoke wafting about his face and head.

"Well, then, tell me. I'd be very interested to learn just what it is I *need* and what I am going to be *getting*."

A quick drag as the man sat back a measure. "Well, truth be told, I'm expecting it's by way a favor I'm doing you, Mr. Riley, to you and to others."

"A favor? Really? The biggest favor you could do for me is put that goddam cigarette out!"

"Christ, in heaven, it's a Yank I've here. Aye, a Yank sure enough, through and through. Strutting about like the Lord High Commissioner himself, barking orders and not knowing nothing of what's to come." He raised his head, several days' full of whiskers on his face and neck. He wore a thick mustache, wide above his mouth, it all pulled together by the sunglasses and his walking hat, it down over his forehead for good measure.

Coming forward again, a deep drag of the cigarette taken and speaking with the exhaled smoke keeping time and pace with the words. "The favor I'm thinking of is getting you and your lad Sean together again! How's that, now, from a man unknown on a cold September's eve?"

Michael Riley had been struck dumb. Sean was five when he'd last seen him, when Maira had thrown him out. He would go over for August back then, sometimes longer, and Christmas when he could, too. It was the way she wanted it, and it was fine by him, as well. Slaving as an associate in a Wall Street firm left little room for a family, even for an American woman raised to expect the early widowhood of the wife of a coming-up lawyer.

The routine was five years and more of 80-hour weeks in the gilded sweat shops about Battery Park and mid-town. Sure, it was no place for a high-spirited Dubliner whose life was the 'cause,' a united Ireland under one flag and one church. A waiter hustling by brushed by Michael Riley's right shoulder, bringing him back to the upper room at Matt Kane's, his eyes now on the man. "Where is he? *How* is he?"

"Well, now, here we are! *Dad of the Year*, he is! Wondering and caring about his lad, gone from him near a quarter century now, not caring a goat's turd all the while..." As the man was lifting his Guinness in mock toast, Michael Riley moved sharply forward, reaching across the table with his left hand, quick grabbing him by the collar of his shirt and landing a full, crushing right just below the man's sunglasses, sending him off his chair against the wall and down in a heap on the floor.

Michael Riley cleared the table from his way, rising to his full height and checking those about, staring off any who might be interested in a piece of it. As he expected, the man was alone, there was no 'we' about him, just one man playing over his game.

Turning back down at him, he could see the man was out cold. He took a full glass of Guinness from a man standing by and emptied it with a thrust of his arm, landing it full on the man's head and face. Returning the glass with a nod of thanks, he reached down and pulled the man up against the wall, holding him with his left forearm and grabbing his face with his right hand, under the chin and up, shaking him. 'Wake up, now. Come on. A thick Irish head like that? Come on, now."

A man to his right moved a chair by the wall next to the man and Michael Riley lowered him down in it, releasing him as he turned to the barman. "A round for any man near, and double for this one." He motioned with his thumb at the man whose Guinness he'd poured on the man and another nod of thanks.

Turning back to the man, now reeling in his chair, Michael Riley righted the chair he'd been sitting on and sat down, reaching for the upturned table and setting it to his left and between them. "You okay?" He reached across and grabbed the man by his left ear, shaking his head hard and banging it against the wall behind him. "You listening? You okay?"

The man nodded as two fresh Guinnesses arrived. Michael Riley passed him one and took the other for himself, taking down a full quarter of it in a pull and putting the glass on the table with a thud. "Now, where were we? Ah, your name, and what you're doing here?"

"Foock off, you…"

Michael Riley's open right hand came across the man's face with a sharp 'Crack!' "What? I gotta knock you out again? Put you on the floor again? I can do it. You know that. And I got all night. Hell, I got all week. Live here, you know. Question is, just how many teeth do you want to lose in all this?"

The man closed his eyes, nodding slightly. Taking a deep breath, he sat up, fixed on Michael Riley as he wiped his nose, reaching for the Guinness and bringing it to his mouth for a pull.

He was young, younger than his voice on the phone, maybe 22 or 23 years with a medium build on a tallish frame, maybe six foot. Putting his glass down, he reached in his jacket pocket for his cigarettes, taking out a pack. Michael Riley snatched it in his right hand, crushing it as he threw it to the floor. "New rules. No smoking. Things'll kill you." He winked at the man, nodding. "Now, let's try it again. What's your name and what are you doing here…and *where's my son?*"

The man looked down at the crumpled pack of cigarettes, then back at Michael Riley as he reached for his drink, sipping then holding it in both hands. "Bryan Canny…"

"And…?"

"And what?"

"…And what are you doing here?"

"That's going to cost you a cigarette, a whole pack."

"Chrissakes." Michael Riley turned to the bar, half standing as he raised his hand to the barman, keeping Bryan Canny in the corner of his eye. "A pack of cigarettes when you get a chance."

"Right…Brand?"

"Whatever will kill him quickest."

The barman turned to a drawer behind and took out a pack of *Camels*, throwing them over. "Here you go. On the tab?"

"Right. Thanks." Michael Riley opened the pack and handed it over. "Need a light?"

Bryan Canny looked over, not answering as he took a *Bic* lighter from his jacket pocket and lit the cigarette, taking a full drag and exhaling at Michael Riley.

"And…?"

"And what?"

"And why are you here? What do you want from me?"

Another drag and a pull on the Guinness. "Like I said on the phone, it's about Sean." He paused, gauging Michael Riley's reaction. "What I want from you is money. Seems you've got your fair share of that."

Michael Riley ignored the remark as he leaned forward, his left forearm on the table surface, his right arm at his side, ready to strike if needed. "Where is he? *How* is he?"

"He's across the border, in the North." A quick drag. "As to how he is, I'm not certain." Bryan Canny sat up, fixed hard on Michael Riley. "He's a hostage. The *Free Ulster Brigade's* got him and they want something in return."

"Money?"

"No. They want a man, a murdering son-of-a-bitch named Liam Halloran."

"Is there a ransom?"

"Are you *listening*? They don't want *money*. They want Halloran and if they don't get him, they'll kill Sean…"

"Then what's the money for?"

"To go in and break him out, for Chrissake…What'd you think?"

CHAPTER TEN
Anonymous

I t was just three years now. A record she'd been told. But there was no way of knowing for certain. Dates weren't marked down on this sort of thing, ledgers kept. Not at all. There were, of course, those before her, each one smart, all attractive, ambitious, yes, this before all else. And all *very* professional. These were women who knew how things worked, women at ease with the *perfect*, unhesitating in their expectation of it and highly comfortable in insisting on it.

Her first real contact with Keith Pierson was at a closing in St. Louis. "*Ground Breaking*" was how the local media had headlined it, an orgy of sorts, print, TV and radio types, all near blinded in the light of the great one, Sam Walton himself, desperate for a quote or picture worthy of a wire service.

It was to be the first 'Big Box' in the state with the media rallying around, singing praises and wondering at the sheer size of it all. Yes, *Sam Walton* at the table, pen in hand, looking up from the contract, flashing his teeth, eyes bright with Keith Pierson across the table, grinning his grin.

It had two sides, it did, a Keith Pierson grin. The outside of it was genial and engaging, even disarming to some. Here was a man who knew how to bring a thing together, how to assemble the properties, work the contractors, arrange the big money, line up the brokers, make a better world.

On the inside, now, the grin was about *the win*, the land owned and held with Sam Walton's name on the building and his signature on a twenty-year lease with adjustment clauses going Keith Pierson's way on taxes,

EPA mandated installations and upgrades, infrastructure improvements and every other thing that could go up. This was Keith Pierson's way and place, in the middle, critical to an enterprise's success, first in line on the cash flow and last in line on the risk.

She had been on the other side of the table that day, just three to the left of Sam Walton. Walmart had taken her fresh out of Stanford Graduate School of Business and put her in site acquisition and development. 'A natural' some had said of her after six months on the job.

Raised in Oklahoma, she had come to the ways and workings of Walmart like a newborn child to its mother's breast. She didn't *work* at Walmart, she had become *of* it. It was all one continuous flow, all twenty-four hours of each day, all seven days of each week.

Feeling Keith Pierson's eyes on her at several of the prep sessions as the project came to closure, she had looked away, avoided engaging. It was at the signing, though, that their eyes had locked for a moment, he nodding a smile, the briefest thumbs-up to her. At the reception following, when all the hand-shaking had been done with thoughts gone to other things, the next project, the flight back, he had sought her out.

Congratulating her on the team she had put together, he took her arm at the elbow and led her to one of the two bars. Catching the bartender's eye, he turned to her, "Scotch rocks, I believe?" Surprised he knew what she drank, she smiled, nodding her nod.

Seamlessly he turned the subject to skiing the high powder at Aspen, knowing that she had just been there, seeming to expect her to know that the hotel she had stayed at was a Mid-America property. She did.

She was to join Mid-America a month later, wooed by an evergreen, two-year contract at twice her Walmart salary with bonuses to boot. An executive vice president in his retail properties division, she soon joined his entourage, never far from his side whether it be New York or London or Dubai or Aspen or wherever else Keith Pierson wanted to be.

Moving to Chicago, she had taken a duplex in Marina City over the Chicago River but found more and more of her time spent in his private floor office and residence at the Blackstone Hotel. In a rare weekend off for a B-school reunion in the year after joining Mid-America, a classmate had asked her which she liked best, the man or the job? She had laughed as she had learned to do, closing the subject.

Fact was, though, she didn't know, not really. In the world of the perfect, *all* was perfect, each element and each part of it coming to be of equal weight, all part of the same *perfect*. She had come to understand that, in the world of the perfect, there can be no confusion, no dispute, because there can be only one answer, only one allowable solution on which there can be no compromise, no retreat – *the perfect*.

But this was all before November 1992 when William Jefferson Clinton had won the presidency from an early-retiring George H. W. Bush. Most improbably, Little Rock, Arkansas, had become a world center, an occasional White House, the official residence of the President of the United States of America.

Yes, Little Rock, home to the leader of the most powerful country the world had ever known. All this and not fifty miles from where Sam Walton had grown up and was now changing how the country was buying its stuff.

Keith Pierson had met Clinton early on at a private fundraiser for the Democratic Leadership Council. A 'comer,' he had told her later. The DLC, now, was Keith Pierson's sort of Democrat - comfortable with business leaders and more than happy to leave the tree hugging and spotted owls to those Democrats who had perfected losing national elections to B-grade actors and weak-fisted vice presidents.

At the beginning of Mid-America's negotiations with Hennessey, she had been in and out of the sessions, depending on whether retail and related properties were on the table. It was at a time, though, when Mid-America was tightening its focus on the Washington market and Hennessey's properties there, and soon he was bringing her to every meeting, making a point of getting her read on Brigit Winslow.

'Player or go-fer? That's what I need to know.'

'Player' had been her call, and Keith Pierson had nodded.

'Townsend thinks John Riley's up to something here, pulling out, maybe…You see anything like that? Get any vibes from her?'

He had asked this in the car on the way to the airport, more a demand, as she now thought about it. She had gotten to know Brigit Winslow well. They had done site inspections together, worked depreciation tables, cash flows, quality of tenants, site demographics, talked business and B-schools. Knew her pretty well. 'No,' she had said, 'not at all. Seems it's been her baby all the way.'

He had sat in his 'I-want-to-be-alone' seat as they boarded the plane, buckling in for the flight down to Bentonville, Arkansas, and the fundraiser Sam Walton was hosting for the Clintons. Going aft, she buckled in on a settee by the small cocktail table, the number three rolling over in her mind, 'Yes, three years…and counting?'

"Ever met a President before?" Keith Pierson had asked her as they deplaned, knowing full well that she had not. "Well, you'll want to watch out," he said with a wink. "This one'll try to bed you if you're not careful!" His laugh here had an edge to it, a harshness, reminding her of when she had first come to work with him.

The Hennessey properties were on Keith Pierson's mind, more so each week, it seemed. Even more certain, Keith Pierson's eyes had turned increasingly to Washington itself, spending more time there, day trips seeing this Senator or that Representative, all with Mid-America's chief lobbyist, Sheila Parkinson, the newly-hired, youngish widow of a Senator from New Mexico. Sheila Parkinson was on his mind as well...

Yes, three years was a record of sorts, she guessed. Time enough, surely. It was at the picture taking, though, that she knew for certain, the grip-and-grin in the hotel lobby between the private reception for the large donors and the ballroom dinner. Sheila Parkinson had flown to Bentonville from Washington and was quickly at home because Washington itself had just flown into Bentonville aboard Air Force One.

It was Sheila Parkinson at Keith Pierson's side, moving him here and there, her hand at his elbow, nodding and smiling, getting him in front of Senators and other notables in attendance, governors and such. And it was Sheila Parkinson at Keith's side for the picture taking with the Clintons and Mr. Sam. Yes, Keith Pierson with the President and the First Lady, Keith and the Keith Pierson grin, two-sided and, from a distance, distant.

Then there were Keith's words to the First Lady, she all a-sparkle, eyes so bright they seemed to light the room, her smile still coursing the far galaxies of Washington and beyond. She and Sheila exchanged smiles and words, a bit of head-back-laughter with teeth flashing white and showy and then Keith's hand out, taking Hillary's in both of his, and a brief word...'We're going to be neighbors just across Lafayette Square...'

They were all forward in the G-IV now, on the way back to Chicago. Sheila Parkinson was onboard, to go to a Mid-America Board meeting the following morning and the talk was of politics in general and public housing finance legislation in particular. Keith Pierson was moving on to new galaxies from which retail property acquisition and development would be at best a fading star, left to burn low and out in the far recesses of a universe past.

Yes, a good run, she thought, three years. Not bad at all, really. Signaling the steward for a drink, she nodded pleasantly to Keith and Sheila and rose, starting for the rear cabin of the plane.

A slight smile came to her face as she sat, thanking the steward for her drink, breathing easier, head back, eyes closed, thinking now of her mother's smile, and her words, 'Now, darlin', just you be sure to remember the one thing your mama been telling you. You know, the *one* thing?'

'Yes, mama,' she had said, 'I do remember, and always will, the *one* thing… Do not expect any more from any man than he is able to give you. *Never, as in, do not ever, do that…*'

CHAPTER ELEVEN
Morning Mass

M aking the 6:30 mass on weekday mornings was not as easy as it once had been. Mary Riley lay in her bed, a dawn glow in the windows of her room facing west toward Connecticut Avenue. She had heard John Riley leave at six, headed for the river and his morning scull.

She had not slept well, Mary Riley hadn't, thoughts of her Michael at Georgetown Hospital, this in time quieted by her murmurings of Hail Mary's and Glory Be's and Our Father's, her fingers working the beads of her rosary on her chest as she lay in her bed.

Raising the sheet and cotton blanket, she sat up, her legs over the edge of the bed, her hands firmly on its edge. Looking down at her knees, she tried to remember which one had gone soft on her. Painful was the word by dinner time, painful and stiff. The mornings, though, there was just a softness, a slight discomfort and a sense that it was not as strong as it once had been, a sense that she'd better not test it too hard, lest it fail altogether.

"Only one way to find out, there is..." She eased her weight forward, her feet finding the cotton rug beside her bed, toes first and then heels as her weight shifted from the bed to her legs. Upright now, she shifted her weight from left to right to left. "Right side, knew it, I did...that's something, I reckon." She shifted back to the right, flexed her knee. "Not so bad as yesterday... a good sign." Leaning forward, she stepped slowly to the bathroom. "Pitiful, is what...grateful to get to the pot by me self without falling over or peeing me knickers."

Brigit had spent the night and had drawn 'Nana detail,' walking her grandmother past the two houses to

Brookville and the short block to Blessed Sacrament. The 'detail,' begun several years ago, usually fell to Eileen. Dr. Peterson had recommended it strongly, saying he 'wouldn't be responsible' if they didn't. Mary had resented it, so deeply at first that she almost gave up weekday mass altogether. In recent months, though, she was glad of it, her hearing weaker and her step less certain. 'Tis for those gone before me that I go, you know,' she'd once confided to Brigit. 'Not so much to pray for 'em, you'll be knowing, as the being with 'em…'

Of the people in Mary Riley's life, far more had passed than were present, and of those still about, she knew fewer and fewer of their names. Bothered by this as it came upon her, she had come to a comfort with it. To her thinking, it was the privilege of the old to smile and nod at those saying to her 'Hello, Mrs. Riley and good day to you, now' without her having to remember or speak a name in return. It seemed to please them well enough to see her getting about without having to help her across a stream or up a stair, this all being just fine with her, as well.

"Nana?" There was a knock at the door. Brigit, no doubt. "Ready for mass?"

"Aye," says she, more to herself, now, just turning on her bureau light and making for the closet. "Yes, yes, a minute, dearie, no more…" Opening the closet door, she reached for her slip that hung just inside it. Lifting it over her head and shoulders, she let it fall down the length of her body, smoothing it out with her hands down the front. "One," says she.

Turning on the closet light, she reached for her Wednesday wear, a red wrap dress. Removing it from the hanger, she opened it, putting her arms through the arm holes and drawing it closed in front. "Two," she murmured to herself as her eyes found the foot of her chaise. Sitting down, she put on her dark brown oxfords, tying them firmly and testing her weight. "Three, four, and no more."

Steadying herself with her hands on the chaise, she sat forward and pushed herself up, holding herself erect for a count before starting for the door. "Pitiful is what…"

They had walked in silence to church, Mary taking Brigit's arm at the curbs and steps, these done one at a time, her right knee soft but still better than she remembered from yesterday and why push your luck?

For Mary Riley, mass had become a prelude to prayer. Prayer had become the being amongst her memories, a feeling that ran deep inside, a sense of self and belonging. In the after quiet of an empty church, she would run through the names, calling them up from within – Paddy and Dennis, her mother Nora and her Da, too, the first man in her life and the one against whom all others would be measured.

Then there were memories and thoughts of Joe Hara and his smile and heart, such a dear friend, and Capt. Kane, too. Aye, Captain Edward Kane, late to her life but a man whose sense of self was greater than that of any other, her Paddy included, this coming no doubt from the forty and more years given to him to sort it all out. And then Kevin, dearest Kevin, and their last days, *then,* their last visit together…his eyes seeming to glow, fixed on the Eucharist, the quiet of the place, the purest silence of it all…

Mary Riley's hands were now at rest, lying open on her lap, full and warm, her eyes closed, her breathing easy. As quick, though, a vision of her Michael came to her, lying still on a bed in a room all white, curtains drawn, empty but for him, his eyes closed, his skin sallow… "No" she spoke aloud, then louder still, "NO! Not my Michael, now!"

She bolted forward, gripping the back of the pew in front of her, pulling herself up by it to her full height, near on her toes, her eyes fixed on the tabernacle, her right arm now raised and a fist made. "You won't be taking my Michael, now! Not afore me, You won't! Not afore me! You've taken my Dennis and my dear Paddy, then Kevin, too, the dearest lad ever there was, You've taken them each in Your wisdom, but You won't be taking my Michael! Not before his new born knows him! You won't be doing that, now, not so long as I have breath in me...!"

Mary Riley froze stiff in her stance, her right arm still raised, a fist still made, no breath taken, her eyes open and blank, unseeing. Coming off her toes, she turned slowly to Brigit, seeing her face struck silent, a horror come to it, her mouth parted, her eyes on Mary.

"What have I done, Brigit? Oh, Dear Lord, what have I done?"

Brigit's hands had come to her face, her head shaking slowly left and right...blessing herself, reaching for Mary...

"Back now, back I say! Stay clear! Stay back...don't be touching me...I've blasphemed the Lord, is what..." Mary Riley looked about the empty church, fixing back on the altar as she eased herself to her knees, crossing herself. *O My God, I am heartily sorry for having offended Thee...*" Blessing herself repeatedly, she cowered forward, her shoulders heaving as she cried, words of prayers mumbling and tumbling out of her mouth.

"Nana, Nana, look at me..." Brigit moved to her. "Stop this..." She moved closer, putting her right arm across her back, pulling her close. "You've done nothing wrong, Nana, nothing." Gripping Mary's left arm, she held her closer still as if to shield her. "You've done nothing wrong."

Moving closer to Brigit, Mary Riley, now silent, braced herself against the pew in front of her, great and deep breaths taken, a moment held.

Separating from Brigit, she knelt forward, her elbows on the pew back, her face in her hands, her breathing eased. She could feel her whole body coming to a balance with what was about her...the pew and the aisle beside her, the vaulted ceiling above and the altar before her. She was now resting on her knees, no weight, no pain...and then the silence, the complete and purest silence of another time, unspoiled. Opening her eyes, she looked about the church, her head held low... "Kevin, now, is that you lad?"

CHAPTER TWELVE
The Trust

J ohn Riley had graduated from Gonzaga College High
School in June 1944, a Thursday afternoon convocation
with him leaving for Parris Island the following week. His
promise to Paddy Riley to finish high school having been
honored, there was his duty to do – to fight for his country
and to kill the man who had killed his father.

John Riley never came to Gonzaga without thinking
about this, about Paddy and the war. This was not in an
emotional sense, just there, a mark in time, a part of him.

This morning, John Riley was expecting to have been
in Chicago, working The Deal. Still waking at 5 a.m., his
normal time, he'd felt strangely unburdened, the sense of
pause that may have come in years past from an avalanche
closing a mountain pass or, today, a fog covering an airport
leaving the world's travelers and shakers stuck in place with
no buttons to push or orders to give. All of a sudden, there's
a block of time unassigned, a hole in the times of a week
when there is nothing to do because nothing can get done.

Is this what retirement is like? John Riley wondered,
the question rolling over in his mind as he made his way up
the front steps of the school. Letting himself in, he breathed
the aroma of the varnished oak woodwork lining the plaster
hallway leading to the President's Conference Room. It was
the fall meeting of the Board of Trustees of the Hennessey
Trust. He had served on it since 1968, the year Mary Riley
had stepped down as Chair of Hennessey Construction.

Jack Hennessey had established the Trust in 1936,
just before his passing. For the last eighteen years of his
life, he had taken under his wing the toughest, brightest
kid in that year's Gonzaga graduating class who was not
able to go on to college. Dubbed 'Squires,' they drove his

car, ran his errands, scanned the newspapers and read at least ten books from his library. Boarded in his basement, there was one day and night off each month to be with family, no girl friends allowed and absolutely no alcohol.

When finished the year, a Squire would have met everyone there was to know in the Washington, DC, construction industry and a fair number of the bankers, lawyers and others of commercial success related to it. The pay was $50 a month, most of which was expected to be saved for college. The Trust had been established to keep this going, to provide college loans for Gonzaga graduates. There was only one unshakeable, unassailable rule: It was a *loan* - and to be repaid, every dime, every cent of it, no exceptions allowed.

Not having expected to attend this morning's meeting, John Riley had no papers. Up from the river and a morning's row, he had stopped by the hospital to see Michael Riley. He was asleep, though, and not scheduled for a wakeup until 10. Stopping by his office for a shower and change, it was now 7:45 and Fr. Frank Kelleher, President of the school and Chair of the Trust, stood by a credenza pouring coffee for two others, Matt Malloy and George Cole.

Matt Malloy had been on the Board since the Trust's founding in 1936. George Cole had come on in the mid-1980s, John Riley having introduced him to the group, where he found quick acceptance. Frank Kelleher was the first to see John Riley and he raised his cup. "Here's a pleasant surprise..." The others turned, smiling as they raised their cups.

"Just couldn't stay away..." John Riley closed on the group, shaking each offered hand and pouring himself a cup of coffee, half decaffeinated, half regular. Raising his cup before sipping, he nodded to Fr. Kelleher. "My Chicago trip was interrupted." He winked at Matt Malloy. "So here I am, no papers to fumble through, but ready to play."

Susan Hayes, Fr. Kelleher's assistant, knocked on the door to the President's office, opening it just enough to peer in. "Mr. Carter just called in to say he'll be delayed and that you should start without him."

"Thank you, Susan." Fr. Frank Kelleher looked at the others and shrugged, nodding to the table. "Shall we?"

As they moved to their seats, the door opened again, full way this time, with Susan Hayes stepping in to lay a briefing book in front of where John Riley was about to sit. "Thought you'd find this useful, Mr. Riley."

"Yes, thank you, Susan." John Riley smiled as he waited for her to step away from the table before taking his seat. Pulling his chair back and sitting down, he turned back the purple cover of the book, reading down the Agenda, his eyes fixing on item four – *Capital Campaign, Mr. Cole*. "Yes," he had heard himself whisper under his breath, "of course, George…Who else?"

Looking up, his eyes found George Cole whose head was turned away as he opened his briefcase for his copy of the briefing book. Of all the friendships of John Riley's life, that with George Cole was the most improbable.

They had first met in the spring of 1968. John Riley, for reasons he had not shared with anyone, had decided to 'hire across town.' Hennessey Construction's books were filling and men would be needed for training in the building trades. It was just after Kevin's last visit when John Riley had spoken to Kevin about bringing men in from Appalachia where Kevin was a social worker. Kevin would have none of it. 'What about men across town?' he'd said. 'There's hundreds of them, looking for work, thousands, even, begging for jobs, needing a start but being kept out. Why not them?'

John Riley had balked. Hennessey Construction Company wasn't an employment agency let alone an engine for social change. He had no interest in stepping up to integrate the Washington construction trades. Before the night was done, though, he had given Kevin his word to 'do what I can.' To his great surprise, Kevin had asked him to shake on it, saying 'Whatever you can do, brother, will be enough.'

In shaking Kevin's hand, though, in giving his word, John Riley had not counted on Kevin Riley dying, and a hero's death, too. A promise made with uncertain prospect as to when it would be honored was one thing. It's a whole other matter when made to one who gives up his life for another. This had become something that John Riley had to get done. But how? John Riley had been at a loss. Not the sort of thing you put in the paper, 'Hey, Hennessey Construction hiring colored. You all come on in, now, hear?'

Upon due reflection, he had called Matt Malloy. "George Cole," Matt Malloy had said without a moment's hesitation. "He's your man. None better that I know of for what you need."

George Cole had been raised near Port Tobacco on the Maryland side of the Potomac, some 30 miles south of Washington. He had gone to Morgan State University, later graduating from Howard University Law School, near the head of his class. After the army, he had joined Haverty, McKinnan and Stein, which had been looking to strengthen its labor practice and make a bow to diversity in its associate base.

Making partner in 1965, George Cole soon led the firm's practice in fair housing and equal employment. It was the birth of the Great Society and some doors were opening, enough at least for a black man with a vise-like grip, a sharp mind and an engaging smile who had figured out how things work, how they get done.

By 1968, George Cole was a rising star in the Democratic Party. And in the smoke and smolder of the riots following the murder of Martin Luther King in the April of that year, white men in high places were seeking out men like George Cole. Washington the Capital, and Washington the city, had been shaken to their collective core, literally, with tanks and armored personnel carriers rumbling through the streets at midnight and troops standing post throughout the city.

Most shocking to John Riley had been the sandbag bunkers marking the corners of the White House facing Pennsylvania Avenue, each with a 50-caliber mount manned by soldiers in helmets and flak jackets with air cavalry units bivouacked across the street in Lafayette Square.

Hennessey's headquarters was on the corner of 15th and K streets, looking down on McPherson Square, its grass trampled and brown from the comings and goings of pedestrians and gawkers since the riots. In the circumstances, John Riley considered himself lucky to have started all this in March, before King's death.

On being alerted to George Cole's arrival, John Riley had stepped into the anteroom of his office, welcoming his guest with a firm shake of the hand. Though he had seen pictures of George Cole, he was struck by his presence – dark, at just over six feet with shoulders broad and full, George Cole needed little assistance in filling a room.

"Welcome, Mr. Cole. Thank you for coming."

George Cole had returned his handshake in kind, his large head nodding slightly forward and his deep-set eyes fixed directly on John Riley. "Very good of you to ask, Mr. Riley."

The voice was deep and, with George Cole's large, brown eyes bearing down, John Riley sensed quickly that this was a man of purpose, certainly power. Releasing the handshake, John Riley stepped back, motioning George Cole to his office. "Would you like some coffee?"

"Yes, that would be nice, thank you." George Cole looked directly at Grace Parker, John Riley's assistant who was standing to his right. "Black, please. Neither sugar nor cream."

"Yes, sir."

George Cole turned back to John Riley who motioned him toward the open door of his office. Stepping past George Cole to behind his own desk, John Riley motioned his guest to one of the two leather-trimmed armchairs opposite his own. As they sat down, Grace Parker brought in two cups of coffee, each on a saucer, handing one to John Riley and placing the other on a small table next George Cole.

George Cole looked up at her, smiling. "Thank you, Grace."

"You're welcome, Mr. Cole." She smiled quickly at him before looking at John Riley and heading back out of the room.

John Riley fixed on Grace Parker as she let herself out of the office, closing the door behind her. Holding his eyes away for a moment, he turned toward George Cole.

"So, Mr. Cole..." He stopped, smiling, leaning forward on his desk. "May I call you 'George'?"

"If it please you, Mr. Riley. Yes, by all means." George Cole had spoken without expression, his legs crossed and his hands folded in his lap.

"Yes...thank you, George..." John Riley had later faulted himself for not having asked Matt Malloy to be at the meeting. "Very good of you to come...how long have you known Mr. Malloy?"

George Cole had picked up his coffee saucer and cup and was just now bringing the cup to his lips. Pausing, he looked over the cup directly at John Riley. "Quite some time, actually. Matt and I were co-counsel in litigation in 1963, a class action dispute." He sipped his coffee and set the saucer back down on the table beside him as he sat back, his eyes now back on John Riley.

"You worked *with* Mr. Malloy, then..."

"Oh, yes...as I said, Matt and I were co-litigators." George Cole sat up straighter, re-crossed his legs, coughing lightly into his right hand before returning it to his lap, resting it atop his left.

John Riley fixed closely on George Cole, suddenly uncertain as to how to begin. Sitting forward, he rested his hands on the edge of his desk, gripping it. "You see...I...Hennessey Construction has been thinking about...has been wanting to take steps..."

Looking across his desk, John Riley fixed on George Cole's eyes, their intensity and, again, their sense of purpose. Moving forward to his desk, his elbows now resting on it, his shoulders forward. "Perhaps I should start at the beginning, explain why I have asked you here this morning."

George Cole nodded as he sat back, his eyes still fixed directly at John Riley.

"I have...had a brother. Name was Kevin. A younger brother, the youngest. He died last month."

"Yes," George Cole said, sitting up a measure, "I read of it...trying to save a young boy...tragic...He has earned our deepest admiration and respect. My sympathies to you and your family."

John Riley managed a "Thank you," as he fought a closing of his throat, an emotion rising in him, "that's very kind of you."

Their eyes fixed, held each other if for only an instant, John Riley blinking, speaking as he looked away. "The last time I spoke with him, Kevin, I made a promise to him to 'hire across town,' as he liked to put it. Truth is, we had had this discussion before, several times before. It was very important to him, you see."

George Cole nodded, as if he had anticipated what John Riley was saying.

"And because of that, and because I gave my word to him that I would, it has become important to me, as well, 'hiring across town'..." John Riley sat up, his hands now flat on his desk as he drew a breath. "I have asked you here this morning to help me, to help Hennessey Construction, to do that, to hire across town."

George Cole was motionless, not the blink of an eye.

John Riley sat back from his desk, his arms extended from his shoulders to the edge of it, his head at an angle. Still no reaction. "Matt Malloy tells me you are highly regarded in labor law. And more than that, a man of influence beyond the law. Here, in the city." He paused now, uncertain of what more to say, words swirling and colliding in his head - 'colored' and 'black' and 'ghetto.' Closing his eyes briefly, now he fixed more closely on the eyes of George Cole. "So, then…can you help me…in…"

George Cole's head had begun to nod slightly. "In...?"

"…in Hennessey Construction hiring across town. It's what I've been talking about…why I've asked you…"

George Cole suddenly sat forward in his chair, his eyes shifting in focus from John Riley's eyes to over his shoulder, fixing harder still, his upper body moving forward, his head now cocked. "I believe, Mr. Riley, that you have a picture of my grandfather on your wall…there, directly behind you."

"Your *grandfather*?" John Riley's eyes fixed on George Cole as he turned slowly in his chair to the wall behind him, now fixing on the spot that George Cole had. It was the picture from the fishing party in 1936 - John Riley at the center, holding a 38-pound rockfish across his chest.

Looking back quickly at George Cole, he turned again, fixing more closely on the picture. Squinting at the forms in it, John Riley could see over Jack Hennessey's left shoulder the image of Charles Ramsey, Jack Hennessey's handyman and barbeque cook. Charles Ramsey was standing by his grill, his eyes down at what he was cooking. Reaching slowly, John Riley took the picture off the wall, examining it more closely as he turned back to George Cole.

"May I hold that, Mr. Riley?"

"By all means..." John Riley half stood, offering the picture. "Here...please."

George Cole reached across John Riley's desk, taking the picture in both hands and sitting back in his chair, breathing deeply, his head moving slightly. "My, my...looky here..."

John Riley studied George Cole, now back in his chair. Sitting forward in his own chair, John Riley nodded at the picture. "Were...were you there, that night, Mr. Cole?"

George Cole looked up for a moment, then back down at the picture. "No. I was not there that night, Mr. Riley. That would not have been possible."

John Riley sat further forward, now against his desk, studying George Cole whose form remained still, his head and eyes fixed on the picture. John Riley cleared his throat. "I don't understand...impossible?"

George Cole continued to study the picture, his right index finger going to the face of Charles Ramsey. "You see, Mr. Riley, Charles Ramsey would never let any of his children or grandchildren see him work as a servant for a white man." George Cole now raised his head, fixing on John Riley. "...Ever."

He looked back down at the picture. "We were raised in Waterside, down river on the Maryland side. The closest white settlement was Port Tobacco. Colored folk from Waterside, they worked, most of them, in Port Tobacco. But they lived with their own, in Waterside." George Cole looked up at John Riley, nodding at him for emphasis.

"Grandfather Ramsey, now, he got good work up here in the Washington town. Paid well, not near what a white man made, but better than what any colored could do in Port Tobacco." George Cole sat forward a measure. "Grandfather Ramsey made learning his life's work. Learned everything he could. Learned how things worked so he could make a living fixing them when they broke.

Learned carpentry and how to work metal and cook barbeques and, of course, how to say 'Mr. Robert' and 'Miss Sue Ellen' to white folk."

George Cole passed the picture back now, across the desk to John Riley. "But he knew he was a man, too, just as they were men and women, and until they treated him as such, he had no interest in having his children see him taken for less than one…a man, that is."

John Riley, his eyes fixed on George Cole, took the picture, moving back from his desk, his eyes now on the image of Charles Ramsey. He remembered the time that Charles Ramsey had taught him how fillet a rockfish at the wetboard beside Jack Hennessey's rear stoop. Turning back to the wall, he hung the picture where it had been.

Sitting back down in his chair, he used his legs to push back to his desk. George Cole was turned toward the window overlooking McPherson Square, his profile showing a high forehead and a full, powerful neck.

Turning back from the window, George Cole re-crossed his legs as he lifted his chin. He nodded to the picture. "Grandfather Ramsey worked for Jack Hennessey for 38 years. At ten or so hours a week, that came to 21,280 hours. That's how 'Mr. Jack' figured it, anyway." George Cole's eyes set fixed away as he continued.

"Well, now, the evening of that fish roast," he nodded at the picture, his eyes now turning to John Riley, "the evening that picture was taken – well, that was when Jack Hennessey asked Charles Ramsey to stop by for lunch the following day. Said Mrs. Kennedy, Jack Hennessey's housekeeper and cook, would be staying special that Sunday to cook it. Yes sir, stayed special for Charles Ramsey."

He looked up now, his face easing, even to a smile of sorts. "…Grandfather Ramsey said it was the best Maryland Shecrab soup he'd ever tasted. He also remarked on the corn muffins. Grandfather Ramsey, you'll understand, had a particular weakness for corn muffins done right." George Cole nodded at John Riley who nodded back.

"Now at the end of that lunch, Jack Hennessey told Charles Ramsey that he was ill and would likely soon die. He thanked my grandfather for all the things he done for him over the years, keeping his place and doing his barbeques, and the friendship that they had shared. Then he reached for an envelope on a nearby table." George Cole leaned closer.

"'Charles,' he said, 'I figure you've been working for me for ten or so hours every week now for 38 years. That's a lot of hours, Charles, a lot of time, a lot of work. And in this time, I was never more pleased with any other person I've had in my employ, and there is no one's company that I more enjoy. You are a gentleman and a friend.' George Cole took a breath here, only one, no more, and continued.

"Then he said, 'Last week, Charles, I asked my accountant to figure up the difference between what a white man gets in this town doing what you do and what a colored man gets. Told him to spend as much time as it took, but it had to be done and done right. Well it did take him some time, and I am confident that it's done right and the number was 13.25 cents per hour difference. That's what he came up with.'

"With that, Jack Hennessey opened the envelope and took out a check in the amount of $2,819.60 and handed it to Charles Ramsey. 'This,' he said to my grandfather, 'makes us *even*, Charles. *Even*, you understand? I hope you will accept it with my sincerest thanks and very best wishes."

John Riley would later remember George Cole's eyes welling a measure as he spoke.

"Well, Grandfather Ramsey took that check to the Oysterman's Savings and Trust in Port Tobacco and with that, and other money he had earned, he put his three youngest children through college and four of his eleven grandchildren, myself included."

George Cole looked away for a moment, then back. "Grandfather Ramsey said that Jack Hennessey was as decent and honorable a human being as he had ever met. He made a particular point of telling each of us this before he died, that we should all know and always remember that there were white men of honor, white men who treated colored men with dignity and as equals...and were their friends."

John Riley nodded.

"And so, Mr. Riley, this is why *I* have come today. I have come to make certain that this company, Hennessey Construction, is worthy of the man who founded it. From what I understand of him, Jack Hennessey was a man who, in our time, would have stepped forward and done what is right...'hired across town,' as you put it."

George Cole sat forward, his right hand made in a fist resting on the edge of John Riley's desk, their eyes locked. "You see, Mr. Riley, it is not you who have chosen me. No, sir. It is *I* who have chosen *you.*"

George Cole, raised up a measure, his head back, his hand off John Riley's desk, resting on his right knee. "The only question now, Mr. Riley, is, have I chosen wisely?"

CHAPTER THIRTEEN
Heroes

"She's sleeping now." Eileen Riley stepped into the kitchen from the hall leading to Mary Riley's bedroom. Her daughter Brigit was sitting across from Mary Kate Rhinemann at the kitchen table, both having coffee after breakfast. They looked up as Eileen fixed on Brigit.

"*What* happened at mass?" Eileen sat down, her eyes still on Brigit. "She was trembling when you all got back, thumbing her beads, whispering Hail Mary's and Glory Be's. Never saw the like."

"That makes two of us..." Brigit shook her head as she rose and stepped to the sink. "Ever seen anyone '*blaspheme*' The Lord?" She looked at each Eileen and Mary Kate, shivering at the head and shoulders as she took Mary Kate's cup and rinsed it and hers before putting them both in the dishwasher, still shaking her head. "Something else, I'll tell you that."

Standing full up, Brigit fixed back on them. "Wouldn't let me touch her... thought she'd be struck dead by the Lord and me taken with her..."

Mary Kate was smiling as if about to laugh.

"Go ahead, laugh if you like..."

Mary Kate looked away, shaking her head, then back, a hand covering her mouth and the lower part of her face.

"Go ahead, laugh away...but in the moment - kneeling next to someone shaking and quaking to the core of her being? Well, let's just say it got pretty real..."

The others laughed as Brigit went to the far counter and opened her purse, her eyes peering inside. "Someone's got to get Mary Kate down to the hospital...and someone has to stay here with Nana..." She looked at her mother.

"I'll stay." Eileen went to the coffee maker and poured herself a cup. "She's used to having me nearby." She turned back to them, both now standing close by the table. "You two go. I'll get down later…Nana's going to have to go, I'll take her, see him then. Your father's going after lunch. Maybe we'll see him there."

"Works for me." Mary Kate rose and went to Eileen, their cheeks touching as she started for the pantry and the back stoop, picking up her purse as she went. Brigit was right behind, her keys in hand, motioning her mother a kiss.

———

Mary Kate Rhinemann settled in the front passenger seat, her purse on the floor at her feet. "Think she'll ever forgive me for naming my Patrick 'Patrick'?"

Brigit was driving, buckling in as she headed east on East Irving. "Mom?" She turned the car right on Brookville toward Western Avenue. "Don't know." Turning right again, she coasted the car along Western toward Chevy Chase Circle, holding there for traffic to clear. "Probably not. I know she'll never understand why I moved to New York so soon after college." Looking left, she accelerated into the Circle, going halfway around and continuing on Western.

Mary Kate resettled in her seat after buckling in. "Bet she blames me for that, too."

"Probably…a little, anyway."

"And why *did* you come to New York?"

Brigit stifled a yawn, stretching her legs out beneath the steering wheel. "Couple of things, really. First, though, was *the* city, the *Big Apple*. No other place like it in the world. Had to be there for a while, anyway. Then there's finance. I knew that's what I wanted to do and that's where it's done." She adjusted the rearview mirror.

"And it was time. I had to get out, get away. Boarding at Georgetown, a whole five miles down Wisconsin Avenue to a right on O Street to Front Gate - well, that's not exactly going away to college. Then there was Dad, too. He didn't want me far away. I knew that. Always spoke about it in terms of Mom, but I knew he wanted me near."

They had come to a red light, her eyes holding ahead, thinking back. "Wasn't so long after they'd put out Patrick, away, at Rollingwood. Didn't seem quite right to leave the house just then." She turned to Mary Kate, forcing a smile. "And, besides, I had a famous aunt on Madison Avenue. Who wouldn't want to play *that* card?"

"Yeah, sure..." Mary Kate shrugged in a New York sort of way. "Fat lot of good that did you on Wall Street... two different worlds..." She turned away, drew a deep breath, letting it out.

Brigit pulled out into the intersection. "Well, you knew where everything was, how things worked up there."

"I guess..." Mary Kate turned, fixed on to her. "Like what, exactly?"

"Like it's all right to jump some horny bastard's cab when he takes his eye off the ball to ogle your legs."

They both laughed as Brigit turned left on 41st Street, accelerating once on it. "It's a big, nasty place for a greenhorn and you were always there for me, my anchor to windward. It meant a lot to me." She paused, expecting Mary Kate to turn to her but she only nodded her eyes ahead. Were they tearing? "You alright? Kay? Have I..."

Kay Rhinemann wiped her eyes quickly with her fingers, drying them on the sides of her slacks before reaching for her purse, taking out a tissue. "No...I mean yes, fine, I'm fine." She wiped her eyes with the tissue and blew her nose. "It's nothing."

"Is it Michael? You know that I called this morning? Spoke to Margaret? He had a good night...a little breakfast, asking about Brendan..."

Mary Kate was shaking her head.

Brigit fixed ahead, on the traffic light at Nebraska, now accelerating to make it just as it turned yellow and getting through. Brigit had never seen her aunt cry before, certainly not from sadness or stress. She pulled to the curb, looked about to make a U-turn. "We can do this later, come back."

"No!" Mary Kate turned to Brigit, reaching for her arm and gripping it. "No, I'm sorry. I need to see him, do you understand? Michael. To hold his hand, to hear him speak..."

Brigit looked at her, their eyes fixing. There was a yearning in Mary Kate's eyes and something else as well, not quite fear, but certainly foreboding, a deep concern that in all their years together Brigit had never seen, her mind now flashing back to a high school assignment – three hundred words on "My Hero." The subject was easy, the problem was keeping it to three hundred words.

It was her Aunt Mary Kate, she was her hero, Mary Kate Riley who wouldn't stay in the house where her mother had denied her the love of Charlie Olmstead, not one night. It was Mary Kate Riley who would not be a model in New York, a walking, mindless cog in a cattle show. It was Kay Riley who would start her own fashion advertising agency in 1962 against all odds and make it work. It was Kay Riley who seemed to know everything, especially when to stay quiet, when to hold her own counsel, when to speak for effect not just to be heard.

It was Mary Kate Rhinemann who birthed Patrick Riley Rhinemann and named him after her father. It was Kay Rhinemann who on her son's tenth birthday flew him to an island in the Pacific where they stood together on a rusting pier over the crystal blue waters of the coral reef where Paddy Riley had died of a sniper's bullet. Yes. Mary Kate Riley Rhinemann was Brigit's hero, a person of character and purpose, and if Paddy Riley's soul was still about them all, it rested nearest to her.

It was for this that Brigit was concerned. Something was wrong, happening, even beyond Michael Riley's operation. Brigit slipped the car into gear and pulled back into the traffic, reaching over to her aunt who took her hand in both of hers, holding it in her lap.

"Can you talk about it, Kay?" Brigit felt Mary Kate's hands tense for an instant, then loosen as she moved her hand back to the steering wheel. Out of the corner of her eye she could see Mary Kate's head lower then rise, look away then fix back ahead.

"It's Patrick."

"Your Patrick?"

"Yes, my son Patrick...He's being recruited to join the Israeli Army. Two of his classmates have already left...in June, right after graduation." Mary Kate reached for the tissue again, bringing it to her eyes. "Nothing I say has any effect."

"And Michael, his *father*?'

Mary Kate caught her breath. "He's...torn...no other word for it, just torn. I think he's more frightened than I. He's been to hell and worse, you know...lived there...The whole thing, the camps, making bombs for those bastards...the Holocaust...the thing that started it all, *this whole goddam mess.*" She looked away, talking to the empty space before her. "Michael lost his whole family in it...Everyone...father, mother, sisters, a brother...just gone...How can he say...no?" She looked over at Brigit.

"And it's tearing *us* apart, my Michael and me. There are nights we hardly speak...working longer hours so there'll be no time to think about it, to fight about it. He could forbid Patrick to go and I believe that Patrick would obey. But he won't, or just can't... I don't know."

Mary Kate was quiet as the car made its way south on Reno Road, rising and falling over the cross hills of Cleveland Park, the morning sun breaking through the trees overhanging the roadway. "He's coming in Thursday, my Patrick. He promised he'd speak to his uncle Michael about it, before he made his final decision. Michael's his godfather, you know..." She turned to Brigit, smiling.

"Patrick adores him, his hero...Michael's why he took up rugby at school, why he's looking at law school...and why not? Knows everyone everywhere, Senators, Cabinet Officers...traveled the world, been everywhere and then marries a beautiful woman twenty years his junior and now has a son!"

Mary Kate smiled briefly then shrugged as she turned back. Ahead, the grounds of the National Cathedral passing on the right side of the car - the Cathedral's tower shining a bright limestone in the sun.

"No way he can talk to Michael about it now, not in the ICU. Margaret would never forgive me if I even mentioned it. Don't know what I'm going to do, who to turn to...Michael was my last hope." She looked through the open window of the car, reaching out with her right hand, cupping the air as they accelerated down a hill.

"It never ends, you know, never stops...the worrying. I was so happy to give my Michael a son. I will never in my life forget his eyes when he first picked up Patrick. I cannot describe the depth, the intensity of the feeling. Until just that moment, I had never truly understood what a *life* is, a human life, and to have *given* it, giving the one, most precious thing that there is, a human life...no idea..." She brought her right fist to her mouth.

"As I fixed on his eyes, looking at his just-born son, it was as if *I* had lived his life, had been in the camps, as if *I* had seen the horror of it. And to realize, to understand, that with this one birth, this one new life, that it was all, in some way, for him, over and done, past. For all the horror of it, the millions killed, butchered, he had made it through, and now, gloriously, had a son, his own son to carry all the rest ahead, forward. And now that son, our son, wants to go *back…into* it…"

Brigit had pulled into a cross street, stopped the car, now fixing on Mary Kate.

"We wanted more children, you know, right away." She turned to Brigit, her head shaking slightly side to side. "But it was not to be." She turned away. "I wanted to see my Michael's gaze again, those eyes on another newborn child, *his* newborn child, his life going on and all those before him with it…just wasn't to be, I guess…" A slight shrug as she turned away.

Brigit Riley Winslow turned ahead, imagining Mary Kate handing her newborn child to Michael Rhinemann and him holding his son, transformed. She slipped the car into gear, heading west on Fulton and on toward Wisconsin, an ache in her growing.

She wanted to be with Bertie, needed to be with Bertie, to hold him and to feel his arms about her, their bodies formed together. She wanted to be alone with him, somewhere together, away from every other living, talking thing, to breathe deep and full, her arms out wide and free with all the things of her life, *The Deal* and every other *thinking* thing, done and gone. Most deeply, though, she needed to have seen what Kay Rhinemann had seen in her Michael's eyes.

CHAPTER FOURTEEN
The Hay-Adams

"One of Brigit's best deals, maybe the best..." John Riley led Bryan Canny through the front doors of the Hay-Adams, an eight-story, Italian Renaissance hotel on the north side of Lafayette Square.

Built in 1928, it took its name from John Hay, private secretary to Abraham Lincoln, and Henry Adams, a direct descendant of presidents John Adams and John Quincy Adams. Closest of friends, Hay and Adams, and their successors, had adjoining mansions on the site from 1880 until the homes were razed in 1927 to make room for the hotel.

"Good morning, Mr. Riley." The hotel manager, Simon de Vries, had been expecting them, his hand out and smile ready. "Your table is waiting."

"Thank you, Simon." John Riley returned the smile, motioning Bryan Canny ahead, toward the elevator bay. "We're a little early, really."

Simon de Vries offered a slight nod, that he understood, as he walked alongside John Riley, only just slightly behind. "Shall I...?"

"That won't be necessary, Simon. Just wanted to show Bryan the view from the meeting rooms on the top floor."

"Yes, of course. If there is anything..."

"Yes, Simon, you'll be the first to know." John Riley stopped, fixed on the manager, smiling. "You're doing a great job hereabouts, Simon. The whole thing–restaurant, meetings, bookings, everything's going just great. Couldn't be happier. Bryan and I are just stopping by for lunch with an old friend, then we'll be on our way. Forget we're even here."

"Yes, sir." The manager offered a slight bow of the head as he pushed the call button for the elevator, standing away with his arm out as the elevator door opened and John Riley and Bryan stepped in past him. Reaching in, Simon de Vries pushed the eighth-floor button as the doors began to close, his smile holding.

"He's first rate." John Riley stood by the closed doors as the elevator started up, his head turning to Bryan Canny. "Brigit found him at the St. Regis in New York-head of catering there. Dutch…speaks six languages…makes me sick." He smiled at Bryan who laughed as the floor numbers clicked on the display above the doors.

"Not sure I would have done very well in the hospitality business. All the sucking up, the ready smile for anyone with the price of a room." The elevator came to a stop, its doors opening.

"Right this way, Mr. Canny."

John Riley attempted a Continental accent, smiling mechanically, a slight bow of the head as he motioned Bryan Canny out of the elevator. Following and then passing him as might a restaurant maître d', he motioned to the right, his step sure as he entered the *Top of the Hay* room. Turning them to the right, he stopped at the entrance, his arms out and about.

"The British Ambassador *insists* on this room for his most important functions." The accent faltering, a forced smile, Bryan Canny seeming not to know what to do. "And why is this?"

John Riley led them across the room, pulling open two curtained French doors, standing aside, his left arm extended, his hand open. "Monsieur Canny, *le Maison Blanche.*"

"Good Christ…" Brain Canny caught his breath, stepping forward for a clearer view of the White House. John Riley moved past him, stepping out onto a balcony that surrounded the top floor of the building at a width of eight feet. He motioned Bryan Canny through the doors, joining him at the railing, now looking out on Lafayette Square. Gripping the railing, standing erect, John Riley caught his breath as well. It never failed.

Before them lay the trees and plantings of Lafayette Square with Pennsylvania Avenue on its far side and then the front lawn of the White House. The North Portico was in partial shadow, a roof-top flag moving easily in the light, midday air with the Washington Monument to the left, framing his view. Now drawing an easy breath, John Riley marveled as the sun played off the Potomac River beyond, bathing the Virginia countryside in a hazel green for as far as the eye could see.

"Brigit got an early call on the place from someone in New York, worked for the Resolution Trust Corporation." He turned to Bryan Canny. "January '89. She bought up the paper on it for chump change and got the rest for not much more." John Riley nodded at Bryan Canny, smiling the smile of the proud father that he was. "The night we closed on the place, she told Eileen all about it, all the numbers. Know what Eileen said?"

"No."

"Told Brigit she should go to confession and give the place to the church."

Bryan Canny laughed hard, looking over to John Riley. "Sure, are you, now, John Riley, that your Eileen wasn't *born* in Ireland?"

Now they both laughed as John Riley relaxed, leaning against the railing, his elbows resting on it and his hands free. Breathing in a measure, his mind drifted back to Monday afternoon in Chicago. Keith Pierson was hosting a working dinner in his office suite on the 21st floor of the Blackstone Hotel. Brigit Winslow had been doing most of the face-to-face work with Pierson and this was the first time that John Riley had spent a full business sit-down with the man.

Keith Pierson as a type was not new to John Riley. He had worked with developers throughout his career and had come to understand that a person had to give them room. They were the idea men, the grinders, the guys who drove the whole thing and he was happy to be close enough to them to get their business, to build their buildings, to help them do their deals, their dreams.

But there was something more to Keith Pierson, something extra. John Riley sensed it in the people he kept around him. Their eyes were always on him. It was as if they didn't know what he was going to do, how he was going to react. And they never seemed entirely sure of themselves, either. Hank Johnson's words on the ride to East Irving came to him now, "How'd a nice fella like you ever mixed with a son-of-a-bitch like this?"

John Riley knew from Brigit that the Blackstone had been purchased out of bankruptcy by Mid-America Holdings in the mid-seventies. A multi-million-dollar restoration was undertaken to return it to its 1920s splendor when it claimed the title 'Hotel of the Presidents.'

As part of this, Keith Pierson had several of the rooms restored to their exact condition of that period. As the meeting had closed on Monday afternoon, Pierson had offered a short tour before dinner. Leading them to a waiting elevator, he ushered them all in, taking command.

"Now, I'm sure you've all heard of the 'smoke-filled room." A knowing smile and nod. "You know, where the politics of our republic actually gets done?" The elevator doors had opened at the eighth floor. "Well, you are now about to see the *original* smoke-filled room." He had motioned them to his left and the group found its way into a large suite overlooking Lake Michigan.

Stepping in after them, Keith Pierson had stood to one side. Before them, perhaps eight or nine chairs were set in a rough circle, some papers and open briefcases on the several coffee tables for effect.

"It was early June of 1920 and the Republican National Convention was in town. They'd been through nine ballots with everybody getting pretty tired of it all. The only thing they were all able to agree on was that, for the sake of the country, a 'return to normalcy' was needed after eight years of Woodrow Wilson."

On his toes, arms moving out and around, Keith Pierson assumed command. "There was all manner of trouble here and overseas, Red Russians killing White Russians, and vice versa, race riots, the League of Nations, a Yankee fear of foreign entanglements reinforced by Red-baiting from the far right.

"So, the leadership all trooped themselves up here and sat around in a circle, it being understood that no one was leaving this room until it was done. Now, Senator Warren Harding of Ohio was a *weak* dark horse when it all began. General Leonard Wood got the most votes in the first ballot. In all, there were a full dozen candidates to get through and sort out.

"Harding had been building steam and gained a plurality in the ninth ballot, but not enough to put him over the top. That happened here." Keith Pierson pointed down at the hardwood floor covered by a deep red oriental carpet fringed at its ends in white. "*This* is the room, restored to how it was at the time." He looked up, pointing them toward a framed article from the Associated Press, speaking from memory of the story reporting that Harding won the nomination in a 'smoke-filled room in the Blackstone Hotel.'

Amid the nodding and looking at the article, the picking up of this and that, Keith Pierson started the group back to the elevator, bringing them all to the tenth floor and another suite, this one not as large. Once inside, Keith Pierson nodded at his Kennedy memorabilia collection, making a point of catching John Riley's eye as the others examined a signed copy of JFK's inaugural address.

And then there were the photographs of Kennedy with his cabinet leaders, most notably Secretary of State Dean Rusk, Secretary of Defense Robert McNamara, and his brother Bobby Kennedy, the Attorney General, all serious and somber, men at work in a dangerous world.

"President Kennedy was sitting at that desk." Keith Pierson had motioned with his head and right arm to a mahogany desk behind which there was a leather trimmed, executive chair. "Rusk had told him that a call was coming in from McGeorge Bundy, Kennedy's National Security Advisor. There had been a report earlier that day of Soviet nuclear missiles in Cuba. They were all standing around Kennedy as he took the call, his face somber. 'No doubt of it, then?' Kennedy spoke into the receiver, his eyes moving among those about him, nodding to confirm the worst."

Keith Pierson had let his words sink in with the others now in the room. "There's a secret entrance to this room." He had nodded to his right. "But they weren't using it that night. No. They were headed back to Washington – to stop a nuclear war." He looked at each around the room. "Big stuff – and all right here in this room."

Allowing a moment for the impact to settle, Keith Pierson motioned his way back to the door, the others falling in line. "If you'll all step this way, there's another suite of interest on this floor. Just down the hall." Leading them into the living area of a large suite, he motioned left and right at more Kennedy memorabilia.

"Now this is the suite that President Kennedy used on another visit to Chicago, here to meet with regional business leaders." He pointed about the room, framed pictures of Kennedy with Roger Blount of US Steel,

Henry Ford II, other notables of commerce and industry. "Perhaps of even greater interest, though, might be found this way…"

Keith Pierson led his guests into the bed chamber, turning as he did to put finger to lips, his eyes teasing in anticipation. Feigning stealth, he tiptoed ahead into the room. Once in, he welcomed the others around as he stood at the foot of the double bed, his arms now extended, each to a photo portrait resting on the night tables beside the bed.

To his left, in evening twilight of the room, lit by the light of a shaded reading lamp, was the image of John Kennedy and, to his right, that of Marilyn Monroe, each picture angled and set toward each other, their eyes seeming to join, to engage.

Speaking softly, his eyes capturing each of his guests. "May we safely assume, gentlemen, *big things* happened here, as well? I think so…yes, most definitely…"

"John?" It was Bryan Canny, pointing to his watch.

"Yes, thanks." John Riley stepped back from the railing, leading them off the balcony to the elevator.

He remembered now that Brigit had turned away as Keith Pierson was speaking, moving to the rear of the group among the snickers and muffled guffaws of the others.

CHAPTER FIFTEEN
Semper Fi

S imon de Vries was waiting by the bell desk when they stepped out of the elevator on the lobby floor. "Mr. Canny?"

Bryan Canny looked quickly at John Riley and then nodded at de Vries, his head up. "Yes?"

Simon de Vries reached for the phone at the bell desk and quickly dialed a number, holding the receiver out for Bryan to take.

"Thank you." Bryan Canny turned away, the receiver to his ear. Nodding several times at what he had heard, a grimace coming to has face, then a slight shaking of the head. Handing the receiver back to de Vries, he nodded a thank you and turned to John Riley. "Server just crashed. We'll be up Saturday midnight, that's certain. There's plenty of time." He shrugged. "Problem is, it's *my* time!"

John Riley laughed as he waved him off. Bryan Canny started for the front door but stopped abruptly, as if he had forgotten something. Turning to John Riley he pointed at him, his finger poking the air between them. "And you're right, now, John Riley."

Halfway up the few steps to the dining room, John Riley stopped, looking back, his hand to his ear. "Right? About what?"

"About being a hotelier..." Bryan Canny glanced quickly at Simon de Vries whose eyes were away.

"Yes?"

"Would've *starved* at it, you would!"

They both laughed well now, Bryan Canny waving and out onto 16th Street and John Riley into the dining room, spying Hank Johnson, already seated at the table John Riley used when at the Hay-Adams.

Making his way among the tables, John Riley's eyes caught the White House from this angle, stately and commanding, larger even than from the roof just above, the yellow-blue sky open and deep beyond and around it. He motioned Hank Johnson back down in his chair and he took his hand to shake. "Good to see you, Hank. Glad you were available."

"Piece of cake. Just across the river, and I don't even have to drive you home...do I?"

John Riley smiled, looking away. "It was a long day, Hank. Chicago, The Deal, Michael in the ICU, maybe just needed a Marine nearby..." He turned back. "You know, *Semper Fi...*"

Their eyes fixed, now, each nodding, each knowing...

"Ah! M. Riley, *bon jour...*" It was Andre, the maitre d'. "A Diet Coke, perhaps, to start?"

"Thank you, Andre, a Diet Coke will do just fine."

"And you, Mr. Johnson, the Jack Daniels?"

"If you insist, yes, that will be fine."

Hank Johnson reached for an envelope resting on the seat beside him. "Here, this came in early." He handed the envelope to John Riley. "It's the wrap-up on the firms in Chicago."

John Riley took the envelope, opening it deliberately, pulling out the report and laying it before him, his eyes fixing quickly, tightly on one of the names - Charlie Olmstead, Partner, *Green, Olmstead and Kuerig*. Speaking Charles Olmstead's name under his breath, John Riley sat back in his chair.

"You know him?" Hank Johnson sat forward a measure, fixing closely on John Riley. "It occurred to me you might, he being from Chevy Chase."

"Sure do." John Riley looked up. "Used to date Mary Kate, years ago, before she left for New York." He scanned the report, coming to the second firm, the second name – Phillip Hastings, Partner, *Hastings Kline*. The same profile as Olmstead – president of Chicago Bar Association, graduate of University of Chicago, BS in Physics. He looked up at Hank Johnson. "Physics from *Chicago* and he's a *lawyer*?"

"Yeah, go figure...went into Rickover's navy. Worked in his office for a while, then law school when he got out. Of the two, he's probably the smarter, just on raw brain power, anyway."

John Riley looked up.

"As you require, John, they both have worked on real estate acquisition and development with the big insurance companies in Chicago – Continental, North American Casualty, Great Plains Life, pick one."

John Riley looked at the spread sheet comparing the two names confirming that they had each worked with the insurance companies participating in The Deal. Closing the report, he laid it on the table beside him, his mind going back to long ago, to when Mary had refused Charlie Olmstead and Mary Kate moved to New York. He had done nothing, stood back and apart, having convinced himself at the time that it was none of his business, only to know later that he should have done something. He turned to Hank Johnson. "Who do you like for it?"

"We only have paper on them. No first-hand contact..." He fixed on John Riley. "And besides, you asking me to pick between these fellas would be like Casey Stengel asking the bat boy who to start in the World Series." He sat back. "Don't know enough, Johnny Boy. Don't know a wren's feather of what I'd need to know to pick between guys in that league."

John Riley nodded, then looked to his left, across Lafayette Park to the White House. "Any more on Pierson?"

"Yeah, there's always more on Pierson." This brought Hank Johnson back up in his chair, his hands on the table. "Turns out, after he was in the big money, he buys his mother a new house – in *Ireland!* Sent her home, that's how her neighbors have it, anyway. 'Wouldn't feel so bad about not visiting her' was how one put it." He sat closer, his voice close now to a whisper.

"Just to be sure, though, he sets up a Title 8 front, some Hispanic he finds in Indianapolis. They do a public housing project right on top of his old neighborhood, like from out of the sky, three city blocks of Moscow Modern, blam splat!" Hank Johnson brought a full open hand down on the table for emphasis, rattling the glasses and coffee cups. "Like I said last night, John, a prince, a sweet-heart of a guy."

"Are we ready, gentlemen?" Andre placed their drinks before them on the table from a small tray he held in his hand. Now standing erect beside John Riley, pad in hand, pen at the ready. "And monsieur?"

"The usual for me, please, Andre."

"Oui, monsieur…" He turned to Hank Johnson, his hands joined at the chest, head at an angle. "Et vous, M. John…"

"What's his 'usual'?"

"Pour monsieur, c'est le Salade du Chef… Excellent…"

Hank Johnson looked at John Riley, shaking his head. "Christ, Johnny Boy, you looking to live forever?" He turned back. "You have any steaks here?"

"But of course, monsieur."

"Good. New York strip, if you have it, but whatever it is, medium rare with fries."

"Oui, monsieur, steak pomme frites Americaine…"

"Yeah, if you say so…thanks."

"That's fine, Andre. Thank you." John Riley looked at Hank Johnson, smiling, shaking his head. "Jesus Christ, Hank, you lived in Europe for how long? You might just as well have been in Pittsburgh."

"Yeah, and that would've been fine with me too, pal. In Pittsburgh, you can say what you mean and mean what you say." He sat up. "Have you ever been over there? Europe? Spent time with them? Chrissakes, all the bowing and nodding and getting out of everyone's way? Never knew where you stood, never knew where *anyone* stood. Never will figure out how people like that got to start the only two World Wars we ever had…"

John Riley laughed, glad for the company and friendship of Hank Johnson who raised his bourbon and drank a measure of it.

Putting his glass down, Hank Johnson tapped the table with his forefinger. "By the way, Pierson's been here, you know. A lot…"

"Yeah, they opened an office a year or so ago next to the Madison Hotel. Fifteenth Street. Some business development, but mostly government affairs."

"No, I mean *here*, in this hotel." More taps on the table. "It's what he uses now. Pays extra for the seventh-floor suite on the Park, the big one – The Truman? Some president, anyway…"

"Really? Now I didn't know that." John Riley made a mental note to run this down - how often Pierson had stayed at the Hay-Adams, meeting rooms used…

"He's been looking at land here, too. In Virginia - Middleburg. In town, too. The Brady estate? Something like that. Anyway, looks like he's fixing to move out here."

"The Brady Estate? Really?" John Riley glanced quickly to his left, fixing on the statue of Friedrich von Steuben in the northwest corner of the Park. "How do you *know* all this?" He turned back to Hank Johnson. "Where do you get it all?"

"You ask, we answer." A smile came to Hank Johnson's face, his right index finger up, wagging left to right. "But no asking *how* we know. That's the deal.

147

Plausible deniability. All part of the service." Hank Johnson nodded a knowing smile. "But we *know*…"

"Well, then, you know that we own this, the Hay-Adams. I mean Hennessey Land owns it. We also own the Brady Estate."

Hank Johnson sat back, surprised. "Really. All 13 acres?"

"All of it. Brigit got it as part of something else. Forget what. It fits with how we've been working Hennessey Land. Pays no dividends because it makes hardly any money at all. We're weighted to unimproved and undeveloped land, like the Brady Estate, with surefire capital growth. The carry, mostly taxes, absorbs what we make in developed properties. So, the company earns hardly anything on an annual profit basis, but the total market value of its holdings just keeps going up." John Riley smiled sheepishly, shrugging before he continued, now sitting forward.

"That's how the Brady piece fit in with Hennessey Land. But Brigit had something else going on, too. She wanted me to buy it, for us to live there. Eileen and me…"

"Christ."

"Yeah, and then we'd build other units on it, you know, a compound."

"Like the Kennedys then…"

"I think that's what she had in mind…" He laughed.

"And Eileen?"

"Yeah, you got it." John Riley laughed again. "Brigit, now, she made the mistake of talking about it to Michael once…forget when it was, maybe a christening or something. Well, Eileen overheard it. Now Eileen, she's good at containment, you know. Didn't say a word until we're in the car, on the way home. Then KABOOM!" He sat back, arms out, high and around like a mushroom cloud. Pulling closer to the table, he spoke in a high voice, feigning the excitement of an irate mother.

"I'd sooner be dead and living in hell for all eternity than spend one night in a mansion on 13 acres off Foxhall Road, just down the street from the Rockefellers! I don't know who Brigit Riley Winslow thinks she is! Foxhall Road...what's happened to the daughter we raised? Where she'd come up with something like that? The Brady Estate, of all things..."

"And you?" Hank Johnson was smiling.

John Riley smiled. "Well, now, this was just after we got the General on Tysons Corner, and a lock on anything nearby that was to follow, not even to mention linking up with Transtar for work outside of Washington, too." He nodded heavily at Hank Johnson. "It was big, a game changer for Hennessey Construction. In the papers and all that." He smiled, sat back. "So, I'm feeling pretty good about myself, and maybe, you know...why not? Just how *bad* could living on 13 acres off Foxhall Road really be? Rockefellers seem like pretty nice folk..."

Hank Johnson was loving it, now sitting forward. "And?"

"Well it was when Ed Kane was starting to fade, which meant Mother Riley would be needing a place and there was no way on God's good earth she was ever going to live on the Brady Estate...and that's for *sure*." John Riley sat back, looking away.

"I was still leaning toward it, though, trying to figure out a way to make it work, rationalizing the irreconcilable." His mind went back to it. A lunch with Michael Riley at Trader Vic's. "Talked to brother Michael about it." He shook his head now, turning back to Hank Johnson. "Know what he said?"

Hank Johnson shook his head slightly.

"Said 'Get over it. You got a better life than you know.'" John Riley looked away, these words rolling over in this mind, thinking back on how they had affected him that afternoon, and since.

Hank Johnson smiled, nodding that he understood, sitting back in his chair. Reaching for his drink, he took a sip, fixed on John Riley. "How *is* Michael?"

John Riley looked back. "Pretty good for a guy whose chest was holed less than twenty hours ago." He shook his head, thinking about it. "Went by the hospital this morning. He was asleep, but fine. I'm going over after we finish here."

Hank Johnson sat up, shifted closer to the table, looking left and right and then fixing on John Riley. "Like I said last night, Johnny Boy, got something on brother Michael you should know about…"

"*On* Michael? What do you mean, 'on' Michael?"

"Well *for* Michael. That's better, yes, *for* Michael."

"Okay, that's better. Now…?

Hank Johnson cleared his throat, looking about. "You remember Skinny Hughes?"

"The driver?" John Riley sat up, pulling closer to the table.

"The same. Well, Skinny Hughes stayed in the 'trade,' as you might say, something of a 'facilitator.' That's how he puts it. Always running across things that one side or the other might need, sometimes even an unofficial 'go between.'"

"Sounds hazardous."

"You could say that." Hank Johnson looked about again, speaking lower now. "Well, it seems he came across an old IRA safe house, some slum in Belfast. Turns out, it was once used by Maira Canny, back in the seventies."

"*Sean's* mother?"

"The same…" He motioned John Riley closer, speaking lower still. "He found her *diary*. She kept a *diary*, for Chrissakes. *Incredible*." His right index finger was up again. "Rule number one in that sort of work is you *never*,

ever keep a diary. But she did…all sorts of stuff - names, places, what was done to who and why for…"

John Riley sat closer. "Do you have it?"

"Yes. Wanted ten thousand and I paid it. Thought you'd be good for it."

"Done. Speak to Grace about a check. Have her draw it on my personal account. And ask her to send it over to East Irving, too."

Hank Johnson nodded.

"Have you read it?"

Hank Johnson sat back. "Yes." He looked away, a thought seeming to have come to him as he gripped the table, fixing back on John Riley. "She was a clever little bitch, paranoid, spiteful…all of it."

"Yes, I know that…we all know that…" John Riley sat closer to the table, his eyes bearing in. "But what's new…You said last night there's something about Michael."

At this, their eyes locked, John Riley's mind racing. What could be in Maira's diary, what would be something she alone, only she, would know and would want to keep from anyone else, anyone near…

Hank Johnson nodded, his eyes closing for a minute, then back on him. "Bryan Canny is…"

"…Michael Riley's son…"

"Yes."

John Riley froze, his eyes now locked ahead, seeing nothing, his ears gone dumb, hearing nothing. Pushing back from the table, he started to rise but held his seat, his legs weak as Hank Johnson's words rolled over in his mind, now racing in a swirl…gripping the table edge to steady himself. Opening his eyes, he pulled himself closer, his voice low but with full purpose, his eyes on Hank Johnson. "That's *impossible…*"

"Easy, Johnny Boy…" Hank Johnson sat back a measure, his head at an angle.

"Then tell me how it's possible. We've seen his birth certificate...I don't understand..." John Riley's head was moving left to right, his eyes now fixed on the linen surface of the table.

"Not like I have DNA or anything, John. But it's in the diary..." He stopped, waiting for John Riley to look across at him, to be certain he was paying attention. "You okay, now, John?"

John Riley nodded a 'yes,' his shoulders bent, his neck in.

"Michael told us there was only Sean when she threw him out in Cardiff, when Sean was five. Now being a little paranoid...no, check that... Being a *lot* paranoid, she throws him out and in two minutes is figuring he's going against her, you know, wanting to hurt her, maybe try to take Sean away..."

John Riley's head rose, his eyes fixing hard on Hank Johnson.

"Like I said, John, she was crazy...Looney Tunes." Hank Johnson put his right index finger to his temple, turning in circles. "So, she heads north, to Belfast. The last possible place Michael would look for her, or even *could* look for her. After a couple of weeks there, in this safe house or somewhere up there, she discovers she's pregnant again, and again with Michael Riley's child.

"Now she's near the edge, here, thinking Michael will be coming after her for Sean and the new one in the bargain. Changes her name a few times and has the kid with a midwife so there's no hospital record. Then she gets the midwife to date the birth certificate three months ahead so that he's down as born a full twelve months after she had last been with Michael." Hank Johnson sipped his drink, his eyes still on John Riley.

"It's all in there, John, in the diary. Says there she never told Sean who Bryan's father was...." Another sip.

"Hell's fire, John, you can have it checked easy enough. If he's Michael's son, he's your nephew."

John Riley sat up now, his hands on the table edge, fixing on Hank Johnson.

"Yeah, that's right, he'd be your *nephew*. All you need is a swab of your spit and something Bryan's touched. A cigarette butt will do it. Get it back to you in two, three days max." Hank Johnson studied John Riley for a moment. "Then you'd know for sure."

There was a welling in John Riley, a rising of something there inside him. A hurt? A loss? Whatever it was, it was not good, tearing at him, closing in on him, as if the whole room was closing in.

"John?" Hank Johnson was forward in his seat, against the table, as if he were about to reach for John Riley's arm.

John Riley shook his head, checking his watch, not seeing the dial. "It's later than I thought...got to go." He took the napkin from his lap just as Andre was placing his lunch on the table in front of him.

"Monsieur...?"

John Riley rose.

The maitre d' looked at Hank Johnson who waved him off as he rose, watching as John Riley started for the hotel lobby. Reaching for the maitre d's forearm, he stopped him from going after John Riley. "He's okay, just needs a minute."

Andre looked at him, his shoulders up in a question.

"We're fine, Andre, just fine." Hank Johnson nodded to reassure him. "But lunch is done..." Hank Johnson peeled a one-hundred-dollar bill from his money clip and put it in Andre's hand. "This should cover it."

"But no, monsieur, this is not..."

Hank Johnson made his way among the tables to the lobby and then quick-stepped through it to the front entrance of the hotel on 16th Street. John Riley was just

153

giving his ticket to the valet. "You going to be alright, here, Johnny Boy? I'm right here, you know that. Got nothing to do."

John Riley looked from the valet to Hank Johnson, a smile coming to his face. "I'm good, Hank. Just got a little stuffy in there."

"Yeah, I could see that.... felt it myself." He handed John Riley the envelope he had given him in the restaurant. "Here, you'll want this."

John Riley looked at the envelope. "Hold that for me, will you? Going to see Michael. Don't want to lose it."

Hank Johnson fixed on John Riley, looking at him as if he were an examining physician. He nodded at the envelope. "Anything you want me doing on this?"

John Riley reached for his forearm, gripping it. "Yes, there is, thank you. I'll call Grace and clear a transfer of $100,000 to Hastings' firm. She'll need you for their contact information, so get over there first thing. Then get to Hastings and set him up for Friday a.m. at National Airport. I *know* you can do that, Hank. Grace can give you the contact and clearance number at ExecuJet. Set up a G-IV. And I want you on the plane, Hank, out and back."

The valet pulled up with John Riley's car, getting out and holding the door for him. Stepping quickly around the back of the car, John Riley got in, looking to Hank Johnson through the opened passenger seat window. "Can you do that, be on the plane?"

"You got it, Johnny Boy, *Semper Fi.*"

"Thanks."

Hank Johnson stepped back, watching John Riley pull his car out onto 16th Street, an engine in another car just now starting.

Some things a person's brain never stops doing. For Hank Johnson, it was seeing how things in a street scene linked up...how John Riley pulling out onto 16th Street started a chain reaction of sorts. The BMW to his left, its engine just now started, pulled out from a parking place, a Mercedes on the other side of the street doing a U-turn, following the first, both turning right on H Street behind John Riley's Explorer.

Signaling a cab in the taxi queue, Hank Johnson got in quickly, pulling a $100 bill from his money clip and handing it to the driver. "A hundred bucks says you can't stay behind that BMW in front of you and drive this hunk of junk wherever else I tell you for the next fifteen minutes."

"Fifteen minutes? You say *fifteen* minutes?"

"That's the number."

"You're on, mister. Hold on to your hat, now…"

CHAPTER SIXTEEN
Sons and Brothers

"**B**ryan Canny...Michael Riley's son..."
The words rolled over and through John Riley's mind as he took a right off 16th onto H Street, away from the Hay-Adams. 'Impossible...Impossible...Doesn't *have* a father...doesn't *need* a father...Impossible.' Both hands fixed on the wheel, now, his eyes blankly ahead, John Riley managed to get to 17th Street without hitting anything or killing anyone. Turning left and south toward the Mall, he thought of pulling over, of closing his eyes, of disappearing. He had to keep moving, though, keep getting away or getting somewhere, but he couldn't stop, something would not let him stop...

Crossing Pennsylvania Avenue, he felt his eyes blink then focus ahead. Taking a deep breath, he shook his hands and arms...stopping at Constitution Avenue, the Washington Monument to his left. Tourists everywhere - short pants and white socks pulled up out of gray and blue and red sneakers and jogging shoes, sun and shade about, kids at their parents' knees, pulling ahead or trailing behind, sullen teenagers loafing along...the light turning green.

Crossing the Mall toward the river, John Riley's mind went back to a spring evening in 1983. It was in his kitchen at East Irving, his brother Michael at the table, Eileen up in New York visiting Brigit. "I have a son, John..."

That's how it started, how the telling of Michael Riley's secret life in Ireland began. For the next hour Michael Riley told of his six-year affair with Maira Canny, and of their Sean, the *Troubles* all about, the romps, the living on the edge, helping her with connections in New York and Washington, envelopes, sealed files left here or there, letters in the hollow of a tree, or the overhead of a bridge...then of the guns. She wanted lots of them, plastique, too, and by this his coming to know that he had to say "no"...his last night there, the last time he saw Sean, his son.

"Didn't know what to do, John. Had no claim to him, none. Wasn't even down as his father. I knew I was though, just knew. I loved him, and more than as part of my life there, I loved him as a father loves a son." He looked up, his eyes tearing. "Had gotten him pretty much out of my mind over the years...till now. Wasn't part of my day, if you know what I mean."

John Riley had nodded. He knew what Michael Riley meant. He had a son, too, and his name was Patrick. His son Patrick was out of his life as well.

"That was till tonight, and this Bryan Canny..."

John Riley had nodded, looking at Michael Riley's right hand, the scraped knuckles.

"I don't know what to do, John." Michael Riley's eyes had glazed for a moment, staring vacantly ahead, lost. "Says Sean's being held hostage, that he needs money to break him out." He turned to John Riley. "Hell, I have no idea who Bryan Canny is, what he is..." Michael Riley looked away, continuing aloud, more to himself it seemed.

"I hired a PI over there to find them back then, in the sixties...went back myself, three, maybe four times. Spent two years at it. Never came up with a thing. 'Disappeared off the face of the earth,' the PI had said. 'Gone...into thin air is where, them in the *Cause*...different places and different worlds is where they live, them in it...'

Michael Riley looked at John Riley, his eyes quickly away as he rose from the table, pacing alongside it, his fingers running across its surface. "Got to get over there, John. Got to get there, be there. Got to find him, got to try." He looked down at John Riley. "This is the first real lead I've ever had...guy says he's Sean's half-brother, for Chrissakes."

Michael Riley sat back down, across from John Riley, his arms on the table surface, his eyes at John Riley, seizing him. "I need help, John. Don't know a tinker's dam about any of it...did back then, a little anyways, nothing now." A pause, then a closer fix on John Riley. "But wait...you know someone who knows all about it. Spent five years over there ...

"Hank Johnson?" John Riley sat back, pushing himself away from the table, rocking in his chair. "Are you *serious*? You want me to call Hank Johnson about this? What are you thinking about?"

"I'm thinking about...no...I'm *going* to find my son, over there, that's what I'm going to do. And when I do, I'm going tell him what happened, why I left, so he'll know what happened, that I didn't abandon him." Now Michael Riley pushed off the table.

"Will you call Johnson? Christ, John, he's perfect. Told me once he was head of security for the whole country, a big deal drug company...Pfizer, I think. He'd know all about it, who's who, where things are, how things get done. Will you do it, John? Will you call him for me?"

"Sure, I can call him. That's easy...Hell, we're his biggest account."

That's how it began, the knowing of Michael Riley's life away, John Riley's mind now drifting back to the door of a small, windowless conference room at Hennessey Construction's downtown headquarters the next morning, his knocking on the door and stepping in.

Michael Riley sat at a square conference table across from a 20-25 year-old man. He wore a dark green windbreaker, opened down the front, a dark sweatshirt beneath, red/orange hair, short and wiry, curling up and about the edges of his cap. His left eye was blackened and swollen, that cheek as well. They both turned to him as he stepped in, closing the door behind him with Michael Riley motioning him to a chair beside his own.

"Here, John. Have a seat." He pulled a chair by its back, his eyes fixing back on Bryan Canny. "This is the fellow I was telling you about." He nodded at Bryan Canny. "Say good morning, Mr. Riley.'"

Bryan Canny turned to John Riley, now seated beside Michael Riley, eyes fixing on him without expression.

Michael Riley sat back, nodding to Bryan Canny, his eyes on John Riley. "Doesn't say much, does he?" Michael Riley turned to Bryan Canny. "Especially for someone asking a total stranger for $40,000, hardly a question asked."

John Riley's eyes fixed on the middle of the table. There was an official-looking paper unfolded and facing up, a seal at its corner, an airline ticket as well, along with several photographs and hand-written letters. Reaching forward, he looked at Bryan Canny. "May I?"

"Suit yourself, *Mr.* Riley."

John Riley picked up two of the pictures. The first was of a twentyish woman with what looked to be her two to three-year son, both smiling at the camera, a great open space behind them. The other was a street scene, a sidewalk café, umbrellas, maybe an afternoon sun, beer glasses on the table with the same boy at Michael Riley's side, they each smiling at one another. He looked at Michael Riley who nodded, mouthing the words 'They're real.'

Returning the pictures, John Riley reached for the official paper, turning it to himself and seeing it was a birth certificate...Bryan Canny, mother Maira Canny, father unknown. He looked again at his brother, and again the nod of acceptance. Leaving the birth certificate in front of him, John Riley now reached for the nearest letter, recognizing immediately it was in Michael Riley's hand. Now looking at Michael Riley he said, "May I?"

Michael Riley reached for the letter and put it back on the table, with the other. "No need. I wrote it. It's mine." He nodded at the picture of the man and the woman, picking up the one of the woman and the boy. "Took this one myself, by the coast in Waterford." He turned to Bryan Canny. "Why not tell Mr. Riley, here, how you knew to reach me, what my name was, where I lived?"

Bryan Canny took out a packet of cigarettes and lit one, pitching the match into the ashtray on the table. "Yes, why not? Like I said - Sean, *your* son." His chin went up to Michael Riley as he turned to John, angry, burdened, sullen. "Maira told him all about the brother here…Rugby touring, rich, smart, that's him, a Yank who was going to help her save Ireland." He turned back to Michael Riley.

"Only you turned chicken, didn't you, now, that's how Sean had it. Had you down for an adventurer who pulled out when the fun was up and the chips were down. Told me though, if I was ever in a pinch, in the States, to ring you up." He turned back to John Riley. "So, here we are…" He sat back, took a draw of his cigarette, exhaling in John Riley's direction.

"I don't see a passport here." John Riley motioned toward the materials on the table. "How'd you get in here? How'd you get across the border?"

"Passport's in the hotel." Bryan Canny took a quick drag from his cigarette, speaking as he exhaled. "Flew into Montreal and walked right on in, partner," his hands were out now, quick and up like pistols in a western. "Bang, bang, you lads are dead, the both of you!"

Fixing across, now, at one and now the other, he sat forward hard against the table, his arms now on the surface of it. "It's a sieve, if you're wondering. Might have Reagan look to that if you've any influence. Can't you just see it? Whole divisions of Russkies, crossing in mufti at midnight, rising up in unison, all over in a day, not a bomb dropped."

A smile and another quick drag, now going serious, Bryan Canny fixed first on John Riley and then Michael Riley. "It'd taken months to get a visa and I didn't have months." He leaned forward. "*Sean* doesn't have months *neither*. Might already be done, gone. They're a loony bunch, the Brigade. Been weeks since they grabbed him…right, enough. Might be done already."

Bryan Canny twitched at the shoulders, looked around the room, then back at Michael. "Look, now, I know this has come sudden to you, a call out of the blue and all, but I've not much time. What I've got to know is whether you're even thinking on it at all. If not, I'll be on my way, do what I can without you."

There were two quick taps on the door, it opening quickly. Hank Johnson stepped through the doorway, careful to secure it once in. Standing now in front of it, as if on guard duty, he looked for a moment at Bryan Canny, then turned to John Riley, motioning to Bryan Canny. "This him?"

"Yes." John Riley sat back as Michael Riley sat forward.

"Hank, meet Bryan Canny." Hank Johnson reached down and over, shaking Bryan Canny's hand. "He's fresh over from Ireland, by way of the Canadian border, he tells us."

Hank Johnson nodded as he looked at Bryan Canny, fixing back on Michael Riley.

"Bryan has a problem back home, Hank, and he's looking for me to help him on it." Michael Riley turned to Bryan Canny, still speaking to Hank Johnson. "He's brought news of a son I have over there." He turned up to Hank Johnson. "Bryan's half brother, Sean. Seems Sean has particular ideas about how things should work over in Northern Ireland."

Hank Johnson raised his head a measure, mouthing the words 'Northern Ireland,' his eyes away for a moment before returning to Michael Riley, motioning him to continue.

"Well, Sean's gone missing and Bryan thinks he knows where he is." Michael Riley turned back to Bryan Canny. "Wants me to help get him back, or out, anyway."

Hank Johnson's face had gone serious, looking to John Riley who nodded back, motioning him to a chair, to sit and be part of it. Pausing for a moment, Hank Johnson nodded back, pulling the offered chair out and sitting at the table, back straight, his hands joined at his chest, looking to Michael Riley who continued.

"So, John and I were hoping you could spend some time with Bryan, here or wherever you think better, and let us know what you think about it all."

"All?" Hank Johnson raised his eyebrows. "This Sean's in *Northern Ireland*, held by a paramilitary force, right?" He looked at Bryan Canny.

"Right, the Brigade."

"Jesus Christ in heaven…"

"You know them?" John Riley sat up, against the table.

"Of course, knew them all." He looked back at Bryan Canny, answering John Riley's question. "What most distinguished the Brigade from the rest of the pack was no one could quite figure out whether they were bank robbers turned patriots or patriots turned bank robbers. Either way they're thugs, animals."

Bryan Canny sat up against the table. "Sorry to disappoint you, Mr. Johnson, but that's who's got him. Don't exactly get your pick of who's to grab you over there, you know."

Hank Johnson nodded, seeming to have liked what he heard as he fixed back on Bryan Canny. "Just what did you have in mind, son?" Hank Johnson was now at the table, his hands down on it, his eyes on Bryan Canny, studying him.

Michael Riley sat forward. "He wants $40,000…"

Hank Johnson turned to Michael Riley, motioning him to be silent as he looked at John Riley who reached for Michael Riley's forearm. Michael Riley nodded and sat back.

"What do you have in mind, Bryan?"

Bryan Canny sat back for a moment, then forward, taking a full draw on this cigarette before crushing it out in the ashtray. "They grabbed Sean after Sean's unit grabbed one of theirs – a murdering bastard named Halloran. They don't want money. They could rob another bank for that. They want Halloran freed and out - or they're going kill Sean. Simple as that."

Hank Johnson nodded, motioning him to go ahead. "So, you want to go in and…?

"Break him out…like I said… "

"And.?"

"And…and…I need guns, a car, money to bribe the border guards. They've got him 30 miles in, a farm house in Enniskillen."

"Really, how to do you know all that?"

Bryan Canny sat back, looking away. "Someone in his unit."

"In your brother's unit?"

"Yes…"

Hank Johnson sat forward, his left forearm on the table. "Look, son, you're all in here. Who else you know has 40,000 American? You've already spent maybe three days getting here and it'll take as many getting back. Near a whole week - and for nothing? You got no choice but to trust us. And you can be damn sure of one thing–you're not seeing dime-one from Michael Riley here unless you can convince me you know where Sean is and you get me comfortable with how you know it."

Bryan Canny fixed on Hank Johnson, his mind churning, reaching for his cigarettes and Hank quicker to grab his arm, holding it. "You got more important things than having a smoke." Hank Johnson's other hand reached into Bryan Canny's pocket and took out the pack of cigarettes. Looking inside the pack, shaking it to see to its bottom, he placed it on the surface of the table, his eyes now on Bryan Canny, his head motioning him to go on.

Bryan Canny sat back, looking at Michael Riley and then to Hank Johnson. "They're all at one another's throats over there, now. Everything's topsy-turvy. Upside down. No one knows who to trust. Seems Sean's deputy's keeping others in the unit from going in because he wants Sean out of the way... thinks Sean's gone mad, like..."

"Like...?"

"No matter..."

"How do you know all this? Are you in Sean's unit?"

Bryan Canny looked up quickly. "Me? No! I'm not in any of it! They're all crazed. My mother got blown up by a bomb she was carrying for them. Some say they set it off early, on purpose, to get her! Her own kind...Given her life to it, and Sean's, too!" A pause, his eyes away, then back. "And the lad gave me all this? A nut job, crazy..."

"Then why do you trust him, this 'nut job'?"

"Sean's his hero, recruited him, trained him. That's how they all are, loyal to the death, especially to whoever brought'em in...gave them a life, something to do, a way to fight!"

"Though you're not in it?"

"No, I'm not! I want out of Ireland, the whole goddam mess of it! I'm on the visa list, at the embassy in

Dublin, to come over here! Got six months to go, maybe less. Haven't seen Sean in more than two years. But how can I leave with him still there, alone…A hostage?"

Hank Johnson sat forward, his arms folded and resting on the table surface, his head now at an angle as he studied Bryan Canny before turning to look at Michael and John Riley, studying their faces as well.

Looking up into the far corner of the ceiling, he sat back, exhaling, his left arm resting on the table, his hand relaxed, finger tips softly down on the table's surface. He breathed in, his head nodding. "And the money?"

"The lad that gave me all this, he has a plan…

Hank Johnson sat back. "A plan? He has a plan? Really? The nut job has a plan?"

"Yes. A *plan*. He's been in and out before. It's what he does. Got some people out, I know one of them. Checked him out myself, said he's the one that got him across….and he's killed some of them…you hear things…you know, who's got the balls to blow someone away at the snap of a finger?"

Hank Johnson nodded.

"Yeah, well he's one of them. He'd wear their scalps on his belt if they'd let him. Said he'll take me in if I can find two or three others to go in with us. And he's going to need the money for the car, the guns, the border guards – both sides – concussion grenades, tear gas…"

"Concussion grenades?" Hank Johnson sat back in his chair, his fingers beating a rhythm on the table surface as he turned to Michael and John Riley, then fixed back on Bryan Canny whose head was down and away, his entire body still, as if spent.

"Bryan, look at me."

Bryan Canny's head froze, his left hand on the table tightening into a fist, quivering slightly…

"Look at me, son…I need your eyes."

Bryan Canny sat up slowly, looking first at Michael Riley, then John Riley before turning, his shoulders now square and up, his eyes on Hank Johnson.

"Bryan, I need the name of the person who told you this, who's going to take you in."

Bryan Canny's face went blank, his eyes slowly closing, a deep breath taken, then "Steven Hughes...goes by Skinny."

"And you know him how?"

"Grew up across the street from us in Bogside, two places over."

"What's his mother's maiden name, Bryan?"

Bryan Canny's eyes opened in a snap, stark and staring at Hank Johnson.

"You've got two seconds, son..."

"McGann. Dorothy McGann Hughes."

CHAPTER SEVENTEEN
Brigit Riley Winslow

S he had forgotten her briefcase at East Irving. Not like her. Dropping Kay off at the hospital, she went back for it. Rush hour traffic. An hour, more than that, gone, wasted. And by the time she had gotten back, Michael Riley was being taken out of the ICU to a private room in cardiology. Kay was able to see him briefly in the ICU but there would be no more visiting till noon.

Half the morning lost, Brigit Winslow had set up shop in a corner of the hospital cafeteria. Her first order of business was a voice mail from Richard Townsend, Mid-America's outside counsel on The Deal: "Mr. Pierson would like to resume discussions on Friday a.m. at his offices in Chicago. Please advise."

"Please advise Mr. Townsend that his message has been a received and that I will get back to him ASAP," was her reply to his secretary, he being not available.

Sitting back in her chair, Brigit Winslow remembered Bryan Canny coming back into the conference room at Mid-Atlantic Holdings, handing John Riley a note. "We have to go," she heard him whisper. In the half count from hearing these words and opening the note, Brigit Winslow had detected the briefest look of relief on John Riley's face, and in her mind a growing sense that John Riley was pulling away from Mid-America.

When she had first approached her father about selling portions of the Hennessey Land's properties, the goals were two - access to sufficient cash to settle the tax consequences if Mary Riley were to die, and to diversify Hennessey's holdings geographically. Mid-America had expressed some early interest, but this seemed little more than sniff-in calls on specific properties until then.

They had been speaking primarily with insurance and private equity groups looking to buy or swap high-value properties, building pieces to grow their profile in the DC market. It wasn't until the summer of 1992 that Mid-America had become more assertive, but still only on certain properties, all middle or low-end.

After the November election, though, Mid-America's interest rose dramatically, hinting here and there that it might even be interested in the whole lot, Hennessey's entire real estate portfolio. Seeming to sense this, two Chicago-based insurance companies started to make similar noises.

By May, Hennessey Land was speaking with only these three, Mid-America and the two insurance companies, and with each it had become an all-in deal. And of the three, Mid-America had emerged as the most assertive, even aggressive, pressing the point that they can "write the check," as Keith Pierson kept putting it.

"It's going to take those big outfits a séance or three with their environmental whiners and at least two board meetings to get this done, John. Two if you're lucky. Trust me on that…"

This was Keith Pierson at his most congenial, most folksy. "Trust me on that. And even then, you'll be dealing with lawyers and second stringers for a couple of years before you see all your money. Maybe longer. You can count on that, too." The knowing pause, a slight shifting in his chair.

"With me? Hell, like I said, I can write the check. You've seen our financials, the numbers. All we need from you is your name on a letter of intent, and it's done. We're writing checks. You're cashing out, all out. Maybe by Christmas."

Keith Pierson had just gotten these words out when the call from Washington came about Michael Riley. Outside the Blackstone, on Michigan Avenue waiting for their car, Hardin Brooks had pulled John Riley aside, Brigit Riley stepping close. "Christmas? He's saying Christmas? This year? Not likely, John… near a billion in real estate? Done and closed in three months? Unlikely at best…we *all* know that."

Hardin Brooks was Hennessey's outside counsel on The Deal and it had been clear to Brigit Winslow from the start that he had not taken to Keith Pierson. It seemed visceral, even, and well beyond Pierson referring to him by his last name as in 'Brooks here can back me up on that, right, Brooks?'

There was a part of Keith Pierson that Hardin Brooks didn't trust. Perhaps it was the power he wielded, the things he could order to be done and know they'd be done…no questions asked, none allowed. For her part, Brigit Winslow sensed in Keith Pierson the soul of a bully and perhaps this is what so concerned Hardin Brooks.

Even still, Pierson's words continued to course through Brigit Riley Winslow's mind …*all out…maybe by Christmas.* "Three months and done…" she heard herself speak under her breath as she sat forward, her eyes closed, arms folded on the edge of a corner table in the cafeteria.

A moment's peace, if that, maybe ten full breaths taken and her mind going quickly to the work-through, the months of passing properties from subsidiary to subsidiary, reviewing and reworking vendor and management contracts. Then the 900 million dollars fresh in Hennessey Land's accounts and managing *that.* There's no end, it will never end, never stop…no way out.

The ring tone on her cell sounded, bringing her up straight in the chair, eyes fixing on the phone, her right hand quick to it and then to her ear. "Yes?"

"Brigit? It's Kay. He's out! No, I mean he's in! His room that is. You know what I mean." Kay laughed. "Come on up. Room 4236. Got it? 4236?"

"Right, 4236…be right up…see you there."

Brigit Riley's eyes sought the schema on the wall to her right, her right index finger tracing the corridors, floor and room numbers. Looking about to get her bearings, she started left in deliberate steps to an elevator bay and up.

Counting the floors tick, her mind fixed on Michael Francis Riley, the who of him, his smile and warmth, emotions in her, contained since Chicago, now rising. She still called him "Uncle Mike" and, holding at six-foot-two, Michael Riley towered over her father and able to kid with him with impunity, something allowed no other human on the planet.

The lawyer in Michael Riley stayed at the office. At home and around them all, though, he was the personality that Paddy Riley had left behind, the spirit still here. Stepping out of the elevator to the nurses' station, Brigit Winslow got the attention of a middle age nurse holding a clipboard, her reading glasses dangling on a gold colored chain and resting against her chest. "Michael Riley? 4236?

The nurse motioned her to the corridor to her left. Brigit mouthed a thank you with a slight bow of thanks and moved down the corridor, her step quickening, hefting her briefcase under her right arm, heavy with its lap top and half the briefing book from The Deal. Marking the numbers above each door, she counted down to 4236 and turned in, halting in mid-step.

Kay Rhinemann was on the far side of the bed, sitting, her hand on Michael Riley's forearm, her eyes fixing on him, soft and warm, listening as he told of something they seemed both to know of, some memory, perhaps. Michael noticed her first, turning to her and speaking in a full and practiced brogue, eyes bright and color strong.

"It's the niece, now, is it? And, sure, the best of the lot! Come here, now, Brigit, darling, won't you, and give your Uncle Mike a kiss, him come back from the brink!"

She stepped to the bed, her eyes misting as she felt the glow of his smile and the brilliance of his Riley-blue eyes. Starting to speak, she felt that her throat might close so she just nodded, taking his offered hand in hers and kissing it, now looking at Kay, her hand out to Brigit, smiling, her eyes misting as well. Stepping against the edge of the bed, she took her aunt's hand, they each looking, one to the other, the words not coming, nor there being any need of them...

"What's this, *Ring around the Rosey*?" The nurse from the nurse's station stepped into the room, clipboard still in hand, going to the foot of the bed, eyes fixing on Kay first and then Brigit.

"Hands off, please, ladies. His heart's all done up new, we've seen to that. The only thing that'll kill him now's the germs." Her eyes went quickly to Kay and Brigit's hands, they releasing Michael Riley's like a hot wire.

Moving around behind Kay, the nurse began checking the drip of an IV as Margaret Riley stepped into the room with the one-year old Brendan Riley held high on her right side. "Well, here we all are!"

Kay rose, walking to Margaret, a hand to Brendan's head and a kiss on Margaret's cheek. Margaret smiled, now looking to Brigit before kissing her on the cheek as she stepped to the bedside, her eyes on Michael. As she bent to kiss him, the nurse cleared her throat harshly, motioning to the child.

"Of course, I'm sorry." Margaret turned to Brigit. "Here, Brige, can you hold him?"

Brigit froze, her eyes going to Brendan.

"Go ahead, they don't bite."

Brigit took Brendan, feeling his weight against her right breast as she fixed on his eyes, an aqua blue against the milk white of his skin and dark of his eyebrows. He reached for her face and she pulled back, turning him in her arms, holding him against her, feeling his legs straddle her upper waist, wrapping her, warming her.

Closing her eyes, her left arm closed around Brendan, that hand finding his head, cupping it to her shoulder. A calm had come to Brigit Winslow, breathing easy now, her body beginning to sway, a rhythm coming to her legs and hips as the child settled against her, snuggling, feeling his hand at her neck, her own hands warming and full and to a purpose…

Footsteps sounded softly now at the door behind her and then the slightest sound of a woman catching her breath. Turning, Brigit Winslow's eyes opened on her mother, Eileen, whose hands were at her face, one covering her open mouth, her eyes on Brigit and Brendan, going from one to the other.

Mary Riley stepped sharply between them, her arms out. "Here's my Brendan! Here's my lad! Give us a kiss, now, Brendan."

Mary Riley kissed the boy, taking him from Brigit and turning him to Michael Riley. "Give your Da a wave of your hand, now, won't you, Brendan."

Brigit Riley's eyes had locked on Eileen's, they each standing motionless, no words said, no smiles offered nor nods done, just them in the space and time of the room, each to their own thoughts and cares and fears.

Brigit was the first to break off, shaking her head quickly to clear it, almost a shiver, as she looked down for her briefcase, hefting it as she stood. Looking to Michael, she smiled a good-bye, he winking back, then a nod to Kay. "I'll be on to the office."

Turning to go, she closed her eyes briefly. "See you home, Mom…" her body leaning to go, aching to be gone, but her head rising as she sensed someone else nearby...

John Riley stood silently before her, his face unsure, his eyes going to Eileen and then back to Brigit. "Brig..."

She started out before he could finish her name, her eyes away, her whole self needing to be gone, to be anywhere but where she was, now moving through the cluttered corridor of the cardiology ward, finding the elevator to the garage below, keys found and fumbled, briefcase in the trunk, car started and now out into the light of the day, the sun brilliant, near to white, squinting at the traffic, crabbing across broad avenues and then not knowing where to go or why, now jutting off to Connecticut Avenue and north on it, away from K Street, the office, now down and under Dupont Circle, the honk of her horn at a pedestrian, gunning to make the light at Florida Avenue, across it and through the yellow light at California Street, to the half circle in front of *The Carthage*, out of the car, the keys to the doorman, a 'Please, Thank you.' uttered and to the elevator.

Brigit Winslow counted up the eight floors to her condominium, doors opening, a code punched, into her place, the door shut hard behind her, a deep breath taken, feet out of her shoes, shoulders working free of her jacket, it dropping to the floor, stepping to her bedroom bath, hands working the buttons of her blouse, it off, the zipper of her skirt found and down, it dropping behind, the door to the bathroom opened, eyes squinting in the brightness of the full glass wall and doors opening on Rock Creek Park, her bra loosened and dropped, her panties pushed down and off, away, hands reaching for the faucet of the rain shower.

Facing up, she felt the water as it coursed down and over her head and shoulders, hands working the shower jets, their streams striking her torso, she turning before them two times to a stop, still now, standing motionless, not a muscle moving, only the sound of the water coursing down and off her shoulders, he arms out straight to each side, feeling the water run down over her breasts, hips and thighs.

Yes, Brigit Riley Winslow uttered, more in her mind than on her lips, *Yes,* a full, deep breath taken and loosed…and another…and still another…*yes, yes*…arms now coming slowly to close across her chest, her legs swaying, hips moving, an unknown melody to mind, her breasts swelling, arousing, a sense of strength, of force, even power, yet still a yearning, a need…to be needed, to give, her arms pressing firmer across her breasts, breathing deep, her head rising, face up…and from the dead silence of her mind…*Where am I? What am I doing…here…alone…*

Brigit Winslow's eyes opened, fixing on the wall faucet, reaching for it, to touch it, her eyes turning left to Bertie's shower. Gripping its faucet, she turned it on, stepping under its stream, both hands against the wall now, pressing it, her legs tensing, pushing, her head up, opening her mouth, tasting the water, her head now down, eyes closed …What am I doing…*here?*

She stepped from the wall, her eyes fixed on the faucet before her, then to the one on her right. Gripping the lever handle of each, she turned them off simultaneously, stepping to her right for a bath towel, she wrapped it around her as she reached for the wall phone, punching in ten digits, listening, three rings…

"Mr. Winslow's line."

"Terri?"

"Yes, Mrs. Winslow. How are you today?"

"Fine, thank you. Is he there?"

A pause. "No…he's flying to San Francisco today. The Cosgrove meeting."

Brigit Winslow bit her lip. She knew that. "Of course. It's on his weekly. Just forgot. When does he land?"

"5:52 our time."

"Yes, that's right. He's to call at 6:30. Thanks, Terri. Sorry to trouble you."

"No trouble at all, Mrs. Winslow. Have a good day."

"You, too."

Brigit Winslow hung up the phone, resting her head momentarily against the wall. "What am I doing to mys…"

Pushing off the wall, she stood erect, turning around, stepping to the glass doors, gripping their two handles, sliding them open and letting herself out onto the balcony, tightening the towel around her. Facing north over Taft Bridge to the Shoreham Hotel beyond, her eyes turned right, up Rock Creek, its trees holding a late summer green, a vast sea of rolling tree tops, north to Chevy Chase and into Maryland and for as far as the eye could see.

Gripping the brushed aluminum rail, her eyes closed as she arched back, taking the midday sun full on her face, her head shaking slightly. "No, no more…" She lowered her head, her eyes now on the far blue of the sky, her grip on the rail loosening, her mind easing, legs relaxed, the phone chime now sounding in the shower room, stepping to it…

"Yes?"

"Miss Winslow?"

"Yes…"

"This is Richard Townsend…"

"Really? How did you get this number?"

"It was no trouble, really. No bother…"

"I'm not worried about you being bothered, Mr. Townsend. But I must say that I'm bothered that you have this number."

"For another time, perhaps…"

"And how did yon know I was going to be *here*?"

A silence.

"I didn't know I was going to be here until I got here. How did *you* know?"

"Yes, how did I know…?" A breath taken. "Well, what I was calling about, Ms. Winslow, was our meeting on Friday…"

"We don't have a meeting on Friday, Mr. Townsend. My message was quite clear. 'I'll get back ASAP', as in 'as soon as possible' and it is not yet possible to get back to you on a possible meeting this Friday. Is that clear?"

"Quite."

"Good…and good day."

Brigit Riley Winslow hung up the phone and turned to the door of her bedroom, passing through it to the living room and her purse on the table by the front door. Finding her PDA, she punched in the name 'Johnson' then dialed the number on her cell phone.

"Johnson here."

"Hank? That you?"

"Why Miss Brigit, you finally…"

"We'll do that later. I need you at the office, now."

"Yes'm."

CHAPTER EIGHTEEN
Over There

T hey were alone.
    Eileen had taken Mary Riley back to East Irving, leaving John Riley with Michael while Margaret dropped Brendan at home with the nanny. Sitting in a bare wood armchair, his back to the window, John Riley fixed on Michael Riley, now asleep, breathing easily, arms lying open along each side, his head and shoulders slightly elevated.

'What you look for is what you see,' John Riley thought to himself as Michael Riley's still profile assumed a near identity with that of Bryan Canny. 'Has Michael's quickness,' too, he thought, 'of mind and body.' Bryan Canny's eyes now came to him, yes, "...near perfect," he spoke under his breath. How had he not seen it before? John Riley shut his eyes, his head shaking slightly. 'And what part of hell is that place, Ireland? A mother changing the date of a newborn's birth to keep him from a caring father? From even knowing he's alive...'

Hank Johnson had taken them for a day/night/day program at Atlantic Security's Virginia training base - weapons familiarization, basic sign language, quiet moving, concussion grenades thrown, gunfire heard, this to be gotten used to. Browning nine millimeters packed and worn tight, fired at targets, birds shaken up and off the ground, chukkas flashing safely up and away, moving things to shoot at and the like. Michael Riley took to it quickly, the prospect of seeing Sean rising in his mind and then, too, a thrill to it all.

For John Riley, it was a ghost trip back to Iwo Jima, Hank Johnson arranging some time with a Thompson gun, just for old time's sake. And he was so quick back to it all that it gave him pause. Was it the rush from the fear of it all? More likely just a slice of a time long-past that his mind had cured to the purest of self - quick-switching clips, hitting targets dead-on from twenty yards, the Thompson braced against his hip, sighting by instinct, dummies ripping apart...

"Picked a good year for it, you did." Skinny Hughes had met them at Shannon, a nervous banter as he took them north, through to Galway and beyond to a cottage by the sea, Connemara being the county. "Killings and bombings all about...up north, here, London, even Lady Margaret's suite at the Grand in Brighton." His shoulders went back and square at the thinking of it. "Lucky she was to miss that, lucky indeed! But they'll get her, by Jaysus, they'll get her..."

Another shuddering of his shoulders in the comfort of a hospital room. 'Insane,' John Riley thought, running over it all in his mind. 'Yes, insane is the only word.' But he couldn't have let Michael go alone on his search for a long lost-son, the newest Riley, now, come at thirty years and more. And then there was Hank Johnson. The only reason Hank was going was for John Riley and how could John Riley let him go without going himself?

And as crazy as it all was by the end, it wasn't near as crazy as when it had started, Sean then being in a Brigade safe house in Northern Ireland, a border to be crossed and then gotten back through, 12 hours as illegals in a land where life was cheap, and lost as quick. It was the early morning of the first full day there, in the dirt-floor lower level of the cottage that Skinny Hughes had arranged, when they learned that Sean had been moved over to the Republic and not far from where they were.

"It's the *Diplock*, you know," Skinny Hughes' finishing words when he'd told of the move. "Second to only one in its depravity..."

"The Diplock?" Michael Riley had fixed on him, almost a challenge.

"In the quick, then, Mr. Michael Riley, 'tis this: One informer, only *one* now, and on no more authority than his own mind and whim, he can bear witness against a man and the fella's picked up and packed away, no trial offered, thank you, and none done, neither. Just gone, Christ knows where."

Michael Riley nodded, his head turning away, a "Jesus Christ" uttered to himself.

"*Second* to one, you said?" John Riley had asked. "What's the *one*?"

"Aye, yes. The 'number one' you're asking, and what can it be but shooting-to-kill-on-sight? Now that'd be the one for Sean, it would..."

"Shoot-to-kill-on-sight?" John Riley's head went back, a quick look at the others and then back at Skinny Hughes. "What's he done?"

"Done Brighton, is what. T'was him, don't you know? Aye, t'was Sean done that...and near got her, too, Lady Margaret, he did! And who else? Aye, Lady Margaret hadn't stopped to chat up the mayor in the lobby? She'd been in the room when it went off, the bomb, that is...and she gone with it."

John Riley turned to Michael here, their eyes holding, then Michael closing his, his head lowering, nodding slowly, a breath taken and let go.

Turning from Skinny Hughes, Hank Johnson looked at John Riley, waiting for him to look at him before speaking. "There are times in these things, John, little pieces of time, when all minds come to the same place." Hank Johnson turned to Skinny Hughes, his eyes fixing on him, seemingly to gauge his reaction.

"And to what place would that be, now, Mr. Johnson?"

"A very gone and a very dead Sean Canny." He turned deliberately now to Michael Riley, fixing on him, his head lowered for effect, waiting for Michael's eyes to be certain he understood.

"Ulster wants him dead. Now Dublin wants him dead. And you can be absolutely certain that Her Majesty's government wants him dead...the Prime Minister now taking a personal interest."

Michael Riley's head nodded slightly, eyes closing again as John Riley stood closer to him, a hand on his shoulder as he turned to Bryan Canny, his chin up, eyes questioning.

"Didn't know it was Sean who did that. Didn't know..." Bryan Canny looked away, repeating himself, now back to John Riley. "I swear it, I do..." his eyes away again as he sat down on a stool, elbows on his knees, head shaking.

"What's this, now? Waking poor Sean before he's even gone, are we?" Skinny Hughes stepped to Bryan Canny, square in front of him, taking his shoulders in his hands, shaking him, pushing him back and looking down into his eyes. "He's a hero, don't you know, your brother is? Near got Lady Margaret herself, now, didn't he? And, sure now, what Son of Ireland wouldn't die gladly for that on his stone."

Bryan Canny rose sharply, kicking the stool out from under him, throwing Skinny Hughes' hands off him with his own, his eyes fixed, lips snarled, his right hand made to a fist and striking his own chest. "This one," he said, the words forced through teeth and jaw, *"this* son of Ireland, me *Bryan Canny*, you crazy-son-of-a-bitch...!" and from nowhere came a right cross that put Skinny Hughes on the dirt floor.

Michael Riley was up in a flash, holding Bryan Canny off Skinny Hughes as Hank Johnson motioned John Riley outside, they now by the vans, speaking close once there. "John, this Sean Canny is radioactive. We can't be anywhere *near* him." His eyes fixed on John Riley, his head nodding. "This deal is done, Johnny Boy, over, finished." He drew his right index finger across the front of his throat.

John Riley looked way. "I'm afraid you're right, Hank." He checked his watch, his eyes still on his wrist. "The chopper is due here in less than ten minutes." He looked back up. "We'll take a swing up north, the same as we laid on, just 'looking for real estate.' Give Michael a while to figure it all out...Bryan, too. Then we'll all get the hell out of here."

It was a Bell Jet Ranger, room for the pilot and one passenger up front and two in the back. Skinny Hughes sat on the left, behind the pilot, his face lumped and still smarting with John Riley on the right. Hank Johnson was up front, to the right. Buckling in, he took out a pre-folded paper map, showing it to the pilot, his finger tracing a line up its surface. "We're looking for a straight line from here, where we are now, north by northeast...not too high, not too low. Want to see the cows moving, if that's any help."

The pilot nodded a 'right' as he looked forward, sunglasses in place, engaging the collective, the pitch of the rotors now raising the craft off the ground as he eased the cyclic forward. The nose dipped now as the Ranger turned north into a blue, cloudless sky, skimming off a slight rise and catching the sea breeze from the west, lifting up and away, north by northeast.

Hank Johnson rested the map on his lap, checking the time, marking it in pencil on the map, head up, looking about, down again on the map, his fingers tracing across its paper surface, repeating this process every two minutes as the yellow and green fields of Connemara passed beneath at a hundred plus miles per hour. His eyes up from the map, Hank Johnson spoke over this left shoulder. "So what'cha have in mind, Johnny Boy? A bit of the auld sod? Hunting and fishing, or is it really for business?"

Checking his own map, John Riley spoke without looking up. "All in the Lord's good time, Hank."

"Great, the old 'In the Lord's good time' bullshit…nothing like flying 3,500 miles to a place I'd already seen four times as much as I ever needed or wanted to see and not knowing what's going on." He wheeled further to his left, looking back. "How's this looking to you, Skinny?" Hank Johnson's head went back, his voice up now, above the thumping of the rotor blades. "Hey you, Skinny Hughes, wake up!" He grabbed Hughes' knee, shaking it.

Skinny Hughes' head stirred, his hands going to his eyes, rubbing them as he turned ahead, then right as he fixed on Hank Johnson, maybe not too sure where he was, his hands finding the armrests as he raised up and looked around. "Aye…"

"So, you're with us now, Skinny?"

"Aye, sure enough."

Hank Johnson's arms waved across the horizon. "Any sense of where we are? Getting your bearings, landmarks?"

"I reckon…" Skinny Hughes leaned forward between the front seats, looking down, pointing to the right. "That's where we were last night, by those large trees." He sat back, looking left out of the helicopter, touching the left side of his face and that temple, now turning back to John Riley, pointing to the bruise on his right temple.

"Had no call to do that…just trying to cheer the lad up? Let him know what a hero his brother is? Where's the fault in…"

Skinny Hughes sat up in his seat, his right arm out now and moving John Riley back in his seat. His eyes fixed down, he reached forward to Hank Johnson, pulling at his shoulder to get his attention. "That's him, that's the place…"

Hank Johnson wheeled to his right, looking down, his binoculars at a farmhouse, then sweeping around it. "You sure?"

"Aye, that's the place, sure as rain's from above."

"You seeing this, Johnny Boy?" Hank Johnson spoke as he scanned the area with his binoculars. "Getting a good look?"

"Yep…"

Putting his binoculars down, Hank Johnson marked the map in his lap, looking up to confirm the compass heading, now checking the airspeed and his watch, his head turning quickly out and down. "Well, well, lookee here…" His binoculars up again, sweeping forward and then as far back as he could see. "What you got over there, Skinny, on that side, out and back?"

"Maybe the same thing you're seeing, now, Mr. Johnson.

John Riley sat up, looked out Skinny Hughes' side, Skinny pointing down to a black car and a van nearby, both beside a small stand of trees, the three figures by it all done in black, a roadblock, several cars held in line…

"Now here's Ireland for you, gents!" The pilot pulled his ear phones down to his neck, sitting back to be better heard above the rotors, his British accent seeming to come stronger than at lift-off. "Beautiful, clear day, it is, and not a car about…not a one! And where they all gone to, you're asking? Where are the men of Ireland on such a day? I'll tell you where…*fornicating*! That's what, that's what I'm thinking, that or buggering their sheep and goats."

"Goats!" Skinny Hughes lurched back, kicking beneath the seat in front of him, punching at it with a closed fist, struggling to get free of his seatbelt, then freezing at the scream of two jet fighters roaring past, the helicopter rocking in their wakes followed immediately by the shock wave and crack of a huge explosion, the helicopter now bolting forward as the shock wave struck it, twisting violently, its tail lifting up, rotors wrenching as the nose dropped down and forward, then veering sharply to the left as the pilot fought to regain control...

"Harriers, for Chrissakes! Royal Navy! Holy Christ in heaven!" Hank Johnson sat back in his seat, his arms braced forward.

Turned completely around and now headed for where they had started, they looked below, the farm house gone, nothing now but a black and brown hole in the ground smoldering in the morning air with bits and pieces of the place landing around and about it...and off to the right two planes, low and level...

"Hang on, now! There's two more...!"

A huge fireball erupted from where the farm house had been, the blackness of the spent napalm defining its shape, another pair of Harriers now roaring in from the sea, more napalm down, exploding inside the same fireball, it rising still higher, the helicopter rocking and lurching as the pilot brought it level and right, away from the line of flight of the Harriers, Skinny Hughes pressing his face to the Plexiglas, his eyes looking aft and down...

"Jaysus, Sean, they got you, now...Dear Jaysus in heaven...Where ya gone, now Sean? Where at all...?"

CHAPTER NINETEEN
The Brudder

"**W**ell, here they are, the Riley boys on their afternoon nap..."

John Riley opened his eyes, fixing on Margaret Riley as she stepped to Michael's bedside, reaching for his forearm, feeling his forehead as mother might check for a fever. Rising, he looked down at Michael, still asleep, and then to Margaret. "I'll use the head here and be on."

She smiled quickly at him, her eyes then back to Michael. "Thanks for staying, John. It was a big help...huge." She looked at him. "Brendan's just getting his afternoon nap down and I didn't want to break *that* up." Her eyes went back to Michael as she reached to adjust the lay of a tube at his shoulder.

John Riley stepped behind her and into the bathroom. Finishing, he flushed the toilet and washed his hands, looking in the mirror, fixing on his eyes and his forehead. 'That's it,' he spoke under his breath, 'the eyes and the forehead,' thinking now of Paddy and Kevin, Michael and himself, and now Bryan Canny. 'Incredible.'

Turning off the light, John Riley went back into the room, stepping to the foot of Michael Riley's bed. His hands resting on the serving table, he fixed on Michael's face, his hands now gripping the table's edge, his head back. "Incredible."

Margaret turned back to him. "Incredible?"

John Riley shook his head slightly, turning to her. "Yes, 'Incredible.'" He checked the time on his watch. "Twenty-two hours ago, Michael Riley's chest was held open by surgical spreaders as four sections of artery were removed from his thighs and calves and sewn into his heart." He looked over at Michael Riley, then back to her. "That's incredible."

Margaret fixed on him, nodding as she blessed herself, her left hand going to her mouth, her eyes welling. "Yes, a miracle, truly God's own miracle."

John Riley reached to her, his arm over her shoulders, bringing her to him, feeling the quiet rhythm of her crying.

"What's this? Someone die?"

They both looked at Michael Riley, his eyes open and on them.

"Is it me? Did I die? Am I dead?" Michael Riley looked left and right, then to his hands, moving them up as he smiled. "Nope."

Margaret reached to him, kissed his forehead. "Not dead yet..." She forced a smile, now one coming full to her face, her eyes beaming. "Not by a long shot."

Michael smiled at her, then looked to John Riley, fixing on him as he spoke to Margaret. "Can you give me a minute with the Brudder?"

Margaret nodded, kissing her fingers and touching his cheek before smiling at John Riley and leaving the room.

Michael Riley's eyes followed her out the room. "Could you close the door, John?"

John Riley nodded, closing the door, stepping to the window side of the bed.

"Have a seat."

John Riley fixed on Michael Riley, his eyes now away, as he pulled the wooden chair by the window to the bedside, sitting down. "What's up?"

Michael Riley shifted in his bed, still looking away, then back at him. "It's about 'over there', Ireland." He took a breath, releasing it easily, seeming to organize his thoughts. "When I was under for the operation yesterday, and later in the ICU, I had dreams or mental wanderings or illusions, whatever - all sorts of things..."

"Your life flashing before you?"

"Yes, maybe. Sure. Why not?" Michael Riley shrugged, his eyes to John Riley, then quickly away. "Years going back and forth, in and out." He turned to his brother, "...but it was mostly about Ireland, my times there, Maira, Sean, the years after...craziness, most of it..."

He fixed on the ceiling. "Anyway, when I woke up and saw Margaret, I had this great fear that I had not told her about it, any of it." He turned to John Riley. "I had, of course, even about '83 with you and Hank." He looked away, smiling. "She couldn't believe that, especially Plan A, you remember, bribing our way across the border...breaking Sean out...guns ablazing, sneaking him back to a trawler."

They were both laughing now, John Riley up quickly to keep Michael from pulling away from his tubes. "Insane, John, that's the only word...especially you, old straight-arrow John Riley. Couldn't believe you, though...working that Tommy gun...at Hank's training facility? Incredible."

John looked at his brother, smiling, his head nodding as he sat down, seeming to be laughing inside at it all, now crossing his legs, hands joined across his chest, quiet.

"What I wanted to talk with you about was...It was about a discussion I had with Bryan while you and Hank were out in the helicopter...back in '83." Michael turned to John, raising himself up on an elbow, fixing closely on him. "Did I ever tell you about that?"

John Riley's mind flashed back to the helicopter skimming over the farmland of Renvyle, hightailing it away from a smoldering black and brown hole-in-the-ground, hoping against hope that they weren't at that moment in some Harrier's gun sights. "No, don't think so. Pretty chaotic piece of time...remember near crapping my pants when that last Harrier roared by at 400-plus."

Michael Riley laughed, relaxing now. "Yes...a day to remember, that's for sure..." He shifted on the bed, his eyes now fixing on John Riley. "About Bryan...well, I'd asked him, you know, what was it like, his years with Maira and Sean? How they lived, got on together...how Maira died...?"

John Riley sat up. "Now that I would've remembered..."

Michael Riley eased back. "Yes, I guess so. Anyway, she'd thrown me out in '60." A quick look. "Told you about that?"

"Oh yeah, the guns and stuff..."

Michael Riley nodded, "Yes, bad day, bad week. Anyway, Bryan could only remember back to '64. They were in Bogside then, moving around inside it and around Derry, some time in Belfast, using different names, in and out of schools. Maira working in pubs to keep them fed and all, sometimes leaving them with neighbors for days at a time while she was on a mission for her unit." Michael Riley paused, his eyes away, now back.

"What Bryan remembered most about this time, though, were the fights, all the time fighting and cursing someone or some group or other. She'd fight with her unit leader, her cell fighting with another cell, other cells, nationalist groups at war with one another, in a pub or at one another's place, pistols and knives at 20 paces on Monday night, one-for-all, all-for-one on Tuesday morning. Then came '69, the 'Battle of Bogside'" Michael Riley paused, looking at John Riley. "Ever heard of that?"

"Not really... I think Mom went off on it for a bit...nothing I really remember."

"Well, it's a section of Derry and it went on for three days, maybe more...A continuing 70-plus hour riot that was beyond the police doing anything about. British soldiers had to go over to straighten things out, restore order. Well, this pretty much did it for Maira, put her over an already high wall." Michael Riley was lying back now, his head at the ceiling, a quick wipe of an eye.

"Bryan learned later that she wanted to blow up the mayor's house, at dinner time, his wife and five children, and the 'traitors' in their service, too, all of them. 'Get'em all in a blow,' she'd be mumbling, 'root and branch.' No one could keep her quiet about it or from trying to do it.

"So, they helped her along, made a bomb for her and all, even mapped a way for her through a wood to the rear of the estate – and that's where it went off and her with it… remote detonation, is what Bryan said."

John Riley tensed, re-crossed his legs, his arms going tighter across his chest.

"Bryan said she'd been crazed by then, mumbling about traitors, eyes always flashing back and about, hearing things that no one else heard, singing the praises of martyrs, 'No greater life led than one given up for Ireland.'"

Michael Riley turned to him, shaking his head.

"This was the fall of '69, Sean was fifteen and Bryan nine or ten, orphans in hell. Jesus Christ." Michael Riley shook his head, looking away.

"He was such a handsome boy, John. Had Maira's red hair, quick eyes - and Sean could laugh back then, when I knew him."

"He was what, then, the last time you saw him?"

"Five, just five…flew over for his birthday. Wanted to bring both of them back, out of that place…she'd have none of it. 'The fight's here, don't you know, not at some swell's bake sale in America.' A pause, eyes away. "Bryan said that whenever Sean disappointed her, she'd chide him with 'What can I expect from the son of a Traitor-man." He looked at John, his head still, eyes blank. "That's what I was to Sean - Traitor-man, that was my name to him…Christ.

"Anyway, the boys were separated then, after Maira 'died.'. Neighbors took Bryan in, later getting him to the family in Dublin that raised him. Sean was sent to

Catholic Services in Derry...bolted the next day, wandering the alleys and pubs of Bogside, living with those in the cause, maybe even some involved in Maira's killing...who knows? It was that sort of place."

The room was quiet now. Through the closed door, sounds of nurses attending their duties, the low and distant murmur of planes coming down the Potomac toward National Airport. Michael Riley took a deep breath, holding it for a moment before letting it out, controlled, his eyes fixed above. "All this was by way of a warning..."

"A warning?"

"Yes, about what might happen that night, going up to Gawlaun, breaking Sean out. 'Be careful' Bryan had said. 'And don't be telling him who you are till we're all safe out, now, and there's others about.'" Michael Riley turned to John Riley, fixing on him, his brogue now gone to a near perfect Bryan Canny. "'Of the people Sean's come to hate in this world...'" Michael Riley turned away. "He left it there...enough said, I guess."

John Riley sat forward in his chair, uncertain of what to do, if anything at all.

"So, I had always wanted to tell you all this...you never know..." Michael Riley shrugged, motioned to the tubes and the hospital room about them. "Might not get another chance. Just wanted to be sure you knew that Sean was dead for me before we even got on the plane, that the Harriers may have saved my life, maybe all of ours...who's to know." He turned away for a moment, seeming to organize his thoughts, now back at John.

"For a while after we got back, all I could think about was what Maira and Ireland and the times had done to Sean. I'd be thinking about the time we spent together, little things, him against me sitting under a tree, napping and then up, running after a ball, tumbling down a hill, laughing...all this wonderment and joy gone to a murderous criminal whose truest expression of life, of his being, in fact his legacy, was the taking the lives of others, killing them." He paused then turned, his arm off the side of the bed, his hand open.

"And then, John, one morning, it was all gone. Woke up and it was gone. Just laid there on the bed, looking out on the park, and it was over, the storm had cleared, calmed, a separation had come from that part of my life. A thing I could not fix and could not escape, was somehow gone, just gone." He paused now, up on his elbow, looking to John Riley.

"And in it all, you were always there, calling, checking in on me, somehow knowing when I needed to be with someone. But when it was over, it was so over that I never thought to thank you, to let you know how important you were in this happening, it getting over."

Michael Riley smiled now. "So, thank you, John Riley. You'll always be the 'brudder' to me, my anchor to windward." Michael Riley's eyes went moist but only that, and quick as a flash opened wide, his head up now, face bright and beaming. "And we did get something out of it all? Didn't we?"

John Riley sat up, struck by the wonder and discovery in his brother's eyes. "Yes?"

"Bryan Canny! Yes, Bryan Canny, over from Ireland. working for Hennessey Construction…a new life for him with us." He looked away briefly, then back, fixing hard on his brother. "Whatever good there may have been in Maira, Bryan Canny got all of it, all of it…and he's all but family to us, now…especially you and Brigit."

John Riley sat up, fixing on his brother, on his eyes, then off them to the heart monitor on the wall above the bed, red and green lines tracing across the screen, rising and falling. "Yes…family…I guess…hadn't thought of him quite that way, but I guess he is…"

CHAPTER TWENTY
Cross Country

T hey'd been right. The first thousand miles was easy, long flat stretches, speed limit signs so much wasted paint on metal.

Patrick Riley Rhinemann was driving a camp-mate's Mercedes 380SL sports coupe, touching past 100 miles per hour any number of times, having to work at times to keep below that. The flat desert of southeast New Mexico had begun to rise, though, getting some roll and character to it as he headed north through Roswell and Vaughn, catching I-40 at Santa Rosa and heading east from there. In the brilliance of a full desert moon, he could make out the Sangre De Cristo Mountains, the southernmost edge of the Rockies.

Now, the Rockies he knew, mostly from skiing with his parents in Aspen on different vacations and breaks. But he had always flown in and out, another destination, roads built, buildings up, golf courses laid out and the grass cut.

Islands of places and people, the same people, in the great expanse between New York and Los Angeles. A "coaster" by birth and soul, the great middle of the country was largely unknown to him, other than at 30,000 feet. He had given himself a full day and a half to cover 1,800 miles of it, two thirds of its expanse, on the ground, its surface a scant five inches beneath the low-slung chassis of the car

In his twenty-two years, Patrick Rhinemann had travelled many thousands of miles, across oceans and times. He had done his junior year abroad at Haifa University in Israel, spending most of the following summer there as well. Learning to read and write Hebrew, he was approaching fluency in it, especially after eight weeks in the New Mexico desert north and east of Carlsbad, where it was the only language spoken, the only one allowed. *Camp Hope* is what they called it, 4,600 acres of scrub desert where the temperatures rose above 100 most of the 60 days he had trained there.

But that was the whole idea. This is what military deployment meant in Israel and that's where he was to serve.

He had first been approached at Cornell at the close of the fall trimester. His language skills and interest in Israeli politics had caught the attention of his academic adviser. And his family history was known to them - his father a survivor of the death camps, and his family - father, mother, sister and brothers - all lost. Can you serve? Will you serve? These were the questions, the easy ones.

Camp Hope was run by the Leader. He had met and married an American physician in Israel, a volunteer at a military hospital in Haifa. Returning with her to the United States, they had carved Camp Hope out of her family's holdings, she returning to medicine and finding ways to help the cause.

An unofficial training facility for American volunteers, the camp had no buildings, only tents, and these would be moved with each eight-week session. The *camp-mates,* this is how they referred to one another, would muster at the Leader's residence, be quickly taken to that session's bivouac area where the tents were to be raised and the camp established.

Here they were under the direction of a training officer, drilled daily and introduced to a rigorous conditioning program, the distances run given in kilometers with all units of measure in the metric system. There were words to learn about military rank and protocol, the rules of it all, and then about guns and aircraft and artillery and tanks and what they could do and how they were used.

And teams, always teams, always the unit, together, each man among them precious. 'You are different from them in this,' they were told. 'We are a *we*, an *us*, and they are *them* – different, scatterings of desert trekkers, thousands of them but each, in combat, alone, without a team, a single person against the right and might of Israel.'

The Leader would meet with each team each week, and twice had accompanied them on night maneuvers. Night fighting was his specialty and they had thrived in his company. He would meet with each camp-mate twice, once each month, each time for two hours. It was he who made the final decision whether a camp-mate was fit to serve, to die, for Israel.

By the time the September sun had risen, Patrick Rhinemann was well into Texas, cutting across the top hat of that state and then into Oklahoma whose distance – less the panhandle – he had covered by afternoon. His mind now expanded to the full size of the place, farm land and fields made over from virgin plains trekked by Asians centuries past and trekked back by them as others from another ocean came west, filling the land and taming it, too, and claiming their place among the nations of the earth. 'Yes…we did that…we did…'

It was harvest time and Patrick Rhinemann breathed in the sweetness of the corn, it seeming to thicken the air with its richness and life as he drove deeper into Missouri. Here the road went east and north, more fields of corn and now cotton, as the Ozarks rose in the low sky to his right. By dusk, he was approaching St. Louis, the Gateway Arch now on his eastern horizon, something telling him to hurry, that he had to get to it.

Pressing forward, the sun now setting on the horizon, shadows gone to evening glow, his eyes fixed on the Arch, working the roads about it. Parking illegally by the entry gate, running, sprinting to the cashier's booth, money paid, the elevator just made, it rising and catching the sun again as it climbed the Arch. The lands he'd just crossed, these now reached out before him, higher and farther and…"My, God," he spoke, "My God…didn't know, never knew…no idea."

Stretching before Patrick Rhinemann was the expanse of the land, the thousand miles he had driven and the thousand beyond to the far ocean… America entire, save that at his back. Turning east, he peered into the darkness. 'Home,' he thought, '800 miles. I can do that now, start tonight, get some rest and right on through. And then…then the beyond from there…Israel.

'But Michael, first, not before speaking with Michael…never.'

CHAPTER TWENTY-ONE
On the River

*I*t was after his son Patrick had been put out that John Riley began sculling. The winter of 1970 was when, the hell of deciding it, and then the hell of doing it, putting Patrick out, that is.

He had lost his taste for hunting afterward, a trip made out west was when, a story heard of the weaker calves of the herd left to wander in its wake and the same, too, for such babes of a tribe. It was told by an Indian guide, the ways of his people, the lives lived on the Great Plains, of the buffalo and the human beings that trailed them. The Sioux called it 'putting out' and putting Patrick Riley out was what they had done.

And in this, a hole had come to John Riley's day. It had started, his day, before 5 am when he woke for his time with Patrick. It would last till 6 when John Riley was to shower and dress for work. Yes, a hole in his time that now needed filling and he could not do it indoors. Something in him needed to be out-of-doors, outside in the air, moving in it. An athlete young and still fit, he had never found the rhythm of the run that carried so many others their miles of it each day.

It was in the early May of that year, an evening at the Kennedy Center, walking its terrace above the Potomac when into his view hove a lone sculler on the silver flat of the river. He watched as the man moved smoothly on the seat of the craft, the oars catching the weight of the water, his legs extending and then his back and arms pulling and again and again, in a precise, silent glide over the water. It had been the motion that caught his eye, not the man, nor the scull, the motion of the thing and he knew he had to do this.

In four classes of time he became certified and bought a scull to be kept at Thompson's Boat House on the river at Foggy Bottom. And by the June of that year, John Riley had found his sanctuary, the place where mind met soul, his body disappearing into a rhythmic force that fueled his being. The stroke was all, legs extending to arms pulling, feathering the paddle of the oars flat, sliding aft in the seat, chest compressing to upright thigh, feathering the paddle square and into the water of the river, and again...

Yes, the stroke. The legs is where it begins and then to the arms, the pull of the oars, the stretch and contraction of sinew, the force of will, and John Riley would escape time and find himself, alone, lungs filled and exhaling as he slid forward, the paddle of his oars digging full into the river and again and again and again until there was enough found of himself to do another day...

It is not every day that a person comes to so piercing an awareness as John Riley had done the day before. Bryan Canny, with whom he had spent every working day for more than five years now, had become in this time more than a part of his life. He had become an *element* of it, something presumed to be always there and of an unappreciated consequence. Bryan Canny was, in fact, a core force in how, and perhaps why, John Riley was living his life. This, and more. Bryan Canny, who until noon Wednesday had no family at all remaining to him, was Michael Riley's son...

John Riley had not returned to the office after his time in Michael Riley's hospital room Wednesday afternoon. He instead found himself driving about the city, along the Potomac, the tree-lined edges of West and East Potomac Parks, past baseball cages and rugby pitches, polo and soccer fields and whatever they called the ground for cricket.

He felt the slight rise in the car as he crossed over Inlet bridge linking West and East Potomac Parks and with it sensed in himself a passing from new world to old. Washington Channel was soon to his left as he drove along the bank of East Potomac Park. Across the Channel were the marinas and tourist restaurants where once had been the Southwest Waterfront of his early years; fishing scows and honkytonk bars, the vibrance of commerce and life at a river's edge, the Rusty Nail and his last day alone with Paddy Riley.

Yet for all the comfort of his memories, John Riley was afraid, as well. Not because he didn't know what to do, but because he did. He had to tell Bryan Canny that Michael Riley is his father.

John Riley had arrived home early that evening to an empty house. Going to his basement office, he did some things that needed doing until dinner time. Mary Kate was there, with Eileen and Mary, a dinner hurried by their talk and anticipation of going back down to visit Michael Riley afterward. John Riley stayed home, saying he'd had a long visit in the afternoon and that he had work to do in the basement. Though awake when Eileen came up later, he lay silent in their bed, she assuming he was asleep, he wishing he were.

But this was Thursday morning, a restless sleep forgotten, a new day altogether. Warm in a full September way, it was still summer no matter the few weeks till fall. An early morning on the river and John Riley felt himself charged by it, certainly relieved. There would be no one to speak to and that was just what he needed - to be alone doing what he always did this time of day, weather and season permitting, and this made him invisible in a most welcome way.

It was two miles from Thompson's Boat House to the tip of Hains Point, and it was to there and back that had become John Riley's morning scull. Forty minutes down and back, a good pull of the oar. But there was more to it today, there was what remained in his mind's eye of yesterday, of the Southwest Waterfront and his times there with his father and mostly Daddy Riley, his grandfather. So today, to test his fitness and strength, he had decided to go to the Point and then up Washington Channel and back, adding two full miles to the normal four.

Soon falling into the rhythm of the thing, the rowing, the fore and aft of his seat on its rails, John Riley came to be a human piston running the course of its cylinder, well oiled and fueled. The still of the water and the rising of the sun soothed him as he slid beneath the arches of Memorial Bridge and out into the open Potomac, the expanse of the water at an early flood tide, the silent movement of bicyclists on the land, and soon the memories of times long past.

Daddy Riley kept a scow in the Channel and among John Riley's earliest pleasures was fishing with him from it. His clearest memory of the time was an 18-pound rockfish he'd caught one evening, later showing it to his father and Jack Hennessey on Mr. Jack's porch. And now the memory of a row in the scow with Paddy Riley, this to the head of the Channel, where rust red iron gates dammed the water of the Tidal Basin.

It was here that he learned of the building and working of the Basin, and the Washington Channel, too, of gates that opened on the Potomac to capture the water of a flood tide, and closed to hold it until the tide was at full ebb. It was then that the gates were to be opened at the head of the Channel, Paddy Riley had told him, flushing out the Channel of the waste of man and beast, carrying it to where the Anacostia met the Potomac and on to the bay and the sea.

It was here that Paddy Riley had said it was 'engineers' that had done all this, figured it all out, laid the plans, drew the drawings and done it, and wouldn't it be grand if John Riley were to become one someday, an engineer that is, and find such wondrous things to do with his life.

John Riley had never heard the word 'engineer' before that day, but he was never to forget it. If it's engineers that build things, then that's what he wanted to be because that's all he ever wanted to do, build things. And for no reason apparent to him, Bryan Canny now came to mind - Bryan Canny in Glover Park getting ready for his day, having forgotten he had a father or any hope of knowing who he was, even forgetting, perhaps, that he had forgotten.

Yes, Bryan Canny on 42nd Street, starting his car without the slightest sense that he had dinner with his father at John Riley's home Sunday evening, and with his grandmother and his first cousin, Brigit Riley Winslow, as well....

'Yes, Bryan's to know and soon,' John Riley spoke under his breath. 'He's the one who must know first, the one to say what's to be done about it all. It's his life that will be most affected.' Michael Riley's face now came to mind, and his telling of it being over, 'over there' being over and done, and his happiness and gratitude for being free of it and that part of his life.

Now one of the cautions of sculling is that, while a practiced sculler in familiar waters knows where he's going by seeing where he's been, he still cannot see what's ahead and coming at him.

John Riley had heard the sound of hard-rushing water, though had no reason to suspect that it was coming off the bow of a very-fast-moving boat, one approaching from dead ahead. The muffled sound of the boat's engines came to him only as the bow of the thing crushed his starboard oar, with the boat's swerving away spraying him full and hard with river water, blinding him as the force of the boat's wake capsized his scull, tossing him into the river, his head down and breath held as he went under the surface of the water.

Free of the scull, John Riley went deeper, fighting the buoyancy of his life belt, furiously working to get away from where be believed the scull to be and the sound he heard underwater of the engines and propellers of the boat now racing away.

Thrusting with arms and legs, he continued as far as he could, finally breaking the surface and drawing a deep breath, clearing the water from his eyes with his hands, the roar of the boat's engines clearer now as it sped south, down river.

"Johnny boy! Behind you!"

John Riley spun around, blinking the water from his eyes as they worked to fix on Hank Johnson standing at the bow rail of a dark blue skiff, another man at the helm behind him. "Christ, Hank. What the hell you doing out here?" He pointed in the direction of the boat as it sped south. "You see what just happened? Son-of-a-bitch!"

"Of course…what d'ya think? I come out here to read the paper?"

John Riley began swimming to the skiff, his right hand striking something on the surface. It was the paddle of the oar that the boat had struck. Picking it up, he pitched it into the skiff as he swam to it, taking Hank Johnson's hand as he got his right leg over the gunwale and pulled himself aboard.

Getting to his feet and shaking the water from his hair and hands, he took an offered towel from Hank Johnson, drying his arms and legs, now pointing down-river. "Hell, if you were out here and saw what was happening, why didn't you stop the son-of-a-bitch?"

"Johnny Boy, Johnny Boy, again, your instinct to gratitude never fails to amaze me. Here you are, flapping around in thirty feet of water, a couple three hundred yards from shore, your craft capsized and useless to you and the first thing that comes to mind is screaming at the guys who pulled your ass out of the water...Amazing...*Truly* amazing."

Hank Johnson motioned the other man toward the capsized scull. Reaching into the water as it came along side, he gripped the leader wire at its bow before moving aft to fasten it to the port cleat of the skiff, the other man heading the skiff upriver toward Thompson's Boat House.

Turning to John Riley, Hank Johnson came forward, shaking his head, sitting against the port gunwale, opposite John Riley. "You okay now, Johnny Boy? Got yourself pretty well calmed down?"

John Riley shrugged a laugh, waving Hank Johnson's smile away. "Yeah, fine. Really, I'm fine."

"And?"

"And *thank you* for the hand."

"Yeah, sure. Touched, I am *truly* touched."

John Riley stood away from the gunwale, looking aft now and finding his balance as he motioned in the direction the boat had taken as the skiff made its way north. "What the hell's going on here, Hank?"

Hank Johnson turned back from downriver, fixing on John Riley. "Johnny Boy, I believe in the Big Money, they call it "IGWIWA.""

John Riley tried to solve what sounded like an acronym, to form the letters into a word, sounding it out - "Ig-w...?"

"Don't bother, it's an old game, just a new twist...I-G-W-I-W-E-T as in 'I Get What I Want *Every* Time.'" Hank Johnson winked. "Yeah, looks like your pal Keith Pierson just promoted himself to National Grand Master."

Hank Johnson stood full up, fixing on John Riley and not speaking until he had his eyes. "Again, I *must* ask…how'd a smart man such as yourself ever get mixed up with a prick like this?"

CHAPTER TWENTY-TWO
Semper Paratus

F irst off the skiff at the boat house, John Riley stepped quickly across the floating dock toward the locker room, Hank Johnson quick stepping close behind. Taking a final rub of his head and short hair, John Riley pitched the towel to the bench in front of his locker as he began loosening his yellow foam life belt. Looking up with a start, he turned to Hank Johnson. "Hey…wait a minute. You *knew* I was going to need a towel?"

Hank Johnson smiled. "Of course. What'd you expect? *Semper Paratus…*"

"That's the Coast Guard."

"Whatever."

"And what were you doing out there anyway?"

"What you're paying me to do – watching out for that skinny little ass of yours." Hank Johnson sat down on a bench, looking about, putting his finger to his lips as he listened for two full counts, satisfied that they were alone. "They've been tailing Brigit, too."

"Brigit?! My daughter? Who's..." He'd stepped to Hank Johnson, his head bearing down on him.

"Easy, Johnny Boy, Easy." Hank Johnson cocked his head, listening for a count, then fixing on John Riley. "I picked up the tail on you after lunch, out in front of the Hay-Adams. Followed them to the hospital, got the license numbers, both of them."

"Both?"

"Yeah, both. A Beemer and Cedes. They weren't taking any chances. Registered to Stuka Security, a private outfit headquartered outside Cleveland. When we track it all down, pretty sure we'll find it's a Mid-America outfit. Likely that the guy running it – Bruce Stuka – was in the army with Pierson...excepting he stayed in. Did twenty years and came out a top kick in Army security service, a lot of it with the MPs..."

John Riley smiled. "Like someone else I...?"

"Don't even think of going there, John Riley...I was an officer in the *Marine Corps*. We'd skewer punks like this guy over charcoal before football games."

John Riley nodded, smiling as he motioned him to go on.

"Anyway - before I was so *rudely* interrupted - he joined Pinkerton for a while and then set up his own shop...Mid-America's their only client."

John Riley looked away as he sat down, his elbows now on his knees, his head shaking. "Christ...what the hell's going on here?"

"Yeah, like I was saying, Johnny Boy, you're playing hardball with the big guys, here...new rules..."

"New rules..."

"Yeah, like in no rules...all's fair in love and war and the Big Money." The sound of a locker opening and shutting sat them both up. Hank Johnson rose, stepped around the line of lockers and returned, giving the all's clear as he sat back down.

"Anyway, at the hospital, I called in support from Atlantic while they were waiting on you with Michael – tailed the tails, as it were. One went with you, Potomac Park, a site Hennessey's working at First and I, Northeast, and on home. The other went to the Capital Yacht Club in Southwest..."

John Riley fixed harder on him.

"Yeah, where Michael keeps his boat, The *Rugger Hugger*? And what the hell's that all about?" A shrug, his arms out, hands up, John Riley waving him to continue. "Anyway, he greased the palm of the attendant and got aboard."

"You mean the boat?"

"Exactly...that's the boat, and that's the message. We know where you are, John Riley...know where your brother keeps his boat. We know when your daughter's to home..."

"Christ...and Brigit, too..."

"Right. So, we have to be careful here...careful and smart..."

"Yes..."

"One thing we got going for us is them knocking you out of the boat just now..."

"Oh, really? That was a good thing, then? Just now? Me nearly getting killed on the river?"

"Sure...count on it. Some one's in deep kimchi over that."

"I don't follow."

"Rule number one in the intimidation game is *you never, ever kill* the fella you're trying to intimidate...ruins everything."

"Sure, I guess..." John Riley fixed on Hank Johnson, their eyes holding. "New game, new rules..."

Hank Johnson smiled, nodding. "Now you're getting it, Johnny Boy."

John Riley stood, pulling his shirt up over his head. "So, what we do now?"

"Like before, we play careful and we play smart." Hank Johnson stood up, started to pace. "First thing we gotta figure out is what this guy wants...he's got buckets of dough, buckets of buckets, for Chrissakes. What do you have that he can't get anywhere else? Is he just looking for a better price?"

"Not sure. Getting Hennessey Land all in a package puts him dead center in the DC market and quickly. But there are other groups, families looking to cash out, same as us. Nothing that his money can't fix."

"You sure? How are you on this deal with him now?"

John Riley rose, slipped out of his speedo swim suit, drying himself as he stepped past Hank Johnson to the shower. "Give me a minute…"

Hank Johnson checked the area once more, picking up a towel as he went to the shower area where John Riley was just turning off the water and taking a fresh towel. "Well, he wanted us back in Chicago tomorrow, Friday. I told Brigit to put them off till next week."

"Right. And that's where I came in. She called me right after she spoke with Townsend. He'd gotten to her on her private home number."

John Riley turned to him.

"That's right. Got her number and knew she was there…as in they were tailing her."

"Whoa…they're pushing the wrong button there. How'd she take it?"

Like you said, they pushed the wrong button. She gave me *carte blanche*, no expense spared 'Check everything, every line, every office. Sonsabitches.' Pretty pissed off young lady."

"She can get there quick when her own's threatened."

"And the deal? You anywhere near closed…?"

"Was moving right along, though I was having doubts…the stuff you were turning up on him…Hardin Brooks from Fox Worthy was getting down on them, especially Pierson, seemed too much like they were rushing to sign, talking about writing checks and getting it done by Christmas."

"And?"

"After this?" John Riley's arms were out. "Running me down in the river, tailing Brigit…it's a HELL NO! I don't want that son-of-a-bitch in the neighborhood. Wait a minute, wait-a-minute…"

John Riley turned away, opened his locker, took out his tote bag. "You find out anything about Pierson and the Hay-Adams?"

"Sure did. Went back there after I met with Grace about Chicago. Spoke with your man Simon de Vries. Pierson's people have been all over it. Tipping staff heavy, asking questions about who's been there over the years, what's happened there, who's sleeping with who. The Truman Suite is of particular interest to them, as in, did he ever sleep there? Why do they call it that? Any memorabilia, in the basement, in a warehouse? Any staff from the fifties and sixties still in town? Had architects in, too. The top two floors are of greatest interest to them."

John Riley had his underwear on and shirt buttoned, now tying his tie. "And the Brady Estate?"

"Have someone running that down this morning."

"Make that a top priority…" John Riley was seated, tying his shoes. "Hank, you know what's going to happen to the Hay-Adams and the Brady Estate if we sell to one of the insurance companies?"

"Haven't a clue…"

"You ever see the inside of an *insurance* company, a big one? The org chart?"

"No…"

"In an eleven-point font, it'd fill the floor of this room. Minimum." John Riley stretched his arms, left and right, back to front. "One of these outfits gets Hennessey Land? Every part and piece of it will disappear to the outside world for a year." He fixed on Hank Johnson. "No, check that. Two at a minimum, maybe three years, even more." He looked at himself in the mirror in his locker, slammed it shut, turning to Hank Johnson. "What about Brigit?"

Hank Johnson smiled. "Well, Bruce Stuka's going to be spending the better part of this morning tearing a new asshole for the asshole who ran you down just now. And then he's going to spend the rest of the day making damn sure Keith Pierson never finds out about it." Hank

Johnson enjoyed a quiet smile. Shaking his head, he fixed back on John Riley, continuing.

"Brigit should be okay. The play's on you, not her. It's you they need. You're the person who makes the decisions."

John Riley nodded. 'Yes, this is true,' he thought to himself. 'It is on me…'

"My guess is they just wanted her to know they're around, maybe knock her off her game…get her a little rattled." Hank Johnson smiled again. "Looks like they screwed up there, too."

"She's a tough one, Brigit." John Riley checked the lock on his locker and picked up his tote bag. "How's your time today?"

"You should know, you're paying for it."

"Great. Let's get some breakfast. I need a meeting with Brigit and Bryan at nine. You too." John Riley just remembered something about Matt Malloy and the National Trust for Historic Preservation. He fixed on Hank Johnson. "You good to go to Chicago overnight, right? Bring Hastings back tomorrow morning?"

"Like the lady said, Johnny Boy, I got *carte blanche…*" Hank Johnson smiled.

"Yeah…I know, I know, 'Whatever the hell that means.'" Come on, let's go. Nothing like getting run down in a river by your own brother's boat to build an appetite."

CHAPTER TWENTY-THREE
The War Room

"We swept this room last night. John's office too." Hank Johnson flicked on the overhead lights in the small conference room in Hennessey Construction's 15th Street office, making way for Brigit Winslow to follow. She placed a file on the table and turned to him.

"I guess we should be flattered…so much attention to a regional construction company…"

"Well, when you're dealing in a billion or so in real estate, people are going to take any advantage you allow them."

They turned to the door as Bryan Canny stepped in, his eyes about the room. "Where'd they put a thing like, now, Hank, under the table?"

"Depends. There, in an overhead light…just about anywhere."

"Find anything, then, did you?" Bryan Canny looked at the ceiling as he stepped to the coffee service on the sideboard.

"Not yet…may not. Just a thing you do when you find out your top guys are being tailed."

Bryan Canny looked quickly to him as Brigit Winslow's eyes went from the thermostat to the overhead top-hat light. "They're voice activated?"

"Generally." Hank Johnson poured himself a cup of coffee at the sideboard. "Coffee?"

Brigit shook her head no. "…Then how do you find them?"

"Spectrum scanners…"

"But if there's no one speaking, they're not on, right? The microphones?"

"Right."

Brigit Winslow looked at Hank Johnson. "So...?"

Hank Johnson fixed on her, his head cocked slightly. "So...the guys doing the sweep? They talk, you know, about baseball, or like they're on the cleaning crew force..." His hands were out slightly as in 'Do I have to draw you a picture?'"

"Guess that'd work." She stepped to the sidebar, poured a cup of coffee, maybe trying to disappear.

Bryan Canny turned to Hank Johnson. "So why the meeting, now, Hank?"

"We're at war." John Riley stepped into the room, a file folder in hand as he closed the door behind him. Placing the folder on the table, he went to the sideboard, poured himself a coffee and sat down. "Shall we begin?"

"War is it, now? Anyone in particular?"

"Mid-America Holdings." John Riley looked across the table, his eyes fixed on Bryan Canny as he sat down. "They've trod sacred ground, Bryan, disturbed peaceful waters."

"Indeed?"

"No. *In fact*." John Riley nodded at Brigit Riley. "They've been tailing Brigit and me, and maybe you, too."

Bryan Canny sat back, looked at Brigit and Hank, then back at John Riley. "And the waters?"

Hank Johnson sat forward. "They ran down Johnny Boy here on his morning scull...close enough to break an oar."

"Dad!" Brigit Winslow and Bryan Canny rose, she going to her father's side, a hand on his shoulder. "Are you alright?"

"No damage, so far...Did get a swallow or two of the Potomac, though...could be fatal."

"True enough." Hank Johnson chuckled.

Bryan Canny, still standing, leaned forward, his hands down and open on the table's surface, his head cocked. "You mean they *ran* you down, liked *varoom?*"

He caromed his right hand off the table surface as a flat rock might skip on a pond.

"Yeah, pretty much like that, a little louder, though…and a lot wetter. Knocked me off the scull, ass-over-tea-kettle into the water. Diving deep to get away from whatever it was." He looked to Hank Johnson. "Good thing Hank Johnson happened by…"

Hank Johnson laughed, sat back. "Well, we figured they were up to something on the water. Just taking reasonable precautions."

Bryan Canny looked at Brigit, then Hank Johnson. "What?"

Hank Johnson fixed on Bryan Canny, motioning toward John Riley. "We were at the Hay-Adams for lunch. Walked John to the front door. As he's driving away, I'm picking up on two cars following him. Grabbed the first cab in the queue and followed *them* following *him* to Georgetown Hospital." He motioned over his shoulder in the general direction of Georgetown with his right thumb and hand.

"Called in Atlantic Security, got some back-up." He nodded a confident smile at Brigit, winking at her. "'Tailing the tail' is what we call it. You can learn a lot that way."

Brigit Riley looked at John Riley and Bryan Canny before turning back to Hank Johnson, her eyes fixing on him, her hand motioning him to go ahead.

"One went to the marina where Michael keeps his boat. Figured they were up to something on the water. Arranged a skiff from Atlantic and was following Johnny Boy at a distance when it all went down." He looked at John Riley and winked, then back at Bryan Canny. "Don't think they meant to knock him in the water, just shake him up a bit…you know, let him know they're around, keeping an eye on him."

"Well there's a comfort, now."

Brigit Riley Winslow stepped to the sideboard, turning back slowly. "So, what happens now? We're at a whole new level here."

"We get even." John Riley motioned Brigit back to her chair. She sat down, opened her file before taking out her pen. "Call Townsend. Tell him Hennessey Land will be at Keith Pierson's office at 10 sharp Tuesday a.m., ready to close."

Brigit Winslow looked up as Bryan Canny sat forward, his head cocked, unsure. "You're going to meet the buggers, then, John?"

"I said 'Hennessey Land'..." John Riley turned to Brigit Winslow. "I'd been giving a lot of thought to Mid-America, to moving off them...and Pierson, too. Not a very nice guy."

Hank Johnson nodded in agreement as John Riley sat back, his hands now flat on the table. "Hank here, well, he's been a real pain about Pierson, keeps asking what a 'nice guy like me' is doing with a son-of-a-bitch like him." He turned to Hank Johnson, winked a quick wink then turned to the others as he opened his folder and took out several sheets of paper.

"I've had Grace work up a schema on when Mid-America first contacted us about several of our properties - it's by month..." He handed out the sheets to each of them. "As you'll see, it links up pretty well with the politicking that's been going on since mid-'91." He gave them a minute to look at the sheet.

"The closer Clinton was getting to the nomination, the greater the interest. When he won it, that's when Mid-America first started talking in terms of taking the whole package, everything that Hennessey Land owned. After the election was when he started with the full schmooze, flying me down to Palm Beach, his executive vice president for retail acquisition practically moving to

Washington, working with Brigit on property visits, getting real chummy…"

Brigit Winslow sat back, an elbow on the arm of her chair, her right thumb and index finger to her cheek.

"What's her name?"

"Melanie Ingram."

John Riley nodded to her as he turned to Bryan Canny. "She was there Tuesday. The blond…kept going in and out for files,"

Bryan Canny nodded.

"Anyway…" John Riley waved his right arm off the table. "Mid-America's gone…but I don't want them knowing it just yet." There were nods of agreement from around the table. They understood.

"So, I've asked Hank to find two law firms in Chicago." He motioned to Hank Johnson to speak.

Hank Johnson sat forward. "We were to find two firms, both under 20 lawyers, each having dealt with senior level executives with the insurance companies and the Big Money in New York, and neither of which have had *any* discernable relationship with Fox Worthy."

Brigit Winslow sat forward, fixing hard on John Riley, her head at an angle, expecting him to speak. He sat forward, holding her eyes.

"Didn't want to bring you or anyone in on this directly, daughter."

"*Daughter?*" Brigit Winslow looked from her father to Hank Johnson and then back.

"Sorry, *Brigit.*" John Riley sat forward. "Hardin Brooks got me aside in the men's room at the airport, while we were waiting for the plane." He nodded to Brigit Winslow. "This is after on the sidewalk in town…gave me a full-court press on Mid-America…pushing too hard, trying to move too fast. Said this was Keith Pierson's game: sign a letter of intent for an eye-popping check, maybe ten percent of the whole deal, then lock it up for years of wrangling and waiting."

Brigit Winslow sat back. "Well, thanks for bringing me in…" She paused, looking at Bryan Canny then back at John Riley. "So, what does Hardin think about Hank here rounding up some new lawyers for us?"

"Doesn't know about it."

Brigit Winslow sat up in her chair for a full count, then back, looking away.

"Plausible deniability…" John Riley sat forward, against the table, his arms folded on it. "Brigit…" He waited for her eyes. "Brigit, Pierson talked about writing checks." He paused for effect. "I'm thinking about *one* check, the whole deal done by Christmas…all in and all out."

"Impossible." Brigit Winslow looked at Bryan Canny, getting a shrug of confusion, ignorance, before fixing back on John Riley. "Can't do it that quick."

"Not even the big guys, the *really* big guys?"

"The insurance companies? *Insurance* companies? Why would they…?"

"Well, first off, they've been talking about it…"

"By Christmas?"

"No, but I'm going to sweeten the deal. First company that writes the check before November 30 gets five percent off."

"Forty-five million dollars?!"

"Yep…about that."

Bryan Canny sat back in his chair as Hank Johnson leaned off the table. Brigit Winslow had frozen in place, her face motionless, her breathing stopped. The first movement was in her eyes, blinking once and then down at her hands on the table surface. "I can't believe what I am hearing…cutting forty-five million in value…" She looked up at her father, at him.

"I doubled the value of Hennessey Land in the last seven years…doubled it…seven years!" Her head shook as her hands locked in a tight grip on the table, her knuckles gone white. "I built over four hundred million dollars of value in this company, in a real estate *depression*, and you want to *give away* forty-five *million* of it to an eighty-billion-dollar insurance company...in Chicago!?"

John Riley was silent, his eyes fixed on Brigit Riley Winslow, his only response a slight nod of the head.

Brigit Winslow shook her head, took a deep breath, holding for a count then letting it out, her eyes fixed fully on John Riley. "Does your mother know what you're doing? How about Kay? Have you cleared this with your sister Kay? What about Michael? And Eileen? Does your wife know you want to *give away 45 million* dollars...?"

"No."

Brigit Winslow's head fell, it now shaking slightly before rising and turning to Bryan Canny, her eyes holding on him. "Just remembered, Bryan. Have a 9:30 call. Oklahoma. Please excuse me." With this, she rose and left the room, closing the door behind her.

John Riley fixed on the door, his head nodding slightly, a deep breath taken and held. Breathing out, he sat back in his chair, now fixing on Hank Johnson. "Hank, I need Hastings at National Airport *tomorrow*. Go to $250,000 if you have to...but I need him there...tomorrow."

Hank Johnson had sat forward, his eyes on the door for a bit before turning to John Riley, now nodding.

John Riley turned to Bryan Canny. "And Bryan, I want you ready to open any and all files Hastings' firm may request and to either or both of these insurance companies. I want a meeting at 10 am Tuesday in Chicago with a fully authorized representative from one of the insurance companies ready and willing to sign a letter of commitment." John Riley's hands spread open and flat on the table, his eyes back and forth on Bryan

Canny and Hank Johnson. "We all understand? Tuesday, 10 am, Chicago time?"

There was silent nodding.

"Good."

John Riley now held on Bryan Canny. "A lot of this going right will be on you and your IT people. Both of these insurance companies have a ton of data already but they're going to want more to sign by Tuesday." He paused, his right index finger down on the table surface. "They must have *every* confidence that we will provide *anything* they ask for and on a moment's notice. I want your people on triple time, bunked at the Hay-Adams and ready to go. And there'll be $10,000 for each on Tuesday if it all goes down right."

"Yes, John. Twenty-four-seven till notice and mum's the word."

"That's right, not a word, not a *syllable*." John Riley looked to Hank Johnson and back. "I need you to get your people on that now. Go over the meetings we've had with them, identify anything they've asked for in the past that we've been holding back on, and have it ready. Put yourself in their shoes, what would you want? Have it ready."

"Right, John."

John Riley sat back, his eyes closed for a moment, then again at Bryan Canny, checking his watch. "It's 9:34. Get going on that now. And something else. I need you to pick up Matt Malloy at the Westchester at 12:10 sharp and bring him to the Hay-Adams...we're having lunch with him."

"We...?"

"Yes, you and I, Bryan Canny and John Riley."

"Right, Bryan Canny and John Riley..."

John Riley stood. "I have some Hennessey Construction work to do...Grace knows about all of this. She's on twenty-four-seven as well and knows I'm to be available to either of you." He looked at each. "We all good here?"

"Aye, John Riley, good indeed."

CHAPTER TWENTY-FOUR
The Promise

"**I**s she in?" John Riley fixed on Brigit Winslow's assistant.

"She's on a call, Mr. Riley. Shall I interrupt her?"

"No...that's alright. Okay if I wait?"

"Certainly." The assistant rose, motioning to an arm chair by the window overlooking K Street. "Would you like coffee, water?"

"No, thanks." He smiled as he turned to the chair and sat down, his eyes closing as his hands rested on his thighs. *Sometime* had finally come, and it was now...

"Dad?"

He opened his eyes, looking up, glad for her smile, but unsure...

"How long have you been here?" Brigit Riley turned to her assistant then back.

"Not sure...maybe five minutes..."

"Dad? Are you alright...?"

"I'm fine..." He gripped the arms of the chair and raised himself, now erect and square, fixing on her. "We have to talk...can we use your office?"

Brigit Riley Winslow stepped back, motioning to her door. "Of course. Did you want coffee?"

He stepped past her, waving 'no' as he crossed the threshold into her office, turning, his hand on the inside door knob. Bringing her in with his arm, he motioned her to her chair by the couch. Closing the door behind her, he followed her in, sitting at the end of the couch nearest to her.

"So, have you spoken to Townsend?"

Brigit Winslow seemed surprised by the question, crossing her legs and resting her hands folded in her lap. "Yes."

"And?"

"Didn't like it. Wanted it tomorrow, then pressed for Monday." Her hands unfolded and rested on the arms of her chair. "But he took Tuesday, 10 am, in Pierson's office."

John Riley nodded. "Good…well done…"

The room was quiet, Brigit's hands joining again on her lap, she taking a breath, he looking away before turning to her, his arm now opening and resting on the arm of the couch between them, his eyes on her. "Couple of things…"

She sat up, nodding back, not smiling, not stern, no expression at all.

"About this morning…"

"Yes…this morning…you mean just now, with Bryan and Hank Johnson?"

"Yes, then. I want to apologize…should have kept you in the loop on what I was thinking, the Chicago lawyers. Mostly, though, for seeming not to respect your interest in Hennessey Land…Your success with it…all that you've done." He waited for a reaction but she made none.

"It's not my world, real estate, finance…that's your world and I may have gotten too far in front…not sure." He shifted in his seat, fixed closer on her, waiting for her eyes before continuing. "What I need from you…" He looked away, listening to his own words, unhappy with how they sounded, thinking now about what he wanted to say, wanted her to understand, working it all in his mind. "Listen, Brigit…look, you have to understand that everything I've been doing on Hennessey Land…"

"Yes?" Brigit Riley Winslow was sitting up, her head turned toward him, her eyes uncertain.

"It's this. Nothing, absolutely *nothing*, is going to happen with Hennessey Land that is not in your interest...is not good for you." He looked away. "It's been your life for the last five years...Maybe more..."

"More..."

"Okay, more..." He almost said 'Maybe too long' but was afraid she'd agree. "When we first spoke about you coming down to work for a while with Bob Hathaway, I hadn't expected you to be so good at it. You were running circles around him in a month...and now it's been more than five years..."

"Eight..."

"Okay, eight years...and now we've got a good chance to be all out by Christmas...maybe even get full price from one of the insurance companies. But the market is off, what? Maybe twenty percent in the last three years?"

Brigit Winslow nodded yes. "More than that, actually."

"And five years from now, if we hold, who knows? Could double?"

Another nod, another yes, this more hesitant, a sense to him of a fear in her that it was true.

"So, yes, a lot more." He sat forward, his eyes ahead. "It's just been in the last six months, the weight of what we're playing with here has come to some reality to me...the amount of it...near a billion dollars...unbelievable!"

"Believe it."

He turned to her, sitting back, wanting to reach for her hand but not. Her eyes were fixed away. "What do you want out of all this, Brigit? Where's the 'win' in it for *you*?"

She had come to an absolute stillness, seeming, for the moment, not even to be breathing. Her eyes closed now, a breath taken. "I don't know. I truly don't...not any longer."

John Riley sat forward. "At the hospital yesterday..."

Brigit's head turned quickly at him. "What about the hospital yesterday?"

Her eyes were on him now, as never before in their lives, warning him, perhaps, challenging, maybe daring him to say more.

John Riley shifted in his seat, now reaching for her forearm, holding it full in his right hand. "There's something you have to know, Brigit."

She pulled away but he held her firm, his eyes now on her, his head nodding. "Brigit, look at me…listen…Brigit…"

Her eyes went to him, her head shaking in the slightest way, her eyes now closing.

"It's about Patrick…"

Her eyes opened wide, back on him. "Don't you talk to me about Patrick…" She pulled her arm away.

Now John Riley closed his eyes, his head lowering, a doubt rising in him, wondering whether to go ahead…but he must. "It was the fall of 1969…a Saturday, late afternoon…one of those times where all the elements of a thing come together…and everything changes…"

She looked at him, her head cocked, her whole body seeming to ease, her shoulders falling a measure, curious.

"I was coming down the stairs, just gotten to the landing when the front screen door opened and Mom came in. She hadn't seen me and started for the kitchen…where you were on the phone. She stopped, we could both hear you speaking…you were upset…explaining to Jerry Davenport why you couldn't go to a dance with him that night…that you had to be with Patrick. Mom's hands went to her face as she caught her breath, her head falling, shaking slightly, eyes tearing." John Riley took a deep breath.

"Then, somehow, she sensed I was there, on the landing. She looked up, reaching for the banister…Taking a deep breath, she started up the stairs, one step at a time, then full up on the landing, stepping to me, her arms down, at her side. 'Hold me, John,' she said, 'Hold me...I need to be held...really need to be held.'

"Reaching for her arm, I held her. She was limp, standing against me, as if her legs were going to give way. I got my arms under hers, drew her closer...She was crying, her arms moving around me, pulling me close as her head settled on my chest...She stopped crying after a breath, just leaning against me...then another breath before looking up at me, her eyes closing. 'Yes,' she said. 'Alright...yes...'

"Turning, she looked down in the direction of the kitchen. You had hung up with Jerry. All was quiet but for you...You were crying...Mom took another breath. 'Yes,' she said again, her eyes away, then on me. 'But you're going to have to do it...And Brigit's never to know about just now, never. You have to promise me that.'

John Riley was tearing now, reaching for her arm, holding it softly, she covering his hand, now, with hers, holding it closer to her. He looked up. "It wasn't that she loved Patrick any the less, Brigit...it was that she loved you as much...you and Katherine and Annie. That's why she agreed to it...If Patrick had been her only child, she would never have given him up, never in a million years."

Brigit's grip on his hand strengthened in the silence, a clearing now, a cleansing of mind and soul before John Riley pulled away. "It was a good promise...the right thing to do." He looked at her, nodding, now finding a smile coming to his face. "But it was about a girl not yet a woman. And now that girl is long gone...in the shadow now of the woman she's become, a woman who has to know the why of the things that happened as she grew."

John Riley rose, taking Brigit's hands as he did, now bringing her to him. "There is absolutely nothing in this world, nor could there ever be, that is more important to your mother and me than your happiness. *Nothing.*" He separated, now holding her face in his hands. "Trust me these next few days…I don't know what I want out of this whole thing, either. We're just going to have to feel our way along…know our luck." He smiled now, broad and full, his hands out, feeling his eyes widen, light pouring in. "Hell, girl, it's only money!"

She laughed, her hands going to her face, eyes tearing, head nodding, her whole face now beaming, laughing,

John Riley smiled, a quick wink and thumbs up as turned to leave, stopping now in mid-stance. "I'm having lunch with Bryan and Matt Malloy. At the Hay-Adams. Why don't you come along, join us?"

"No thanks." Brigit Riley Winslow wiped the tears from her cheeks, still laughing quietly. "Things to do. You know, calls to make…" She shook her head clear, working her hair with both hands before a final quick shake of the head and a full smile at him.

"Besides, Mom said she'd be taking Nana to the hospital about noon. Maybe I'll catch up with them up there."

John Riley smiled as he nodded, turning on his way out, another thumbs up as he passed through the door.

CHAPTER TWENTY-FIVE
The Truman Suite

J ohn Riley had walked the two blocks to the Hay-Adams. Several minutes early, he had called on the manager, inquiring if the Truman Suite was occupied. On learning it was being readied for occupancy that afternoon, he requested a key and asked that it be held available to him until 2 pm. As he returned to the lobby, Matt Malloy and Bryan Canny were just entering.

He took Mathew Malloy's hand, shaking it firmly, nodding to Bryan Canny, "Matt, good of you to come. Appreciate you being available on such short notice."

"The pleasure's all mine, John." Releasing John Riley's hand, Matt Malloy looked about the lobby. "Haven't been here in years...looking pretty sharp." He turned to John Riley. "Did I see that this is a Hennessey Land property?"

"It is, as a matter of fact." He motioned Matt Malloy across the lobby toward the dining room. "Brigit got it out of a bankruptcy for a few box tops and a promise to be good."

Matt Malloy laughed, shaking his head, smiling at Bryan Canny.

"Seriously, never quite figured out how she got it for what she did...amazing, really. It was a three- or four-way swap. We had a few pieces in Foggy Bottom that someone needed to complete a multi-housing site there and then someone else was aching for some air rights we held in Silver Spring, over an old railroad yard...that and assuming a very manageable note and...Bingo!" John Riley snapped his fingers. "The book of what we had to put up was less than three-and-a-half million."

They took the several steps up to the dining room where they were greeted by the *maître d'*, Andre. A welcome smile and nod of the head, he led them to a table in the southwest corner of the room, the White House here visible through the maple and oak trees of Lafayette Square. John Riley seated Matt Malloy facing to the Square with himself opposite and Bryan Canny to his own left.

"My, my, this does bring back memories…" Matt Malloy seated himself, opening his napkin and placing it on his lap, his eyes taking in the full vista of the park, from east to west, before fixing on Bryan Canny. "Been here before, Bryan?"

"First time was yesterday. John had me up to the top floor and the view. An eye-popper, that, looking down on the White House and all."

"Yes, quite a view…" Matt Molloy looked out on the park before fixing on John. "Last time I was here was for Brigit's wedding, what five years, now, John? How is she? Any children?"

"No, not yet, anyway. But she's fine. Maybe never happier than right now." John Riley checked his watch. It was just past noon.

Andre returned, a smile each around, running the specials of the day and taking the order for drinks.

Matt Malloy fixed on John Riley, his eyes bright. "John, I must have told you about the time I was here with President Truman…and Dean Acheson?"

John Riley nodded, smiling. "Yes, you did. But I'm sure Bryan here would love to hear about it. A story well worth the telling."

Matt Malloy turned quickly to Bryan Canny, his small frame leaning in that direction, eyes quick and bright. "Well, Bryan, it was 1946 and everything's still shaking itself back into shape after the war." Matt Malloy, nodded a wink at Bryan Canny.

"Well, John L. Lewis is running the United Mine Workers back then, thinking he's King of the World, maybe the entire known universe." Matt's arms out, now, and around. "There's no one bigger in Big Labor, that's for sure, and he wants his 'more' and thinking a Democratic President is going to go along with anything he wants...it being that the unions were key to FDR winning in '32 and keeping him in the White House for three more elections.

"And Harry Truman? Why he's just some nobody from Missouri. 'President Accident from Independence' is what they called him. Most folks in Washington still trying to figure how he got the job in the first place. So, Lewis is talking about a national strike and he doesn't give a good tinker's dam what it's going do to the national economy or anything else." Matt Malloy reached for Bryan Canny's forearm.

"You have to understand, Bryan, back then, this country *ran* on coal. No coal meant no electricity, no home heat, no trains running, no factories operating, no *jobs*." Matt Malloy sat back, motioning up with his right thumb. "Well, *Big* John is up in an eighth-floor suite...no, check that, Big John has the *whole* floor. And looking *down* on the White House, just across the street." Matt Malloy points through the window behind John Riley, to Lafayette Square and beyond.

"And he's got these big bushy eyebrows like some *Michelangelo* mural looking down from heaven or up from hell, depending on your leanings." Matt Malloy allowed himself a little chuckle, winking to John Riley.

"Of course, Big John has no idea who he's dealing with here. This is Harry Truman and Harry doesn't like this son-of-a-bitching union boss one bit to start with. And here he is, Big John Lewis, threatening to shut down Harry Truman's whole *country* for Chrissakes!

"Now, remember, this is the Harry Truman who hadn't even heard about the Manhattan Project till after FDR had died and before you know it, he's dropping *atomic bombs* on whole cities! They were looking at 250,000 American casualties if it came to invading the mainland and here's a chance to end it quick. A no-brainer to Harry Truman..." Matt Malloy shifted in his seat, now leaning closer to Bryan Canny.

"So, we're in the White House figuring our options...national strike...tens of thousands of coal workers looking for 'more'...*and I'm there, in the room*! The Oval Office! Special Assistant to the President for Labor...Incredible!

"Now, we're getting bits and pieces of what Lewis has in mind, committee chairs from coal states in the Senate and House saying this and that, all aquivering and ashaking lest Big John speak his mighty roar and shut the whole deal down - Maine to Mexico! Visions of riots, mines closed, burning this and that, and Harry's just sitting there. Pretty soon he's done thinking and turns to Acheson. 'Mr. Secretary,' he says, 'where *is* this son-of-a-bitch, I mean *right now*?'

"Well, now, Dean Acheson sits up, surprised by the question, looking a little afraid to give the answer. 'Why Mr. President, I believe he's at the Hay-Adams, just across the street.' Now as soon as he's said this, Acheson knows what Harry's thinking and Dean Acheson, Secretary State, Wall Street power-broker, at Yalta with FDR, diplomat *par excellence*, well he just shudders and goes a little white. Before he can say anything, Harry turned to me. 'Matt, I want you to call up Mr. Lewis and tell him we'll be calling on him...in fifteen minutes." Matt Malloy is tapping his wrist watch.

"Now, Bryan, this is eight o'clock on a Tuesday night in March. It's pitch black out. We have no idea whether Lewis is even in the hotel. But I get up, go to Harry's secretary, and ask her to call over to the Hay-Adams and advise Mr. Lewis that the President of the United States will be calling on him in fifteen minutes.

"So, we walk on over, across Lafayette Square, Dean Acheson clearing his throat the whole way, still trying figure out how this whole thing is going to play out as we come into the lobby, just right over there." Matt Malloy motioned to the entrance of the dining room and the lobby beyond. "The three of us. So, we got in the elevator, Harry Truman, Dean Acheson and yours truly with one Secret Service Agent and we go on up to the eighth floor where Harry leads us to Lewis' suite and knocks on the door. The door opens and it's Big John Lewis himself. "Why, Mr. President, so good of you to call..." Matt Malloy nodded the nod of a man who was there.

"It was a short meeting, never even sat down. Harry informed Big John square up that he was calling for an emergency joint session of Congress to announce that if the UMW voted to strike, he would draft into military service the entire union membership, order them into the mines and, as Commander-in-Chief of the U. S. military, sic the U. S. Army on them if they refused." Matt Malloy sat back, a sure nod of the head before leaning forward again.

"Well, Bryan, John Lewis near crapped his pants standing up! Spit is coming to the corner of his mouth as he starts harrumphing and hollering, but Harry Truman was having none of it. He shook hands with others in the room, thanked the King of the World for his time and led us to the door. In three minutes time, we're all down to the lobby and on out to 16th Street.

"Yes, sir. That was a man who knew his mind and who knew what being a President of the United States in 1946 was all about. Couple of weeks later, I overheard Secretary Acheson telling someone about it. Said that when we were walking back across Lafayette Square you could hear Harry's balls clang!"

Bryan Canny burst out laughing, but no louder than Matt Malloy. John Riley laughed as well, sitting back, watching the two of them, a good story well-told, the wonder of a good laugh, the freedom of it. Bryan Canny wiped his eyes now, a quick look to John Riley then back at Matt Malloy who clapped Bryan's shoulder and started laughing all over again.

"Tell me, Matthew, then you knew President Truman well?"

Catching his breath now, Matt Malloy wiped his eyes with his napkin. "Proud to say I did. Started in the White House in '45 and stayed on till '49." Matt Malloy paused for a moment, his eyes away, then at John Riley before returning to Bryan Canny. "The best man I ever met, bar none." Matt Malloy sat up. "No taller than me but he took guff from no man. He had a genuine aversion to Big - Big Business, Big Labor, Big Anything. But you know what he wouldn't tolerate…at *all*?"

Bryan Canny sat up, fixed closely on Matt Malloy. "No, sir, I don't."

"A bully, that's what. Some tough son-of-a-bitch pushing the other fellow around for the pure pleasure of seeing the poor fellow's discomfort."

John Riley relaxed in the wonder of Matt Malloy telling tales of Harry Truman and his years in the White House, Bryan Canny hanging on his every word as the lunch came and cleared. Bryan Canny having to leave before coffee to take a call, John Riley took this opportunity to invite Matt Malloy to the Truman Suite on the seventh floor.

Letting them in, John Riley walked to the windows facing south, looking out over Lafayette Square and the White House. Pulling the French doors open, he stepped aside, offering the view to Matt Malloy.

"Does take your breath away, John." Matt Malloy looked at John Riley, studying his face for a moment and then turning back, out of the doors. "The beauty and the power of it all.…"

"Yes, it does catch your breath...even scary in a way...looking down at it, on it." John Riley shook his head. "Lived my whole life here, in the shadow of it all...booking work...building buildings. There's so much I don't understand, so much of it I have no sense of at all...None."

John Riley could feel Matt Malloy's eyes on him but avoided turning to him, his own eyes now on the trees of the Square, their tops moving easily in the September afternoon air. "This is what he wants, you know. This..." John Riley open his right hand and arm in the direction of the White House.

"He?"

John Riley now turned to Matt Malloy, uncertain for a moment, then said "I'm sorry...Keith Pierson, Mid-America Holdings."

"Ah, yes..." Matt Malloy looked again over Lafayette Square then standing back a few steps, viewing it from inside the suite. "Yes, I can see it...Keith Pierson in his suite looking down at the White House...Yes, that *is* the man."

John Riley turned back into the suite, motioned Matt Malloy to a chair at a card table, taking a seat at the corner to his right. "Had Grace track Mid-America's attention on Hennessey Land..."

"And?"

"Marginal, really, until Bill Clinton started to move out of the pack. Picked up a bunch when he got the nomination, then came heavy and often after he won the election." John Riley looked out on the White House for a moment, then back at Matt Malloy. "This is not a nice man, Matt. Not someone I want in the neighborhood. Especially across the street from a third-tier governor who just became the most powerful man in the world."

Matt Malloy sat back.

John Riley could feel his eyes on him as he turned to him. "You've been inviting me to the annual reception for the National Trust for Historic Preservation...."

"Yes. I'm on the Board."

"For reasons I do not want to get specific about, we are pulling away from Mid-America on The Deal. In fact, we're re-thinking the whole thing. One thing for sure, though, Keith Pierson is never going to own this property." He fixed on Matt Malloy, his head moving side to side. "*Never.*"

Matt Malloy nodded. "How can I help you, John?"

"I want to make an irrevocable commitment to deed this property over to the National Trust and I want the National Trust to issue a press release at 3 pm ET Tuesday, in effect accepting it. Is that doable?"

Matt Malloy caught his breath, cocking his head. "Are you alright, John?"

"I'm fine. I'll be even better if we can get this done."

Matt Malloy sat forward, his left arm on the surface of the card table. "I expect so. I'll need Hennessey Land's outside counsel on it right away, like this afternoon. Who is it, Fox Worthy?"

"Yes, Hardin Brooks."

"I know him. Good man." Matt Malloy sat back, looking away, his mind running, churning, now the lawyer. He leaned slightly toward John Riley, reaching for his forearm, his hand now resting on it. "Now you're going to have to be prepared to guarantee the note on this property. They'd probably want that from you personally, not Hennessey Land."

"No problem...Done."

"That'd be about it, I think...knowing how you folks run your business."

John Riley sat back, their eyes locked. "Thank you, Matt. That's a great relief...great relief." John Riley looked away for a moment, thinking back to Matt Malloy taking the photograph hanging in his office of the fishing party with Jack Hennessey, Paddy Riley and the rest. Shaking his head slightly he rose. "Better get right to Hardin on this. Can we drop you back home?"

Matt Malloy rose, smoothing his blazer down the front. "No. I'll want to make a few calls to the Trust, get them started." He looked at John Riley. "Besides, this is the afternoon of my annual visit to Mt. Olivet Cemetery."

John Riley stood erect. "Really?"

"Yes, it's my grandfather's birthday…his 155th."

John Riley looked away, his mind fixing on the Riley plot on Mt. Olivet, then to Bryan Canny. "That's odd…"

"*Odd?*"

"Sorry, Matt. I meant *extraordinary*…I'd been thinking about taking Bryan there. Why not come back to my office, we'll both make our calls and go from there?"

"Done."

CHAPTER TWENTY-SIX
A New Place

T hey had taken a taxi to Mt. Olivet, John Riley and Matt Malloy. Bryan Canny was to catch up in his car, all of which suited John Riley's needs very well. Passing through the main gate of Mt. Olivet on Bladensburg Road, Matt Malloy directed the driver to take a right along Mt. Olivet Avenue. After several hundred yards, he asked him to stop. "Can you wait for me? By the main gate?"

"Yes, sir. The main gate it is."

Matt Malloy let himself out of the car, making room for the driver to execute a U-turn, watching as the taxi moved slowly over the pavement back toward the main gate before turning to John Riley. "So, have you ever been to Section 43?"

John Riley stood erect. "Section 43? We're in Section 43?"

Matt Malloy motioned with his right hand along a narrow stone path. "Right this way, Mr. Riley." He smiled, looking about, the land sloping down on his right, building high to his left. The higher the eye followed, the larger the statues of angels and saints and stones altogether. "They called them *necropolises* when they first came into fashion and necessity…'cities of the dead'."

John Riley nodded as he kept pace.

"Technically they were 'extramural cemeteries', outside the walls of the city. They started in Europe in the late 1700s and became popular over the next 100 or so years, and necessary, too." Matt Malloy spoke as he walked the path, his eyes fixed ahead on a bare spot of ground. "It was when cities started to grow geometrically with the people in them dying exponentially. The practice of stacking the dead in graves three and four deep in a quiet church yard by the neighborhood chapel became impossible, and hygienically toxic." He stopped, opening his arms to the stones and monuments around him.

"They were parks, in a way...folks coming out on a weekend in fair weather to have a picnic. They built light-gauge railroads to them in London. And the paths of them were done as mini-avenues in a city, winding among the hills and grave stones, families out with their children to be with those close to them who had passed." He pointed to the hill at the center of Mt. Olivet, turning to John Riley.

"And it was done on a class basis, you see. Up there, that was for the swells, them that had done well. Here..." He motioned with his hands at the area where he had come to a stop. "This is where the tradesmen and lower government workers took their rest."

Now pointing up and beyond the hill, Matt Malloy continued, speaking away. "Over there, that was mostly for shop owners and such, and the near-well off." He turned further to his right. "Over there is where you'll find the Blacks." He fixed on John Riley. "Mt. Olivet was the first Catholic cemetery in the city to receive African-Americans. Had a place marked off for favored slaves and freedmen."

Matt Malloy paused, a breath taken before bowing his head, his eyes fixing on the ground at his feet. "And here lies Thomas Francis Boyle, born in Limerick, 1838, died in Washington, DC, 1919." A deeper breath now taken, and it held for a moment before he turned to John Riley.

"He was father to my mother, Rose, his first child and only daughter." Another pause, a slight nodding of the head, his eyes still down. "By God, she loved him...as did we all." Matt Malloy turned to him. "My father died young, you see...I was just six...and Dada...well, we moved in with him and he was my father for most of it, till I was nineteen." Another breath, this one deeper still. "Born in one calamity – Ireland – and died in another –

the flu of 1918. Took that to kill him…worked right up till he caught it…paid my way through Gonzaga."

Matt Malloy's face came bright on a thought, now turning to John Riley. "He knew Jack Hennessey, you know." His eyes now fixed down on the stone. "Yes, kindred spirits of a sort, always had good words together at a St. Dominick's picnic or breakfast."

John Riley cleared his throat. "Would you like to be alone, Matt?"

"Alone?" Matt Malloy raised up, smiling as he fixed on John Riley. "No, not at all, John. The last thing I want to be is alone." He stepped back from Tom Boyle's stone, his eyes going from it to a large stone with the name Boyle across its face, the stone leaning a little forward, it marking the twelve graves purchased by Thomas Boyle in 1873 for $103.50. Matt Malloy turned back to John Riley, a smile coming to his face.

"Would you like to hear about my fondest memory of him, John?" He nodded at Tom Boyle's marker, at his feet. "Might be the fondest memory in all my 93 years."

John Riley smiled, a slight nod of the head

Matt Malloy nodded back, taking a deep breath. "Yes…well it was his 75th birthday, so that's what? 80 years ago? Yes, well, anyway, the families around had got together and scraped up a round-trip ticket to Cork and $750 spending money to send him back to Ireland for the summer. And they'd gotten together on a party, too - May of 1913 - at the Ancient Order of Hibernians Hall in Swampoodle." Matt Malloy stood a little taller, getting into the story now.

"Now he knew about the party. But the trip? That was the surprise, and it really did surprise him. Hadn't a clue." A smile now came to Matt Malloy's face, perhaps he was remembering Tom Boyle's face coming alive as he spoke of it.

"So, we've all been at it, having a grand time, with evening coming and the toasting and roasting running its course, stories of him doing this and that, and how he got on and got better. Then Rose shushed us all quiet. She has an envelope in her hand, the thickness of the thing showing that it was of some importance, more than just some greeting card.

"'So, Da,' says she, 'we were all trying to figure on what we could be giving to a man who already had everything he ever needed or wanted, who had never once in anyone's memory complained about anything. What's to be done with such a man? So, says we, let's send him back to from where he come, let's get good Tom Boyle a summer in Ireland. And the only thing you need do for it, Da, is to promise us all you'll be coming back!'

"Well now, John, as you can imagine there's applause all around, a few hoots of good cheer, several courses of 'For He's a Jolly Good Fellow' rising and falling. Tom, though, he's dumbstruck by it all, eyes blinking, his head shaking, half squatting now to his seat, then rising with Rose pressing the envelope into his hands and Tom taking it, looking at it, feeling its heft, all now coming to a quiet, not a peep to be heard.

"Rising to his full height, near six foot still at 75 years, he looked about, tapping the envelope in his right hand on the palm of his left. "Ireland, you say? Packing me off to Ireland, are you now?"'

"'Yes, Da,' says Rose, she being the closest, her hands joined at her bosom, the full light of a May morning in Limerick on her face and in her eyes. 'Aye, Da, Ireland!'

"Well, John, let me tell you what happened then. Thomas Francis Boyle looked at his daughter, caressed her face with his hand and a wink of the eye. 'Shall I tell you, then, about my last day in Ireland, Rose? Shall I?'

"'Yes, Da, do, now. Your last day there', her face near bursting with anticipation." Matt Malloy paused, looking away, maybe wanting to be sure to get it all straight.

"'Aye, the last day...Well, it'd be at dockside in Cork, now. March 21 being the day and 1850 the year. I was just 12 years. An early tide to make, a mist settling on us all...pressing through our clothes, such as they were, deep down to our skin, damp and dank.

"'We're all making our way up the gangplank to the main deck of the thing, a water-soaked hulk whose bare masts stuck into the gray overcast, broken fingers scratching across the heavens.' He looked up here, John, seeing the masts again, he was back there, now at quayside in Cork, you could see it in his eyes.

"'There was the crying all about, now, you know, on the ship and the quay, too, muffled some of it, and some higher, whines at the sky and times. Then, on the captain's call to cast off, a voice there rose from a pile of rags and refuse on the quayside. Aye, a voice and the man it come from, hair on all parts of him to be seen, rags falling from his arms, teeth yellow, what there was of them, now standing full up but for the one shoulder broken and bent. All eyes turning, now, all silent but the voice, it coming to a deep, broken growl.

"'Be gone, now, the lot of ya! Be gone from me, won't ya. I am *Erin,* I am, don't you know? Aye, Erin I am and I'm telling ya, now, be *gone*! I'm drained dry by ya, all of ya, sure exhausted is what, the millions that scraped at my soil and soul, that sucked me dry of my life's blood and water, only then to die on me in thanks, laying about by the tens of thousands, the stink and mess of it all...be *gone*, now, won't ya? And don't be thinking o' comin' back, now, neither. There's no room here, don't you know...no room at all. My only thanks to ya this fine day is ya didn't drop and die on me for the cleanin' up after...So be gone, now, you cursed of Erin, find yourselves a new place to die and rot, but for the love of God, now, *be gone*, and *don't be coming back!'*

"Tom Boyle's eyes came back, now, fixed on all and each of us, his head nodding. 'I was the only one out, you know. My Da, God bless him, he'd talked to my Ma, and his brother Dennis, too. They had the place together, Da and Uncle Dennis, his family already gone to ground, all of them in the dirt. They'd scraped together near ten pounds, you know, selling this and that…and the food all but gone. I was second born, you see, to my sister Rose…'

"He smiled here at his daughter, taking her hand. 'Then there was the boys after me, the two with us still, laying by, their stomachs out and the hair coming to their foreheads like the dark fuzz of a peach. "You're the one, now, Tom," says my Da. 'You come from God made stronger than the rest. No sense in sending your sister out, only to die on the boat over, no sense at all. And Tim and Emmet, they wouldn't live to Cork. So, it's you, it is, now, Tom, my dear son Tom.' He caught his breath here, holding it for a moment.

"'Go now, Tom, and remember us all.' Da held me then, more like a clinging, it was, his voice breaking, so weak from it all. 'Knowing that you got out, now, son, that you'll find a life there, in America, that'll be something for your Ma and me, and the rest, for God knows there's nothing here but the dying.'

"Tom Boyle wiped his eyes and blew his nose, then reached for his Guinness, taking a pull. Raising his glass and then finishing it, and from some spot of sun in his soul there came a smile to his face that lighted us all, our breathing now come back and our faces bright.

"'Aye, lads, and out I got, I did! And to this fair city! Aye! And all those about me, my children, now, carrying the names of those I left behind and their spirits and hopes, too!' A fresh glass had been passed to him and he near emptied this one as well, raising it high.

"'So, now, lads, I won't be going back. I was sent *here,* don't you know!' He pointed to earth at his feet. 'Aye, here, to *live* here, in America! That's why I come. Aye, a life lived and a family built, with no choosing among 'em as which was to live and which to die. The only 'here' to me, the only *home* I got, the only *hope* there is in me, is here, in *America*!' He paused, looked down at the ticket and the cash, then back up, his broad, full smile holding.

"'Tell ya what, lads...' We could see his brain working, now racing even, you could just see it in him, John, the sparkle now come to his eyes. Yes, Tom Boyle alive as I'd never seen him before, his eye fixed on my mother. 'Now, tell me, Rose, did you get this, the ticket, now, at O'Halloran's, on H Street? Is that where?"

"It is."

"Good girl. Now, knowing him as I do, I'll swap it off for a train ticket to Chicago. Aye! Chicago! St. Louis, too. And then San Francisco, and maybe to Portland and then to Dallas and I've never been to New Orleans, don't ya know, never been. How's that? I'm gonna see the rest of where I've been now these last 62 years! What do you think o'that, lads?"

Matt Malloy let a tear fall now as he turned to John Riley. "You should have been there, John Riley." He nodded, his eyes fixed and sharp. "The whole world should have been there to see that, to know what the human spirit is, to know what *we* are, what America means and is." He looked down at Tom Boyle's marker. "Yes, John, that's when I discovered America, came to understand what it is, what it must be."

Matt Malloy nodded to himself. A final look at Tom Boyle's marker, he made the sign of the cross then started along Mt. Olivet Avenue for the main gate. John Riley walked beside him, his arm now reaching out and resting across Matt Malloy's shoulders, holding him as they walked in silence. Coming to the rear door of the taxi, they stood apart, Matt Malloy looking up at him. "I'm very glad you were with me today, John. Yes, very glad, indeed."

Reaching for the handle of the rear door of the taxi, he paused, looking away, then fixing back on John Riley. "I meant to ask you John…when you were at my place on Tuesday, you mentioned that you'd been to Keith Pierson's place in Palm Beach, the one Pamela Harriman once owned."

"Yes?"

"When was that?"

"November. A week or two after the election."

"I see…" He looked away and then up again. "What time of day?"

"Well, he flew me down in his jet, set me up at one of his properties in West Palm. Sent a car over at 6:30."

"Then it was dark, when you were there?"

"Yes, not even a moon."

"Have you ever driven around Palm Beach in daytime, John, on a nice, sunny day?"

"No. Can't say that I have."

Matt Malloy thought about this for a moment then fixed back on John Riley, holding his eyes. "You need to go back, John. You need to drive around the place in the daylight."

John Riley shrugged. "Right, if you say so. I'll put it first on my list after all this…"

"No. You have to do this *now*, before all this with Hennessey Land is settled, played out. Tomorrow, do it tomorrow. I checked the weather. A fine, sunny day is predicted. Mid-eighties."

"Yes, but…"

"On Tuesday night, at my place, I got the sense Hennessey is signed up with one of the executive jet leasing deals – 'Anytime, anywhere. Call us, you're flying? That sort of thing?"

"Yes, we did. Just for this, getting Brigit around, back and forth to Chicago."

"Then the ticket is already paid for, John. You can be back here by mid-afternoon." Matt Malloy fixed on John Riley, ticking things off on his fingers. "You clear National Airport at 7 am, you're in West Palm Airport by 9:30. Get yourself a convertible - has to be a convertible. Go across Flagler Memorial Bridge, takes you right on to Royal Poinciana Way.

"Take it as far as you can, and then go left on North County Road, holding to the oceanside, get to the inlet and come back to Royal Poinciana on the inland side. This'll take you right by Pierson's place - on your right, just after the golf club. You'll be back at West Palm by eleven and touch down at National by 2.

"Do it, John. That's an order. And after you've done it, call. Call me from West Palm. Yes, John Riley, you give me a call and tell me what you saw."

John Riley was holding a smile, mentally re-arranging his next two days, now seeing that something behind him had caught Matt Malloy's eye. Turning, he saw Bryan Canny coming down from the highest ground on the cemetery. Turning full around, he smiled, waving Bryan Canny to stop, that he'd be right up.

He turned back to Matt Malloy, offering his hand. "You know, Matt, six or seven hours away from everyone in this deal might be just what I need, anyway."

"Good on ya, lad. Have a good trip, and remember to call…from West Palm."

"Consider it done, Matt, and thanks…thanks especially for sharing that day with Tom Boyle."

CHAPTER TWENTY-SEVEN
Twins

I t was a summer afternoon, a crystalline sky above, his ticket in hand, the man tearing it in half as the turnstile clicked them into the dark, under cavern of the ballpark. Now mixing with a river of men in dark hats, eyes up on the section number signs, they stepped ahead in quiet anticipation of the game amid traces of hot dogs and mustard, peanut shells cracking under foot, now striding up the ramp and...

WOW! There it was - the ball field, yes, the diamond seen from the shade beneath the upper deck, a brilliantly lush green, so green, boxed by raked gravel and sharp white baselines, the stands on the far side basking in the yellow of a full July sun, the sky above made all the more blue by the brilliance of the colors below...

It was to Michael Riley as if they just stepped onto another planet, a new world. People everywhere, grazing off his shoulder, his hand gripping Paddy's as they came down the aisle to the box seats behind the Senators' dugout.

Yes, this was his day with Paddy, *his* day, before Paddy shipped out, his day to be alone with the most important man in the world, the *only* man, alone and without encumbrance of siblings and mothers, grand or otherwise. And now down the aisle, to the fourth row, seats C-3 and C-4, the stubs to be kept on his dresser till Paddy got home to claim them.

Michael Riley was drifting in and out, wanting his hand to grip Paddy's fingers harder but his hand not responding as his mind saw the field from the box and then back from there, from behind him and Paddy, watching as they rose to the sharp crack of Cecil Travis' bat on a fastball, it now screaming down the first base line, Paddy picking him up so he could watch Travis round second base and beat it out for a triple…and then…Then a fluorescent ceiling light…a nurse walking by the door.

"Michael?" His name was being called, softly, then a bit stronger. His eyes blinking and again, "Michael?"

It was Mary Kate's voice, from away, in and out, now here, his eyes turning to his left, her eyes on him…searching…now smiling as she saw him recognize her.

He felt a smile come to his face as he swallowed, fixing on her. "Hi…been here long?"

She smiled back, shifting her chair closer, reaching for his hand, taking it in hers. "I guess, don't know really." She looked at the clock on the wall. It was 2:30. "Yes, I guess so. Eileen and Brigit left a little after one, Mom, too, when you dozed off."

"And you've just been sitting here?"

"I guess…no where else to go, really. Just wanted to be nearby you…you know, being twins and all."

He smiled, a fullness coming to him, a comfort as his body relaxed down the full length of the bed. "That's nice. I like that." He covered her hand with his own, now looking away. "I just had the most wonderful dream, Mary Kate…wonderful…so real, like it was happening just now, exactly now."

She sat closer. "Tell me about it…"

He turned to her, his eyes on her for a moment but now just past her. "I was at Griffith Stadium, with Paddy. That time he took me just before he left?" He fixed on her. "You know, *my* day…"

She smiled, now, remembering, perhaps, her own day with Paddy, at Peirce Mill. "Yes, I remember when you came home that day. The Senators won…And Dad had taken you to the locker room after…got you a ball signed by…"

"Cecil…"

"…Travis! Right? Am I right?"

"Absolutely."

"How did I come up with that!" Her face suddenly went still, her eyes away. "There was a picture of the three of you, Paddy and you and Cecil Travis, all smiling, that ball in your hand, you wearing a Senators cap. It came after he'd left…Dad. It's the last picture we have of him with one of us…" She turned away, her right hand to her face. She was crying now, reaching for a tissue on the nightstand. "I'm sorry, Michael."

"Mary Kate?" Michael Riley shifted up in the bed, tubes moving about, he reaching for her arm. "Mary Kate, what is it?"

"Nothing…"

"Yes, I can see that. We're just sitting here having a chat, you remember a baseball player's name from 50 years ago, and then burst into tears. Sure, why not? Simple as pie…" He sat up further, squeezed her arm more firmly. "Come on, now, Mary Kate, for Chrissakes, it's me, your twin, fresh off the boat, now, from Fourth Street Southwest…don't be telling me, now, it's nuttin."

She turned back to him, braved a quick smile as she wiped her eyes and cheeks, blowing her nose, letting the tissue roll off her hand into the trash can and looking away, catching her breath. "I can't…"

"Mary Kate? Hey, listen, I nearly died two days ago…remember…gone to dead…" He squeezed her arm again, gripping it now. "I'm feeling pretty good about being alive, as in not being *dead*. Maybe I can cheer you up, you know, help?"

She turned back to him, slowly, her arm taken from his grip, her eyes on him for a moment, then down, her hands resting in her lap. "Please…I can't speak about it."

Michael Riley looked across at this sister, her head down, closed now to the outside world. This is how she got through the tough spots. Hunker down and in, find your stuff and get on with whatever you've got. The picture came to Michael's mind now, of him and Paddy and Cecil Travis, then to Paddy Riley's leaving from Union Station, going to war…never coming back.

"It's about Patrick, then?"

He caught the slightest shudder in her arms, then to a complete stillness, not even a breath taken and, in her time, the slightest nod of the head.

"Going to Israel?"

Another nod, turning away, a hand out to be taken, held.

He took it. "How can I help?"

She looked up at him, rose in her chair, her other hand on his. "He's coming to Washington, some time today, then to New York and then Monday to…'"

"There?"

She nodded yes, her left hand now to her face, covering her mouth.

"When was the last time you spoke with him?"

"June…" She looked away. "Just before he left for New Mexico or wherever…some sort of boot camp."

"Any letters?"

"No…not allowed. Total immersion. He called it Parris Island with all the matzo balls you can eat." She laughed now, gripping Michael's hand, her breathing gone easier.

Michael Riley sat back, his head resting for a moment on the pillow, then turned to her. "Sometime today…and for how long?"

"Just the night." She fixed on him. "He's coming to Washington mostly to see you…promised me he'd talk to you one last time before he left."

"Well, yes…we'd spoken about that. What day is it, by the way, today? I've lost track…"

"Thursday. All day, it's Thursday…"

"So? I'll see him tomorrow. That's right, said we'd talk Friday, September 19. Right? So, we're still on. I'll talk with him tomorrow morning."

She looked at him, sitting back. "Yes, but now?" She motioned about the room.

Michael Riley sat back, his arms out. "What? This?" He fixed on her, his head at her. "This is nothing, for Chrissakes…nothing." He reached for her hand. "Mary Kate, now, look at me…look at me."

She turned to him.

"There's an old boys rugby game on the Mall the day after Thanksgiving and I'm going to be playing in it."

"Please, Michael…"

"No. I'm serious." He sat up, motioning to the hospital room and the tubes. "This is no more than having your appendix out…not like I have somebody else's heart in my chest or anything. They're going to have me doing heavy exercise in a few weeks. Ask the doctor. I did. Told me if I'd lived till Thanksgiving, *if* I had lived, the game would have *killed me for sure*. Don't you see, now I got a good chance of living through it!"

She laughed a chuckle or two, a smile of resignation more than comfort.

"Listen, I'm going to talk with my godson tomorrow morning in this hospital room. At 10 am. You set it up. You drive him here. He's going to be sitting in that chair." He motioned with his hand to the chair she was sitting in. "Do you remember what Matt Malloy said about me after I won the Tilden case? You remember, the rendering plant in Georgetown?"

"Yes, I guess…" She tried to smile but got only halfway there.

"Matt Malloy, the Lion of Malloy, Henderson and Ryan, advisor to Presidents of this Republic, *Presidents!* Well, Matt Malloy said I could talk a starving dog off a gut wagon!"

Mary Kate Riley laughed now, so hard she had to stand up to catch her breath.

"Mary Kate Riley Rhinemann, do you seriously think for one minute that I'm going to let a few tubes and pulse tapes stop me from a full court, Irish-break-his-balls press on your son, on *my* godson, about service in a foreign nation's army in a centuries-old war!? Do you really think that is at all *possible?*"

"No…Yes…but Margaret, what about Margaret?"

"Margaret? Hell, Margaret has a son of her own now. She knows what it means to have one in danger. What do you think she'd think of me if I didn't try to talk your son out of flying full bore into harm's way? I mean, really, Mary Kate…"

Mary Kate Riley's eyes were on him now as never before, her head now coming to a slow nod. "Yes, yes, of course. It's what she'd *want* isn't it…Yes, she would…"

"Good, that's done then. We're agreed." Michael Riley looked at the wall clock. "They're in here between 8:15 or 8:30 to check me out, see how I'm doing, the IVs and all. Rounds have been at 9ish. You have Patrick Francis Rhinemann in here at 10 am sharp." He looked at his sister, his twin.

"Know this, Mary Kate Riley, if there's a way that boy can be talked out of it, Godsword, I'll find it."

CHAPTER TWENTY-EIGHT
Nightmare

P atrick Riley Rhinemann was ahead of schedule. He'd only slept two hours in St. Louis, waking in a full sweat, shouting, his throat sore from it. It was about *Cage Day*, the last test, the final hurdle before qualifying, scenes and sounds of it racing through his mind and away.

Camp Hope was unlike anything he had ever experienced. A foreign land, a chaos of sorts, all previous structures and anchors challenged and a few new ones found. Opening in classroom settings, it turned increasingly into a war zone, a growing sense that you were not safe.

Unity and Nation were the dominant themes, a two-part mantra driven into them day and night. Unity and Nation were what made them different from the gutter goats of the refugee camps. But for all this there was, everyday, a challenge to your loyalty, to your commitment, that only the loyal and the committed would succeed, were worthy.

And for Patrick Rhinemann, beyond the pattern of the mantra and the searching to understand the metric against which he was being measured, there was Mica Harwitz. From the first day, Harwitz had an edge and a focus on Patrick Rhinemann. Russian-born, he'd emigrated in 1970. Officially a tourist in the United States, he was an Instructor at Camp Hope.

It had started with *Pa-hattie*. Said derisively and with purpose, it was clearly meant to grate on him, and so it did. It wasn't until the close of the third day, though, that Patrick Rhinemann came to understand it was 'Paddy' spoken by a Russian Jew attempting a brogue. And, so, it was to be *Pa-hattie* this and *Pa-hattie* that, all said in

Yiddish, and somehow still with a brogue, driven to 'how dumb can so smart a person be, to have survived thus far in life, so ignorant about so many simple things.'

There were no ranks in Camp Hope. The instructors were to be addressed as 'instructor' or 'mister.' For Patrick Rhinemann, though, not even these words were acknowledged by Harwitz when spoken to him by Patrick Rhinemann. It was not until after two weeks in camp and his first meeting with the Leader that he was to learn why.

'To Harwitz, you are not Jewish,' the Leader had said. 'This is because your mother is not Jewish. To Harwitz, being Jewish can come only through a person's mother.' Patrick Rhinemann had nodded on hearing this, his mind running through the names of his father's family who had perished in the camps. Certainly they were *no longer* Jewish... they were no longer anything.

'You must try to understand, Patrick Rhinemann,' the Leader had continued. 'Mica Harwitz can trace his family back more than three centuries, the name of each man and each woman over twenty generations, and each one Jewish, both sides, all sides, only Jews.' Patrick Riley Rhinemann had nodded again. It was clear to him that further discussion of the matter was pointless. Mica Harwitz was Jewish in ways that Patrick Rhinemann would never be. In fact, in the mind of Mica Harwitz, Patrick Rhinemann would never be Jewish in *any* manner or means. To Mica Harwitz, it was simple - the world was composed of Jewish people and those who were not, those persons not born of a Jewish mother.

It was during Patrick Rhinemann's interview at the close of week three that Harwitz had asked him why he had chosen to serve in the Israeli army...rather than join the IRA. Patrick Rhinemann was so stunned by the question that he was not able to respond, eventually stammering that joining the IRA had never even occurred to him, offering that he'd never been recruited by the

IRA. 'And if they had recruited you? What if? Do they recruit you *now*?'

It was from this point that Harwitz had ignored him completely, even to a shunning, leaving a table Patrick Rhinemann might sit down to join. But there were others such as himself, a person with whom one instructor or another had an issue. And each week they had changed tent mates, from one group of ten to another, from one instructor to another. And with each change the adjustment came easier. More important was the close of week four. This was when martial arts had begun and, in this Patrick Rhinemann, had excelled.

Co-captain his senior year of Cornell's rugby team, he had led it to the Ivy League championship that year, made all-league as Third Row. Always athletic, Patrick Rhinemann had come to love the contact of the rugby pitch, the crashing into a mall, tearing the ball out of an opponent's hands and working it back to the scrummy.

This was something he could do all day. And at Camp Hope, few could match him in the weekly ten-kilometer forced march, all in 100+ degrees of heat with 10 kilograms of sand in a backpack. More than anything, it was this that had marked his success there.

By the eighth week, Harwitz had all but disappeared from Patrick Rhinemann's life at Camp Hope. His Yiddish had become fluent - he could argue in it and shout in it. Even curse in it. So entrenched had the language become in him that his mind no longer had to translate his thoughts from English into Yiddish because his thoughts were now in Yiddish. It was the language of the *cause* and all he had come to think about was the cause.

He had, in fact, come to a complete understanding, a knowledge, that Israel was the last, the *only* hope for the Jewish nation. That should Israel fail now, it would be gone and *forever*, that there would never be another

Israel, no center, no *place* for his Jewishness, this thing that had come to share his mind, even his soul. Should they fail now, they will have failed their God, *the* God, and all of it...the pogroms, the chained ghettos of Europe, the mind ghettos of home, the *Holocaust*, 5,000 years and millions upon millions dead, all to dust, all for nothing.

And it was at Camp Hope that Patrick Rhinemann had done his genealogy, on his grandfather's side back to the early 1600s in Poland and on this grandmother's side back to 1638 in Austria-Hungary. All Jewish, each and every one. And as in the Bible, he could recite them in order, by name, more than one hundred names by count.

But it was not until his final interview with the Leader that he came to realize what had happened in his eight weeks at Camp Hope. He had come to know the Israeli persona - how it thought, how it lived, why it fought - and he was now at one with it. At the close of the interview, the Leader rose, extending his hand across the table. 'Are you ready, Patrick Rhinemann, to fight for Israel? To *die* for her?'

'Yes' was his answer. There could be no other.

'We shall see, Patrick Rhinemann...tomorrow. Good luck and may God be with you.'

Tomorrow was *Cage Day*. Waking at dawn, breaking camp by noon, all tents were packed for the next group to start its journey. Each camp-mate was told to pack his personal belongings in one duffle bag and to have a change of clothes in a kit bag tethered to it. What did not fit was to be discarded.

Dressed in combat boots and desert shorts only, the camp-mates were ordered to board two of four buses that had arrived the night before, along with two trucks, one for the duffle bags and a larger one for the tents and equipment. There would be no midday ration. The bus Patrick Rhinemann was on had two large containers of one-liter plastic bottles of ice-chilled water. At precisely one pm, the engines were started.

On the closing of the door of the bus that Patrick Rhinemann was in, an instructor had risen from a front-row seat and turned to face them. "All rise," he said, and they did. "Bow your head and place both your hands at the center of your chest." They did this, as well. "Now repeat after me…" A pause, now complete silence.

"I swear by my ancestors never to disclose to any person anything about which I am now to engage." They all repeated after the instructor on which he raised his head, motioning them to sit down and the driver to proceed.

On the eastern edge of Camp Hope there was a cluster of low mesas. As the two lead buses approached the mesas, they separated, one bus going left to the north, the other going right to the south. The two other buses proceeded directly ahead, as did the trucks. The first two buses were soon out of each other's sight. Patrick Rhinemann was in the bus that had turned to the south, which soon pulled up to a narrow, gated pass. The instructor rose again in the front of the bus as the engine was turned off, the driver stepping out, going to the gated area.

The instructor bowed his head, his hands raised and open at shoulder level. "May we each be worthy of our fathers and the enemy we face within. Give us each the courage to succeed, to go forward." His head slowly rose, looking across the thirty before him.

"This is your final test. All depends on your success here." He paused, taking a deep breath. "You have been called to defend Israel from her enemies. You will be serving shoulder-to-shoulder with her sons, those who have seen battle, who have lost comrades, who have killed enemies, Israel's enemies – some with their bare hands." He paused, looking at those before him, inspecting, observing.

"While your training in Israel will continue after you arrive, you begin your deployment there on the front lines, either on the Strip or the Heights. You will be at war, in a war for Israel's survival." He paused now. "They want us dead, gone. *Each* one of them wants *each* one of us, each one of you, all of us, *dead.*" He paused, motioning now to the gated pass to the right of the bus.

"Through that gate is a chain-link cage, ten feet high and fifty feet across, open to the sky and the God you wish to serve. You will access the cage through a series of holding rooms. In this, you will be separated from each other and prepared for the cage." He reached for his belt.

"Each of you will be given a knife." He now raised his knife above his head, black in color with a nine-inch blade of hardened steel and a composite, cross-hatched grip. "You've been trained in its use. You've stuck it through burlap bags, thrown it at wooden targets." With this, he stepped forward, his arm back, now hurling the knife with the full force of his arm and shoulder, it flying, tumbling between the rows of camp-mates the entire length of the aisle into a wooden target at the far end, striking and sticking a red circle painted on a wooden gate across the back of the bus. Walking the length of the bus, he pulled it out, stepping forward toward the front of the bus as he spoke.

"In the final holding room, your chest with be coated with chicken grease. Keep your hands off it. It will affect your grip on your knife." Reaching the front of the bus, he turned to face them, his knife still in hand. "You'll also be fitted with a schutzhund bite bar. It will cover the arm and shoulder of your off-arm." With his knife in his right hand, he traced the length of his left arm from wrist to the shoulder. "There's a grip inside so you can lift it for protection and keep it from being torn from you."

He motioned now with his left arm, raising it to protect his chest and neck while thrusting several times with the knife under it and upward, stepping forward with his left foot as if to meet an attacker. "In addition to the schutzhund, you will be given a lacrosse helmet and a lacrosse glove...for your other hand.

"After your time in the cage, you'll go to another holding room. If you pass, you will return to this bus or the other bus. If you fail, you will be escorted to one of the other two buses you saw as we left. Those who fail, they will be driven out of Camp Hope. If you pass, the bus you will be put on will take you to one of two dinner ceremonies at two separate locations on the camp grounds. You'll have accommodations for the night and be discharged in the morning with itineraries and passage to your unit in Israel ten days from today." He paused, looking across those before him.

"Now, some things you *must* understand." He paused, taking a deep breath, assuming the posture of a Lord High Commissioner. "You were *never here*. Camp Hope *does not exist*." His eyes seemed to reach each of them separately. "Those of you who pass cannot know who failed, cannot know all who passed. There is no reunion. You met *no person here*, you know *no names*. If you encounter a camp-mate in Israel, that is where you met him. If you encounter a camp-mate later in life, that is where you met him. Do not *ever* speak of Camp Hope because *it does not exist*. Never speak of *Cage Day* because it *never happened*. Do you understand?" The nodding heads spoke of yes.

"DO YOU UNDERSTAND?"

"YES!" all shouted.

He nodded in satisfaction before motioning to the four camp-mates in the first two rows. "You four, follow me."

Patrick Rhinemann rose, first in line behind the instructor as they passed through the gates, now each assigned his own instructor and separated from the others. While the face of his instructor had not moved a muscle,

Patrick Rhinemann could see in Mica Harwitz' eyes a sense of anticipation. Following him through a low door that Harwitz closed silently behind him, Patrick Rhinemann found himself in total darkness, an all-encompassing black, a silence so complete he wondered if Harwitz was still in the room.

On entering, and before the door was closed, Patrick Rhinemann had seen a table in front of him and he shuffle-stepped to it, crouching slightly and reaching out with his hands, finding it and moving against it at his crotch.

"So, *Pa-hattie*, it is at the finish we are now, eh?" He could feel Harwitz move behind him and step to the other side of the table, now in front. "I am not still understanding why you are here, *Pa-hattie* Riley Rhinemann." There was the sound of something being placed on the table.

"It is of your Jewish father's Irish woman that you were born. Why are you not exploding bombs in London department stores?"

Patrick Rhinemann's mind was trying to gauge the distance to the voice, his brain trying to remember if Harwitz had a weapon on his belt, whether he was left-handed or right.

"Here. Your helmet. It is you who is to be first."

Patrick Rhinemann reached out his hands, felt the skull piece of the helmet and put it on, buckling the strap.

"Your glove…"

His hand out again, he took the glove, working it on, his fingers flexing under the hard-plastic knuckles.

"You are quiet today, *Pa-hattie*. Not like the other drunken sons of Irish whores I see across Europe. Yes, wherever Israeli patriots needed bedding, there was always an Irish whore."

Patrick Rhinemann stood motionless except for the working of his fingers in the glove, the sound now of barking, high-pitched barking.

"They are coyotes, you know. Captured by Indians…fed full for three weeks with desert game…it's to twenty-five kilograms that they get."

Patrick Rhinemann flinched, stepping back and forward as a heavy brush with chicken grease swathed across this chest, three times.

"They haven't eaten in two days." He paused for effect. "They are quite hungry now, keeping them we are in cages separate or they kill each other…to eat. The barking gets very loud…" There was the sound of something being lifted. "Put out your left arm…"

Patrick Rhinemann felt the schutzhund being slipped over his left forearm, hiked all the way to his shoulder as his left hand felt the grip inside and held it, moving it up and down to test its weight.

"There! All done. Our great gladiator ready to fight for…Israel? But you are not Jewish. Why would you fight for Israel if you are *not Jewish*?"

The lights snapped on, glaring, blinding, Patrick Rhinemann stepping back from the surprise of it, his eyes squinting in the brightness, searching for Harwitz, finding him to his left, his 9mm Glock in hand.

Seeing Patrick Rhinemann's eyes on the gun, Harwitz waved it slightly. "For the coyote, 'just in case.' I think you say."

Patrick Rhinemann stood to his full six-foot-one height, working his shoulders to feel the shutzhund, moving left and right with it, raising it up and down as the instructor had done on the bus.

"So, *Pa-hattie*. Now we are ready…" From his belt, Harwitz removed a knife, raising his arm, he stuck in the table's wooden surface, motioning Patrick to take it. "Now you have all things necessary…Yes, but the intelligence…the enemy… yes, who is he? And how do I fight him?"

Harwitz took a step back, went into a slight crouch. "Enemy is a twenty-five-kilo coyote. He bites like a wolf, maybe stronger." He smiled here. "His stomach is vacant – no food, two days since. Your purpose to his life is to fill his stomach…with *you*…your arm, your leg, maybe…something to stop the pain in his vacant stomach." A pause now, the nodding head of a person who knows, a person in complete charge, control of another.

"You begin in the center of the cage. The animal, the enemy, come in, directly in front. Simple, no?" He smiled. "If lucky, you get a stupids. He see you, he smell chicken grease, he attack!" Harwitz lunged forward, feigning an attack, stopping three feet short. "He jump up at you, bite at your arm, you raise your arm, like so…" He squatted, raising his left arm, as if a shield, his right hand and arm thrusting beneath it and out, up. "Drive knife into his flank, at the shoulder, like here."

Harwitz stood to his full five feet, nine inches, motioning to an area under his left arm, breast high. "Like so." He motioned the thrust of a knife. "The blade go into lungs and heart, pffft! He dead. Blop." Harwitz motioned with his arms as the coyote would drop, then clapped his hands. "All gone! Coyote dead! You go to dinner…all happy…"

Harwitz fixed on Patrick Rhinemann now, his face stopped, his eyes up on Patrick Rhinemann, bearing in, challenging. "So, *Pa-hattie*…" He motioned Patrick to the door behind him, reaching for the door knob. Opening the door a crack, the brilliant sun of the New Mexico summer streamed into the room. Harwitz gripped Patrick's upper arm, holding him back as he looked outside.

Patrick Rhinemann was now able to see the edge of the chain-link cage.

Harwitz turned back inside, a smile coming to his face. "Too bad, *Pa-hattie*. You not lucky today. The big one, you get the big one…some wolf maybe I think in him, maybe a lot…"

Mica Harwitz guided Patrick Rhinemann through the door, closing it behind them as he led Patrick to the cage door, a large coyote in a holding pen on the far side of the cage, barking and lunging against the chain-link fencing, his eyes fixing at Patrick Rhinemann. The animal was darker than the coyotes Patrick Rhinemann had seen in camping trips outside Aspen, and larger too…

Opening the cage door, Harwitz motioned Patrick inside, closing it after him. "I'll be over there." He motioned to his right, holding the Glock up for Patrick to see. "If going badly, give me clear shot…I save you for IRA."

Patrick Rhinemann ignored this, starting for the center of the cage, his eyes fixing on the animal on the far side of the cage, it now lunging at the door. "NOW!" Shouted Harwitz and the door of the pen sprung open, seeming to thrust the animal at him.

With the full diameter of the cage for a start, the coyote bounded at him, launching from ten feet, maybe more, heaving itself at Patrick Rhinemann who now braced his legs, raising the schutzhund like a shield, lowering it at the last instant to get under the coyote's flared jaws.

Taking its full weight with his protected left arm and shoulder, he lifted under the animal, flipping it over him into the wall of the cage behind him as he scrambled now to the middle of the cage, squaring himself to the animal, it regaining its balance, setting low on its forefeet, its eyes at Patrick, snarling, nostrils flared, darting and feigning at him, raising on its hind feet but holding its distance.

Now in a squat, Patrick Rhinemann worked his legs, thrusting at the animal, growling at it, shouting, matching its moves to the left and right, now closing on it, the coyote darting left, suddenly breaking right and in two bounds launching at him, higher this time, higher than Patrick had any idea it could get, flying at him as Patrick set his feet, raising the schutzhund like a shield, this time taking the animal's full weight square on, stepping into it to break the animal's charge as he drove the knife into its side.

The weight of the animal now falling on Patrick's left arm and shoulder, he hefted it with the schutzhund and the hilt of his knife with his right arm, thrusting it away from him, watching it fall to the hardpan floor of the cage, dead…a stillness coming, silence.

And now a roar from Patrick Rhinemann's lungs and throat, a bursting of power and force, a sound such as he had never made before or even had heard, his head shaking as every muscle and tendon in his body flexed to the maximum, his head and throat seeming near to exploding from it.

Stepping to the carcass, Patrick kicked dirt on its flank and spat on it. A few deep breaths taken and loosed over it, the animal's eyes open, staring blankly, blood at its tongue and covering its left flank, spreading now on the hard pan floor of the cage.

Patrick Rhinemann cast down the schutzhund and knife as he turned to the cage door, now held open by Harwitz, a glance at him and no more as he walked out of the cage, ignoring completely another man who had been watching.

And nothing need have been said. It was all in their eyes, what they had seen…the death of a desert scavenger and the birth of a warrior, of a new-made force born to the earth, bestriding the face of the planet.

What they could not know, though, what Patrick Rhinemann himself was only just now coming to, was that he had *thrilled* at the kill, that he wanted to do it again, *right now.* But this time not with some desert junk dog snared in an Indian trap. No. This time he wanted to do it with Harwitz. This time he wanted to *kill* Mica Harwitz, to thrust his knife into *Mica Harwitz'* flank, to see *his* body lying still and dead on the dirt floor of the cage, leaving it to balloon and burst in the heat of the desert sun...

That was the nightmare.

CHAPTER TWENTY-NINE
Homecoming

J ohn Riley started up the hill to Section 24 at Mt. Olivet Cemetery, looking up, catching Bryan Canny's eye, a quick wave to keep him where he was. Flying to Palm Beach at 7 am tomorrow was not going to happen. He had an 8 am meeting with a lawyer at National Airport, maybe done by 8:30 and off then. Whatever there was to see in Palm Beach would be seen by 1 pm and getting him back in DC by 3:30-4:00 pm.

And now The Deal running the courses of his mind, maybe going too fast, too fast. It's not your world, John Riley thought, real estate, then thinking as quick that being all the more reason to be away from it. Yup, got to do it, got to do it. If Mom were to pass any time in the next three years, her estate would have to come up with two hundred million, more than that, and do it in eighteen months. No telling where the market would be. Could be a real mess, a calamity. Got to do it...

Section 24 was as close to a 'mount' as there was on Mt. Olivet, the highest ground there, topped off with soaring maples and an oak tree that seemed to attach the whole thing to the sky. Looking left, he could see the Capitol and to the left of that the sun off a turn in the Potomac, just beyond the Tidal Basin. Hard to believe he was in the water there just eight or so hours ago. Time flies when you're having so much fun...

"So, John, now, you made it, did you?" Bryan Canny's hand extended and John Riley took it, happy for the grip of his hand and the pull up a high curb to the marble bench Jack Hennessey had placed there nearly seventy years previous. Stepping to the bench and turning south to the

River, John Riley sat down, his eyes closed, taking a deep breath, it coming to him now what's to be done...

"Here lie Christine McCarthy Hennessey and her son, Gone to God, July 19, 1892." Bryan Canny read the inscription on the large stone before them. "Not been up here before now, John. Drove Mary Kate here once, she and her Patrick." He looked over at John Riley. "Stayed with the car, you know...thought that best."

John Riley held Bryan Canny's eyes for a moment. "Well, you might have come up...I'm sure Mary Kate wouldn't have minded." His eyes went to the river. Rising, he stepped to the large stone with Paddy's name written large across it. 'How does this happen?' he thought to himself. A quick look at Bryan, whose eyes were on him, curious...

"Hank Johnson was back in Ireland last month, Bryan...some golf, and to see friends...came across Skinny Hughes..."

"Skinny Hughes, now! Well, knock me down...Skinny Hughes!" Bryan Canny roared a laugh, pointing at John Riley and laughing all over again, doing a jig in a circle.

"Last we saw Skinny Hughes, he was stealing the wrong van! Scared shitless, he was, ducking under Harriers long gone, a dash from the chopper to the van that was full of our suitcases and not a five-dollar bill anywhere in it! Michael's forty thousand in cash in the van to the right, and another ten thousand in electronics!" He laughed again.

John Riley was laughing, too. Hadn't thought about that part of it in years. Couldn't laugh about it back then, though, not with Michael in a state of shock. All hope of seeing his son gone forever. Still chuckling, he chided Bryan Canny. "Not much of a fella, your Skinny Hughes."

"Hey, wait a minute there, now, John Riley, wait a minute..." Bryan Canny was still laughing, softer now.

"Might not have been the IRA assassin I had him down for, but he did find us Sean, now, didn't he? If we'd been there a day earlier..." He stopped now, looking away and then back at John Riley. "But we weren't, now, were we?"

"No, we weren't." Now John Riley looked away. "And God only knows what would have happened if we'd gotten him out, Sean..."

"True enough, true enough..." Bryan went to the bench, sitting down, forward, his elbows on his knees, he eyes fixed on the ground before him for a moment, then up at John Riley. "So, how is old Skinny Hughes? Getting by, is he? Put on a few pounds, perhaps?"

John Riley turned, looking down at Bryan Canny. "Hank didn't say..." He turned away. "Did say that Skinny's come across a journal, a diary really...found it in an IRA safe house..."

Bryan Canny looked up, sitting back, his eyes now hard on John Riley, his head cocked, his brain working, maybe racing now...

"It's..."

"My mother's, right, John Riley? Right? Maira's?" Bryan Canny was up now, his eyes past John Riley. "She'd be scribbling in it, now, mumbling to herself..." he fixed on John Riley. "Tis Maira's, right?"

John Riley's silence was his answer.

"And where is it?" Bryan Canny stepped to John Riley, at him. "Where is it, now, John Riley? I got..."

John Riley reached out, holding Bryan Canny at the shoulders. "Hank Johnson has it...it's to be dropped off at East Irving this afternoon."

Bryan Canny started for the path to his car.

"Bryan, wait..."

"Wait, yourself, now, John Riley."

"Stop!"

Bryan Canny stopped, turned around, facing back.

"Hank's read it..."

"All the more...I've got..." Bryan Canny turned down the path.

"Bryan! Stop!"

Bryan Canny stopped again, his shoulders slumped, not turning back again.

"Bryan, look around you, now. Come back up here...look around you. *Read* the names...Bryan, read them."

Bryan Canny turned slowly toward John Riley, now coming back, his head shaking slightly, coming to stand at John Riley's side.

John Riley motioned to Paddy Riley's stone. "Read the name, Bryan...Out loud..."

Bryan Canny turned to the stone, his eyes on the letters and words cut into it. "Patrick Francis Riley, born March 17, 1900, died November 21, 1943." His eyes looked up and ahead for moment, then turned to John Riley.

"Bryan Canny, you just spoke your grandfather's name...welcome home..."

Bryan Canny caught his breath, his eyes fixed on John Riley, questioning, doubting, torn, stammering. "What are you saying, now, John Riley? How...how is it possible? How...My grandfather, you're saying? Here? In America? Impossible..."

"Believe it, Bryan...it's in the book...in her own hand."

Bryan Canny turned back to the stone, his legs buckling as he kneeled forward, then his hands before him on the ground, the green grass of Paddy Riley's grave.

John Riley kneeled down beside him, his arm across Bryan Canny's shoulders, speaking to his ear. "It's all in the book, Bryan...she had your birth date moved forward by the midwife...so there'd be no possible link to Michael, so she could keep you from him...but he's your father, Bryan, all the same. Michael Riley *is* your father…it's in her book, in her hand, that you are…"

Bryan Canny raised up, sitting back on his calves, his hands to his face, rocking back and forth, deep breaths taken. "God in heaven, thank You…thank You for the knowing of it." His hands now found his thighs as he stared at the name on the stone before him, his lips speaking the name Patrick Francis Riley.

As his breathing eased, his eyes turned to another stone, speaking the name. "Kevin Riley". He looked at John Riley.

"Your uncle…" John Riley smiled, his arms out, hands open. "And Mary Riley's your *grandmother*…"

Bryan Canny mouth dropped open. "My grandmother…" His eyes drifted away…

"Mary Kate's your aunt, her son Patrick your first cousin…"

Bryan Canny's eyes came back to John Riley's. "Then Brigit's…"

"Yes, your first cousin, too, Katherine and Annie as well..."

They both rose now, Bryan Canny standing before him. "Then you're…"

"I'm your uncle, Bryan…though…"

Bryan Canny breathed deeply, his head now nodding, understanding, their eyes locked, sharing, they now closing to an embrace, Bryan Canny now crying, John Riley, too….

In time, John Riley stood back, wiping his eyes, looking away and then back at Bryan who was wiping his face with a handkerchief, now blowing his nose. "Christ, John, now, the help'll be having us down for two of the lads on an afternoon tryst…"

John Riley laughed, shaking his head.

"I can see the headline now in *The Post,* "Necrophiliac gays seen trysting on Mt. Olivet…Cardinal refuses comment…"

John Riley laughed all over again, stepping away as he breathed a deep breath, waving Bryan Canny quiet, now fixing on him. "As of right now, Bryan, the only people who know about this are you, me and Hank…oh, and Skinny Hughes…"

Bryan Canny laughed, a great shrug of his shoulders. "Don't be too quick to that, now, John Riley. Maira's writing was chicken scratch and Skinny could barely read large print." They both laughed.

John Riley looked away. "It's your call, Bryan, what you do with it, you being Michael's blood son." He turned to Bryan Canny.

Bryan Canny looked back at him now, his eyes returning to Paddy's stone, silent, his head nodding.

"It would be nothing but good news to Mary…the more grandchildren the merrier…" He fixed on Bryan Canny. "You think about it, Bryan…seems there's twists and turns in it you might want to think through…happy to speak with you about it anytime."

Bryan Canny's eyes went to the river, the Capitol to his right, then to the city to the right of that. "Been a citizen, John, now for four years, and been with Nan three, thinking hard about getting married." He turned back to John Riley. "Couldn't want a better situation at work, couldn't dream of it." He looked back down at Paddy Riley's stone.

"That was the only missing piece, you know…Aye, knowing my Da's people." Bryan Canny lowered his head, now turning back to John Riley. "I thank you for this, John Riley, for the knowing of it, who my people are, that there's a plot I can come to, and know 'tis my home." He took a deep breath, shaking his head, smiling at John Riley.

"And I'll be by this evening to see the book, Maira's scratchings." A broad, full smile now came to Bryan Canny's face. "But what I need more than anything just now, exactly now, is to see my Nan, you know, to hold her in my arms, to take a deep, deep breath…Aye, that's what's needed now."

To John Riley, there came a fullness of being, a completeness. No word seemed adequate. No word seemed needed. Sometimes it is enough to just smile back and nod, which is what he did.

"So, then, Uncle, can I drop you to the office, now, as I get on to Nan?"

"By all means, *nephew*, by all means, indeed."

CHAPTER THIRTY
Mothers and Daughters

M ary Kate knocked on the door to Mary Riley's suite off the kitchen at East Irving Street. There was no response. She knocked again, her ear now to the door, listening. Still no answer. Gripping the door handle, she turned it softly, easing the door open.

Mary Riley was asleep in her armchair, her head back, her hands on her lap, holding a rosary. Stepping back, Mary Kate was about the close the door when her mother's eyes opened.

"Yes...who's...oh, Mary Kate, now...come in...come in, won't you..." Mary's arms waved Mary Kate in as she sat up in her chair, now motioning Mary Kate to the near end of the settee beside her, her eyes coming bright, even eager. "So good to see you, now, sit down, sit down...." She patted the cushion of the settee.

Mary Kate stepped to her mother, kissing her on the forehead before sitting next to her, taking her left hand in her right and caressing it, feeling a full smile come to her face.

Mary smiled back, looking away. "Not often a person gets to see that, you know...a mother and daughter close, now, after so many years..."

Mary Kate pressed her hands firmer. "Yes...a wonderful thing to see...I was so happy for Brigit, and Eileen, too, so happy..."

"Aye, 'tis as much a mother can hope for, it is..." Mary covered Mary Kate's hand now, drew herself closer. "The miracle of the thing is that, all the years between? Well, they just go away, now, don't they...or somehow come back, richer, maybe...Who's to say? Who's to know?"

Their eyes joined, each nodding what they knew of such miracles, of their own years apart, and the wonder of their years since, their second life together. Mary sat up. "And where'd they go, now, after the hospital?"

"To Brigit's place, I think…"

Mary sat back. "Aye, a special day indeed."

"Really? How so?"

Mary let a quick smirk. "Not sure she's ever been there, Eileen hasn't"

Now Mary Kate sat back. "Really? Then it's high time!" She laughed and Mary laughed with her.

"And your Patrick, now, he's to come today, is he?"

'Your Patrick' was Patrick Rhinemann, Mary Kate's son, the words said so close it was if there was no space between. To Mary Riley, Patrick Riley Rhinemann was *Yourpatrick*, and that's all there was to it.

"Yes…" Mary Kate looked away. "There was a voice mail when we got back from the hospital…said he'd be here by eight, maybe nine." She looked away. "He's been driving near non-stop since Tuesday night, I think…I'm not sure when…Don't know, really…" Her hand went to her mouth, covering it.

"Ach! Now what's the worry about that? A strapping lad like your Patrick, an all-whatever rugger? He'll be in, we'll each get kisses and hugs and he'll be out as quick to the pub with some of the lads about."

Mary Kate turned, her head now going to Mary's lap, speaking away. "Oh Mom, it's not the getting here, the driving…it's what happens next…"

Mary covered Mary Kate's shoulders with her arm, her head down at her ear. "What can it be, now, this 'next'? What's the lad up to?"

Mary Kate sat up, looking away for a moment, drawing a deep breath before facing her mother. "He's joining the *Israeli* Army…He's to be there for a full year…leaves next week."

P.D. St. Claire

"Ach! The army, now! What's this, the *Israeli* Army? He's off to war, is he? Your Patrick gone to war, now?"

Mary Riley struggled to her feet, looking down at her daughter. "How can this be, girl, him off to war, and fighting in another place's army?"

Mary Kate's hand went back to her mouth as she fought the tears, looking away. "They recruited him when he was over there last year."

"And is this all legal, then, is it? Your Patrick being American and going off to fight, now, for another country? How can this be?"

Mary Kate looked up, then away again. "He's explained it all to us...showed us the regulations. He can serve in another country's army for one day short of a full year, so long as he's not an officer, and not lose his passport."

"Lose his passport, is it, now!" Mary Riley's arms went out and up, her doing a full turn and back at her daughter. "Jayus, Mary and Joseph, Mary Kate, what's the lad thinking, now? Is he thinking at all, is what I'm thinking..."

May Kate shook her head, looking up now and patting Mary's chair for her to sit down, reaching for her hand as she turned to sit. "Sit. Mom...He's not going to lose his passport. It's just what the law is."

Mary Riley looked at her, her head nodding. "So, then, that's the law, is it... the 'what' of it, and no more. Aye, 'tis the 'why' of it, that's what I'm wondering, now..."

Mary Kate shook her head, looking away. "I don't know... at all," she said, her eyes away. "He'd changed when he got back last year, after his junior year there. Made new friends at home, in New York, brought new friends down from school, took a minor in Middle East..."

279

"Bah! Took courses, did he? Learned all about it, did he? All the books, now…" Mary shook her head, waved it all away. "The books don't tell the hell of such things… the books is what keeps it all going."

Mary Riley looked away, then sharply back. "And his father, now, *your* Michael? What's he been saying about all this? His only son going off to war and all?"

Mary Kate looked up, shaking her head, unable to speak.

"His only son's to go to war, and he says nothing, now, nothing at all? What sort of father is this, now!?"

Mary Kate looked away. "How can he…after all…"

"Pigs leavings! He can say 'don't go!'…Aye, and for all the 'after all' of it you're talking about, now? Jaysus, Mary and Joseph…Aye! 'tis why he *shouldn't* be going, not 'after all,' but all together, now!"

Mary Kate shook her head. "We've stopped talking about it." She turned back. "We've practically stopped talking at all…it's why I went to Los Angeles…made up something about a client there...just had to get away…" She closed her eyes. "It's been awful, tearing us apart, tearing me apart…I just don't know."

Her eyes on Mary Kate, Mary Riley reached for her daughter's hand. "Aye, Mary Kate, poor girl, what's to be done at all I'm wondering…"

Mary Kate turned to her mother. "My only hope left is Michael…Patrick promised to speak with Michael before he made his final decision, before he left…"

"*My* Michael, is it? In the hospital, tubes and such sticking in and out of all parts of him, now?" Mary Riley's eyes fixed on Mary Kate. "And when's this to be, then, him being so sick, now?"

Mary Kate sat back. "Tomorrow morning…"

Mary Riley sat back, her face off, a breath taken.

Mary Kate squeezed her mother's hand to reassure her. "It's fine, Mom…He's fine with it…insisted…said he'd never forgive himself, or me, if he hadn't a try at talking him out of it." She held her mother's stare.

"Well, I guess, now…" Mary Riley looked away, then back again, her nodding the confidence of a knowing and proud mother. "Aye, if there's a man alive who can talk the lad out of it, 'tis Michael Francis Riley, himself." She looked at Mary Kate, a sure wink of the eye. "There you go, now, girl, my Michael's your man…"

"I hope…" Mary Kate looked away.

Mary Riley fixed on her daughter. "You can pray, now, too, you know, Mary Kate. No regulations against that."

Mary Kate turned back, her mother's eyes holding her.

"Aye, girl, times like this, Mary Kate, 'tis what praying's for…" Mary Riley fixed on Mary Kate. "And when's the last time you've spoken with your Patrick?"

Mary Kate's right hand, made in a soft fist, went to her chin. "Early in July. He's been in some training camp out west…Couldn't even tell us what state…God, I hate it."

Mary's head went to a nod, now shaking slightly. "And the last time you spoke to your Michael, now?"

"I…I can't remember…"

Mary Riley sat back, her eyes closed for a moment, now open and on her. "I'm sorry, Mary Kate, sorry for your troubles, I am…But there's time yet, and your Michael's a good man, as good as any."

She gripped Mary Kate's hand firmer, pulling it close. "Trust the ones you love, girl, and the ones that love you, too, for surely he does…trust and pray…"

Mary Kate looked into her mother's eyes. They were tired, almost to closing now, tired but true…Mary Kate looked away. 'There *is* still time,' she thought, turning back to her mother. Her eyes had closed.

Loosening her hand from her mother's soft grip, Mary Kate rose, kissing her mother on the forehead before stepping quietly to the door. As she reached for the door knob, Mary spoke.

"Like as not I'll be down for the night before your Patrick gets in...can you ask him to walk me to mass in the morning, now?"

Mary Kate stopped, turning back to her mother, now up and starting for her bathroom door. "I will...I'm sure he'd like that...sleep well, Mom..."

"You, too, now, Mary Kate." Mary's eyes were fixed on the bathroom doorway. "Get yourself a good night's sleep, now, girl, and remember to pray, now, won't you?"

"Yes, Mom, you may rely on it..."

CHAPTER THIRTY-ONE
Nana

T here was a soft knock at the door, two light raps of a knuckle. "Nana?"

'Aye, 'tis time,' she thought, putting down her rosary and blessing herself as she shifted forward in her armchair, easing herself up, standing now and dressed for the morning. 'Aye, Mary Coughlin Riley, 'tis time…'

Turning out the light by her chair, she looked west, toward Connecticut Avenue, the dawning light in golden hues off the white clapboard house across the garden and driveway. 'What's their name, now?' she's thinking, 'Two years there and barely a 'hello' in the street.' Her eyes now back on the door, making her way to it.

"Is that you, now, Patrick?" She gripped the handle, pulling open the door to behold her grandson, Patrick Riley Rhinemann…Aye, all six feet plus of him standing tall in the brilliance of the dawn's light through the kitchen, a smile now come to his face, all the more striking by the white of his teeth against the near brown of his tan.

"Morning, Nana…"

To her surprise and wonder, he stepped toward her, holding her for a moment, even a bit of a squeeze, now, then back and that smile again, sure a Riley smile it is, she's thinking.

"So good to see you, now, Patrick, lad…" She patted his chest, looking at his shirt. "And aren't we looking smart in our crocodile shirt and linen pants." Her eyes fixed on him, she holding back, near tearing at the sight of him. "So good it is to see you, now, Patrick, so grand."

Smiling with a slight nod of the head, he offered his arm and led her through the house to the front door, out the brick walk to East Irving and the two blocks to mass.

Now it had occurred to Mary Riley as she was dressing this morning that it was half her life that she had been going to mass at Blessed Sacrament, forty-six of her ninety-one years, near 15,000 times her quick numbers made it, give or take…and then thinking of the silliness of such things, the 'how manys' of this or that in a life.

It was each time the value was there and taken, that's what counted in a life, each time there to pray, to think, to be with those gone before, and then to be with…herself…She had come to this some time ago without knowing just when, just happy to be in these years and her awareness of it, a comfort with just being.

The celebrant this morning was the pastor, as kindly a man as Mary Riley had ever known, late to his calling and the better for this, him knowing the ways of how things get done, and all. The homily was brief, speaking of the parable of the loaves and fishes, Mary thinking how such a thing could happen, five fishes and two loaves and twelve apostles to hand it all out. Ach, even how one man's voice could carry to five thousand, or who made the count, just so many more 'how manys.'

They sat where Mary always sat at daily mass, half up to the right, the church quiet now with mass done, Mary now just being, her mind at rest, and her soul.

"Nana?"

Mary Riley's eyes blinked at the sound of her name, sitting up a measure as she took a breath. 'Aye, Patrick, now…' She turned to him, "'Tis time.'

"Didn't mean to distract, you, Nana," he smiling his smile. "Just, you know…"

"Aye, lad, just wondering if I was awake or what, now…" She patted him on the thigh, smiling. "And sometimes, now, I'm even wondering myself…"

She looked toward the altar, the glory of the morning sun through the stained-glass windows of the nave, the comfort of the church, the rows of wooden pews before them, all leading up to the muted golden door of the tabernacle. 'Aye,' she thought, 'and to Patrick, tis come...'

Looking at Patrick Rhinemann and smiling, she rose, pulling herself up on the back of the pew in front of her, Patrick now rising as well, making room for her in the aisle, his arm again offered as he turned toward the rear of the church.

Taking his arm as she stepped into the aisle, Mary Riley turned her grandson toward the altar, Patrick taking her lead as she walked them to the front row, motioning him to sit there, in the left front row, at the aisle, as she genuflected and sat in the second row, just behind. Sitting forward, she spoke softly, almost a whisper. "Let me tell you, now, Patrick, of the grandest day in all me life..."

Patrick Riley Rhinemann turned toward her, the trace of a smile on his face...curious, eyes open wide, expectant...

"I was sitting just where you, are, now Patrick...Aye, the place of honor, don't you know. And on a day just such as this, bright with a full sun, the air dry and the sky blue and clear...a glorious day altogether, now." She turned toward the back of the church, speaking over her shoulder.

"And the place was packed, it was, don't you know, folks from all about, and flowers too, on the altar and at the pew ends, most of them, white rhododendrons, and bows of satin, music coming from the balcony above, the grand organ there, and the voice of an angel as well, so clear and pure it was..."

She turned to him here, her eyes closing, the sight of it all as clear in her mind now as the day of its happening. She took a short breath, letting it out as her head shook, her eyes now on him, a wink offered, her face coming to a smile as she pulled herself closer to him.

"Then the music goes from hymn to march and we're all standing now, smiling and fidgeting with this and that, programs and such, turning to see them coming up the aisle, three brides maids and the maid-of-honor, all being from New York, now, and then she comes, my treasure, now, your mother, my Mary Kate, and so grand she is! Aye, in her high-neck collar and the lace veil I wore me self and me mother before me in Ireland. Such a sight, Patrick, you've never seen.

And son John, now, him in his white collar and tails, walking at her side, an inch or two off her height, she wearing her heels and all, you know, and up they come, she smiling left and right and her eyes coming forward now and...and now taking to themselves a special light." Gazing away, now, she turned to Patrick.

"Aye, Patrick, a light in her eyes and they going right to your father Michael's, he standing opposite me, by his best man, his eyes, too, all alight. Aye, a sight I'd never before seen and not since, her eyes of green on the green eyes of your father, another green it was, sure, but green all the same and never a blink from either of them, now, nor a waver, and now they're here, they are..."

Mary's eyes went to the floor of the aisle at her feet, now turning to him. "Aye, Patrick, standing there, the two of them, and not another person in the place, not to them, anyways, just the two of them, looking into one another's eyes, Patrick, all eyes. And then he says, Father Hara, he does, 'And who gives this woman in marriage to this man?' And don't you know, Patrick, I pop up, I do, and 'tis in the aisle, I am..."

Mary Riley rose now, stepping into the aisle, with Patrick Rhinemann up as well, in the aisle with her, at her side, taking her hand, his eyes on her. "And then, Nana, then you said 'I do, *the Mother*. I give this woman to this man...'

Mary Riley froze as if struck in the face, her eyes clear and on Patrick, her mind coming to a wonderment. "Then you know, now, Patrick? They told you?" She stepped toward him, holding him, leaning into him, his arms closing around her.

"Yes, they told me, each separately, each saying I was never to speak of it, that it was a sacred moment, one for only the three of you, and me because, I am the child of it all…"

Mary Riley reached for the pew end, gripping it as Patrick held her other arm, steadying her as she slid in the pew and Patrick now sitting beside her, she holding his hand, kissing it, leaning into him, her eyes closed, her left hand now covering their joined hands, looking up at him and then to the altar ahead.

"It was, Patrick, as if a black crepe had been taken from my mind that day. A revelation, a transformation, a new world opened, a new light…a new freedom. Everything changed, everything…. there were no enemies, no fears…no places to hide because no hiding was needed. Aye, everything open…and clear…so clear...

She looked up at him, their eyes joining. "The greatest man I ever met in my life was Jack Hennessey."

Patrick nodded that he understood, that he knew who Jack Hennessey was.

"Aye, Jack Hennessey, no greater man ever I met. He tried to explain all this to me one afternoon, what he'd come to know about love and living. It was his last week with us, near sixty years ago now…Aye, Jack, dear Jack…" She looked away, then back.

"He left none of his own blood, you know…none. And I was so sad for him in this…But he told me, he did, that blood's only a part of it, and the lesser part, too…that it's the people you come know and build your life around - that's the greater part of it, and it was love at the bottom of it all. Love, Patrick, simple love."

287

Mary Riley looked up toward the altar. "Aye, love...love is all..." Turning now, she fixed on Patrick Rhinemann. "I never knew what love was, not as deeply as I come to understand that day, until I saw it in the eyes of my Mary Kate and your father as they took their vows. That was love, and it is to this day. *Love,* Patrick, it is all, a miracle, is what."

Mary Coughlin Riley's eyes fixed ahead now, toward the altar, but not seeing it, not seeing anything, hearing now in her mind the low murmurings of those about, a teeming rain, her own mother at her father's side, holding his arm, and uncle Dennis, now, walking, head down, the magistrate speaking out over the damp of it all 'It being found...' and other words a six-year-old girl had no knowing the meaning of, and then Uncle Dennis walking up the platform, his hat taken from him and a rope over his head to his neck and a sack too, more words now from the magistrate and he drops, gone, her father growling, a long, low sound, a moan that had haunted Mary Riley the whole of her life since, her mother holding her father at his arm 'Steady, now, Sean, steady...' she's saying to him and then men wearing peaked hats pushing among them, 'Go on, now...no more to see here...off to your places, now, the lot o' ya...'

Mary Riley turned away from the altar and the black of that day, now eighty and more years ago, her eyes finding those of her grandson, on her, waiting.

"'Tis a miracle you're here, now, Patrick Rhinemann, a miracle, sure." She held his eyes, gripping his hands more fully. "Aye, tis a miracle it was your father's uncle, found him in the debacle of war's end...you can have no knowing of what that was to do...among the millions lost and living...millions upon millions...and then the miracle of your father finding my Mary Kate and they finding the love that fulfills them to this day. Their love that I have come to cherish in a way I would *never* have thought possible."

She felt the grip of Patrick Rhinemann's hand tighten in hers. "And there's miracles to come, now, too, Patrick Riley Rhinemann, miracles of your own life, of your own finding." Her eyes fixed beyond him for a minute, in her mind the miracles of her life, her times, times with Paddy and Kevin, dearest Kevin, her eyes now again on Patrick's.

"And if you're looking for miracles, now, lad, be looking where the love is…the love…don't be spending your time looking for miracles where there's nothing but hate…miracles are hard to come by, now, where there's nothing but the hating…"

Patrick Rhinemann's eyes held hers for a moment then looked ahead, still.

"And there's another thing, now, lad, you'll be needing to know, too…"

Patrick Rhinemann's head held firm, his eyes fixed on whatever was running the courses of his mind.

"To a man, now, Patrick, a country's like a woman, it is. You can love more than one of them, you can, but not at the same time…"

Patrick Rhinemann's head turned sharply down on Mary Riley, at her, then slowly away, fixing ahead as he quietly stepped into the aisle, turning to her, offering his arm.

CHAPTER THIRTY-TWO
Getting Out

J ohn Riley turned left off Connecticut Avenue and quickly into the half circle at the front of the *Carthage*. Brigit Winslow walked out to the car, the glass and wrought iron front door held open by the doorman who stepped smartly around her. Opening the door of John Riley's Explorer, he took her briefcase and overnight bag, putting them in the back seat.

Half getting out on his side to greet her, John Riley sat back in the front seat, his eyes on her as she rested her purse on her lap and turned to him, smiling, at ease.

"Morning, Dad. And how are you this fine day?"

This was the 'how' of their lives these last eight years, since Brigit Riley Winslow became President of Hennessey Land Company. They were in business together, partners of a sort, the only hint this morning of anything else being that she addressed him as 'Dad' and not 'John.'

They had had dinner here last night, at her place, John and Eileen and Brigit. Sitting, eating, drinking and speaking in the evening glow of her balcony, watching as the sea of tree tops filling Rock Creek Park turned from green to musty to a soft, quiet dark against the lights of Taft Bridge.

John Riley cleared his throat. "Quite well. And yourself?"

"Just fine, thank you."

John Riley nodded, smiling as he put the car in gear, turning left and just making the light back onto Connecticut Avenue, now heading south toward the city, checking his watch – 7:15, plenty of time.

They were to meet Phillip Hastings of Hastings and Kline in a conference room Hank Johnson had reserved in Butler Aviation's offices in the General Aviation terminal at National Airport. John Riley checked the rear-view mirror. "What do you see happening at this meeting?"

Brigit Winslow sat bolt upright, her open right hand to her chest, looking left to right, then back at him. "Me? *Moi*? Are you talking to *me*? Are *you* talking to *me*? Brigit Winslow?" With her right index finger, she began jabbing at her breast bone, thumping for emphasis, her voice rising with each strike of her finger as she turned in her seat at him, continuing...

"What do *I* want out of this meeting? This meeting *you* called so *you* could open the bidding on how you are going to give an eighty-billion-dollar insurance company forty million dollars of *our* money, as in one thousand times one thousand times forty American dollars." She sat back, square to the windshield, her eyes fixed ahead. "*Pul-ease!*...and we were just getting along so well..."

John Riley laughed. Really laughed. He had expected no less of her. "Okay, okay, let's just say, for purposes of discussion, that *I* set the meeting up...just for the sake of argument..."

"Fine, let's just do that."

"Okay, fine, good..." John Riley accelerated to make the light at K Street. "So, we have this meeting...it started way back when Mid-America was still at the table and pushing hard for us to sign a letter of intent...and maybe reading me right that I was thinking about it..." Pausing now, he gave a quick look to Brigit. No reaction.

"So, we get the call from Nana about Michael, the meeting breaks up and we come home. Now Hardin Brooks speaks to me on the sidewalk in Chicago about Pierson, and Hank all along giving me reports on what a son-of-a-bitch this Pierson is, all topped off, or bottomed out, with the son-of-a-bitch's people following you, calling you on your private number and then *running me down on the river.* So, Mid-America is out, gone, history..."

John Riley pulled up to a stop light at Constitution Avenue, checking for pedestrians as the light changed..."So...where was...yeah. So Mid-America's gone, but the issue that started the whole Deal remains...nearly a billion in real estate hanging on the health of a ninety-one-year-old woman..."

John Riley eased the car around the traffic circle at the Tidal Basin, heading east now for the Fourteenth Street bridge, moving to the right lane.

Brigit brought her hands down softly on each knee, sitting back. "Is this where I get to say – again – that I told you so?"

"Yes, be my guest..."

"Okay, 'I told you so'..."

"And that gets us?"

"I'm not sure..." Brigit Riley Winslow looked to her right, toward the Tidal Basin, across to the Jefferson Monument on its far side, his statue standing tall and clear amid the columns and rotunda of it all. "Remember yesterday, Dad, you asked what I wanted out of all this..."

John Riley stole a quick look at her, his foot off the accelerator, now for a traffic light, stopped at it. "Yes..."

"Well, I know the answer now..."

Their eyes met for a moment, she now turning ahead, her eyes fixed forward. "Out, I want out...out..."

John Riley reached for his daughter's arm, gripping it firmly, her eyes to him, locked. "You show me how, Brigit, and it's done. You tell me how, and we'll do it."

A horn sounded from behind them and John Riley accelerated ahead, bending right toward the access ramp to the bridge, and on up over the river, his eyes fixed ahead. "Like I said yesterday, Brigit, 'It's only money' all this, The Deal, all of it…You show me how, and that's what we'll do."

Brigit reached for his shoulder, cupping it in her left hand…the morning air off the river washing through the open windows of the car, memories coursing John Riley's mind of old Southwest and fishing with Daddy Riley and Paddy Riley and Jack Hennessey, too…now turning right for the underpass on the George Washington Memorial Parkway and on to National…Brigit now pulling her arm back.

"What's wearing on me, Dad, is that we're still in the trough of the thing - the recession. We're down maybe 30 percent in market value in the last three years, and in another three, we'll have that all back and more, and in five years, *tons* more…that's been the model."

John Riley nodded, mouthing a 'Yep. That's the model…'

"But if Nana passes in the next two years, selling it off to meet the taxes…half of it'll go up in smoke …a waste, just a waste." Brigit Winslow sat up, her left hand now gripping John Riley's forearm, turning sharply to him.

"So, here's what…Pretty simple really. I'm working on getting out. You let me take care of that, okay?" She paused, waiting for a quick look off the road from John Riley, he giving it and a nod. "Good, so I'll take care of that." She sat back.

"Next, we see if this Hastings is all that Hank's got him cracked up to be, whether we can work him, his horsepower to set a meeting. We'll know that at 8:30 today, i.e., *now*." She paused, fixing on John Riley. "Right?"

"Right." John Riley turned right to the General Aviation Terminal, slowing to get in the left lane.

"If he's all that we're hoping for, we authorize him to set a Tuesday meeting with one of the insurance companies, get aimed at working a buyout in, what, three to six months for the whole deal, maybe even by the close of this tax year. That's what a big outfit like either one should be able to do. Write the check." She'd paused, eyes ahead. "We'll have to give them something for that."

John Riley nodded. "Yes, go on. I like the sound of this…" He was biting his tongue, fixing on what Matt Malloy had once told him about diplomacy being the art of letting the other fellow having it *your* way.

"Yeah." Brigit Winslow was smiling now. "Thought you might." She turned to him, "but not five percent."

"What works, works. Anything's better than kicking ourselves raw for the rest of our lives for having to go to a fire sale to pay off the IRS."

"Right…we'll see…" Brigit sat forward now, her right hand on the dashboard, turning to John Riley. "I can go back to Chicago with him…"

"When?" John Riley eased the car to the right now, pulling into the parking lot and heading for an open space near the terminal entrance.

"Now, this morning …the plane's booked already. All you have to do is set up the meeting, you know, be the top dog and confirm to Hastings that I speak for Hennessey Land and can order up any information he needs. Hank has him down for being able to get into either top floor. We can get a lot done in the two hours to Midway. I have the rest of the morning with him, maybe see his office." She looked ahead. "I have something in Chicago anyway…"

"Sounds like a plan…" John Riley turned the car off, removing the keys from the ignition as he turned to her. "But this gets you dead center in the middle of the workout, that'll take months, maybe a year…maybe more…and you wanted…"

"Dad, John, listen to me, trust me..." She fixed on him. "Let me handle me getting out… I'm already working it." She reached for the door handle, gripping it as she turned to him. "It's going to get done, and it's going to get done soon."

CHAPTER THIRTY-THREE
Homeland

T hey had hardly spoken on the way to the hospital. Patrick Rhinemann had arrived at East Irving Thursday night after ten, exhausted by the twelve-hour drive from St. Louis, lengthened by a three-hour traffic jam in western Maryland - a late summer deluge. He had been behind the wheel for more than thirty hours of the last thirty-eight.

There were pleasantries while Mary Kate fixed him a sandwich, looking for a time tell him of Michael in the hospital, the words coming out badly and Patrick Rhinemann's face stopping, then he finding a stool to sit at the counter and saying, more mouthing, the words "heart attack…"

"No, not a heart attack, open heart surgery."

He had stood, challenging. "That's worse! Where is he…?"

"At Georgetown Hospital." She had put the sandwich in front of him, reaching for a paper napkin, sliding it to his plate. "And it's not worse, not now…that's what your father said, anyway."

He sat back, his arms propped against the counter top.

"That's what he said. I spoke with him Tuesday. The major risk now is infection. He spoke with Margaret about getting him out of the hospital as soon as possible."

Patrick's head had gone back at this, questioning…

"That's where all the germs are, in the hospital."

"Oh, I guess…" Patrick Rhinemann's eyes had gone back on her now as he sat back down. "Well how bad is he?"

"Not bad at all, really…certainly not for what he's been through. If they hadn't caught it…" She looked away, now back. "His doctor said he was a walking dead man…needed a *quadruple* by-pass." She reached for her coffee, sipping it. "Partial blockage in four arteries."

"Four…why didn't you…"

Mary Kate Rhinemann had turned sharply at her son. "'As in why didn't we call you'? Is that where you're going? Well, don't go there, because there's been no way to reach you…for two whole months."

Patrick Rhinemann had raised his hands, shaking his head. "Yes, yes…I'm sorry…wasn't thinking…" He reached for his sandwich, nodding to her. "Thanks for this, just what I needed." He had looked away, reaching for his ice water.

"Yes…well, you're back now, anyway, for a while at least, that's something." She paused waiting for him to look at her. He didn't, and she didn't want to get into it, where he'd been, the whole thing, the whole damn thing. She turned to the counter and rewrapped the turkey and cheese, and the bread, putting them all back in the refrigerator. Wiping the counter clean, she rinsed the sponge, hanging the dish towel on the bar handle of the range as she turned to him. "Michael said he can see you at ten tomorrow."

Patrick Rhinemann looked to her, nodding. "Thanks."

"I'll drive you, if you like…"

He had smiled at her now, eager. "Yes, I would like that…that'd be great…had all the driving I need for a while."

She wanted to go to Patrick, to hold him, to never let go…But she was afraid to, of what she might say, where it would all go. 'Get through tonight' she kept telling herself. 'Get him to Michael in the morning without a fight…Michael will fix it…there's still time…'

Mary Kate turned left off Reservoir Road, now, into the hospital complex, staying in the right lane, pulling to a stop under a portico, checking the time on the dashboard clock. "It's just five minutes till ten…" She kept her eyes fixed ahead. "He's expecting you up there now. I'll catch up." She heard him open the door and get out, now closing it and speaking through the open window.

"Thanks, Mom…do you know the room number?"

She shifted the gear lever to neutral, looking at him briefly, then ahead, avoiding his eyes. "4236…the elevators will be just to your right, inside."

"Thanks."

She shifted into drive and pulled ahead to the parking garage, coursing aisles, thinking she should have used the valet, but more than anything just grateful for having gotten Patrick to the hospital and out of the car without having words. Parking the car, she made her way to the elevators, a word on the floor display catching her eye – *Chapel*. 'Yes,' she thought…

It was not large, maybe ten pews deep, a center aisle with seating for perhaps five or six on either side of it. Alone now, Mary Kate Riley stepped instinctively to the right, stopping midway to the altar, genuflecting before sliding in, staying at the pew-end, her shoulder finding a comfort in pressing slightly against it, a place, a silence, a calm, and now the memories of the mind, of chapels and places and times long ago, of St. Dominick's in Southwest and summers in the streets and the parks of the place, and friends and brothers, John and Michael, always Michael, and Kevin, too, trailing them then and now in front, gone…

Mary Kate Riley was crying now, and wondrously so, there, just there, just being in the quiet and peace of her mind and now Paddy Riley himself by her side, unseen, untouched, somehow there and their last time at Peirce Mill and the truth of it, of what was never asked and never spoken but taken and later found - that he had to go, that to be Paddy Riley, he had to be in the war, in the fight, or there'd be nothing left of him, nothing left at all…

It was in speaking with Fr. Hara that she had come to this, after the war, after Fr. Hara had come back and they had moved to Blessed Sacrament. They had become friends there, she and Joe Hara, and what bound them was Paddy Riley, they each loving him so, each in their own way, each owning their own mind of him, at least their memory of it. And it was in the knowing of Joe Hara as a man that she had come to understand her father as one as well, a man, a person separate from being her father, of being a father at all.

And of all the times they had spent together, she and Joe Hara, none was more enduring than on the porch at East Irving Street, a summer's afternoon with Mary moving about, getting ready for people to come, no matter that it was all done and set out, she having her pace, nonetheless, and Fr. Hara smiling as he nodded to Mary going by, back to the kitchen, somewhere for something, but off and Mary Kate seeing in Joe Hara's eye that he understood her, Mary, that is.

"Why is she like this?" Mary Kate had asked, her eyes on the front doorway Mary had just passed through.

Fr. Hara had turned to her, the warmest of smiles on his face, speaking in a slight brogue, ''Cause that's how she come, now, girl, don't you know…'

Mary Kate had nodded, her eyes gone from the doorway to Fr. Hara then to her hands folded in her lap. "She hardly speaks to us of Paddy at all, you know, not when we're alone with her, anyway…and it's not nice when she does, a lot of it…him going off to war to be 'shot by a heathen'…leaving her all alone…" Her eyes had gone up to Joe Hara, hoping…

Again, the smile, the warmth of it, even now, and his eyes.

"She's selfish, Mary Riley is. Yes, selfish…selfish in the way a mother has to be selfish… 'Family first' is how they think, mothers, the good ones anyway. Family first, yes, the core love, the love given a child, the thing of a woman's love and loving…and then there were the two of them, Paddy and Mary, two halves of the same whole…and to the half that's left, after a passing? Well, there's *nothing* left, nothing at all but a torn half, now without purpose, a torn half looking for…" Joe Hara turned away here, then back. "…looking for another way to love…another way to love. It's the way of it, Mary Kate, living and life…the heaven and the hell of it all."

Mary Kate Riley knelt forward, now, blessing herself, her elbows resting on the pew-back in front of her, her head bowed against her joined hands, her mother's words coming now, 'Pray, Mary Kate, pray…' and as she sought to pray the words of Joe Hara from another time, and another place, a time when Mary Kate Riley had come to understand love and loving…

"Don't pray to God for something to happen, Mary Kate, to get something, or for Him to do something for you, no. When you pray, pray for the strength to live with whatever it is that happens, to accept that which is beyond your capacity and power to change. That's a prayer worthy of you and the God that made you." He had stopped here, waiting for her eyes, then holding them with his own. "We are what we *do*, Mary Kate, not what happens to us."

She looked up now, a breath taken, her eyes on the things about her - the altar, the sanctuary candle, the altar rail, now sitting back. Another breath taken and then realizing that the last time she was in this chapel was when Joe Hara was dying, a pure heart finally failing…and his last words to her "It is to love as best you can, this is all that there is."

301

"Yes," she mouthed, "all that there is…," her head coming to a nodding as she gripped the pew-back and raised herself up, stepping into the aisle, blessing herself as she genuflected, "Thank you," she spoke, "thank…" A chime struck on the wall clock to her left, her eyes quickly to it…"Ten-thirty!"

Turning, she quick-stepped to the rear of the chapel, one hand on the door bar, the other dipping the holy water, blessing herself as she stepped into the corridor, her head up now, getting her bearings, going right to the "2" corridor, the elevator bay coming quickly to her right and on up in the first car to the fourth floor, nearly running to 4236, stepping through the open door. "Patrick?"

Michael Riley looked up from a book. "Mary Kate, and where have you…"

Seeing that Patrick was not in the room, Mary Kate stepped back into the corridor, looking left and right and then back into the room, her arms at her waist. "Where's Patrick?"

"Gone…" Michael Riley sat up in this bed, motioning her to him. "Mary Kate, relax, relax. Come here…" He patted the edge of his bed. "Come on…"

Her shoulders slumping, now up and back, Mary Kate Riley Rhinemann stepped to the bed, her eyes on him. "I don't understand…did you speak with him?"

"Well, in a way, I guess…"

"You guess!" She was at the bed now, standing erect, her hands clenched and at her waist. "You guess? After what we spoke about yesterday, you 'guess' you spoke with him?"

"You have to relax, Mary Kate…"

Cocking her head, she closed on the bed, her left thigh against it…

"*Relax*, Mary Kate…." His eyes were now at her, fixed and stern, his voice low and forced, easing her back from the bed. "Good. Now pull that chair over here and I'll tell you what happened."

302

Mary Kate reached for a metal desk chair under the serving table, pulling it next to the bed and sitting down, their eyes locked.

"He was only here for five minutes, maybe not that long, as I think about it...told me he'd changed his mind...that he wasn't going..."

Mary Kate's jaw dropped, her eyes opened wide, now sitting back, her hands to her face covering her mouth, her breathing stopped. Unable to speak, she reached for Michael's outstretched arm, half standing toward the bed. "Thank you, Michael, thank you...how can I ever..."

Gripping his sister's hand harder to get her attention, Michael Riley eased her back, their eyes meeting. "Mary Kate, listen...I didn't do anything...hardly spoke at all..."

"Then...then what...?"

"I don't know..." Michael Riley now leaned toward her. "Something's happened, Mary Kate...wherever he's been...knocked him over. He spoke in circles, saying he couldn't tell me anything about where he'd been or what he'd been doing there. Then the drive here from there, thirty plus hours near non-stop...then about the Arch in St. Louis...has he ever talked about that?"

"No, never..."

Michael Riley shook his head. "Probably nothing...don't know, really..." Michael Riley looked away, a quick shake of the head, now back at her. "Said he'd never seen anything like it, going up into a sunset, seeing it again, the sunset, and 'for as far as the eye could see and seeing only a small part of it, had no idea how big it was'"...He fixed on her. "He repeated that several times."

Mary Kate was relaxed now, her hand in Michael's, warming her as she imagined Patrick atop the Arch, his face into the sunset, his eyes, so like his father's...

"Then he said he had to see his father, that he had to tell your Michael of his decision and how he came to it,

303

that it was something he thought only your Michael would understand, and that he had to tell him first, in person, just the two of them…"

'Yes' Mary Kate thought, a smile now. 'Yes, the two of them.'

"Then he left."

She fixed on him. "Left?"

"Yes, left. Like that." Michael Riley snapped his fingers. "Gone…asked me to tell you not to worry, that he's well-rested. He's going to take a cab to Irving Street and leave for New York right away, to see his father…said he needed to speak with Michael before he spoke to you about it."

Mary Kate eased back, breathing deeply, exhaling now, wondrously free of fear, her eyes wide, drinking in the light of the room, Michael Riley's smile, feeling the warmth of his touch. Rising now, she sat on the edge of the bed, leaning toward him, his embrace, feeling his arms about her. "Thank you, Dear God" she heard herself say, another deep breath and then back, holding each of Michael's hands.

"He said something else, too, Mary Kate…that his grandmother, *our Mom*, Mary Coughlin Riley herself, is the *wisest* person he's ever met in his life or ever expects to…that his time with her at Mass this morning will be with him forever, wherever he goes, for as long as he lives…and beyond…" Michael Riley nodded now. "That's what he said."

Mary Kate sat back, then forward, her eyes on her brother, a sense of wonder coming to her… "*What* did she say to him?"

"That's what I asked him…Said it was between him and Mom…" Michael Riley looked into Mary Kate's eyes, holding them, a slight nodding of his head now. "Whatever it was, Mary Kate, it's why he's not going. She did it, Mary Kate, Mom…she did it."

CHAPTER THIRTY-FOUR
Matt Malloy's Eyes

H astings was all that John Riley had anticipated and more. An athletic build with a thick, commanding handshake, it was clear from the start that this was a man who got things done. Within five of the thirty minutes they had together, Phil Hastings had figured out that Brigit Riley was the person he had to speak with. John Riley's only contribution from that point on was to excuse himself at 8:30 for his flight to West Palm Beach. A nod good-bye from Brigit would have been nice.

John Joseph Riley boarded his plane at 8:45…with no work to do. Copies of the Wall Street Journal and the Journal of Commerce were available in the terminal, the New York Times and Washington Post, as well. But he had passed them all by. What he did do was borrow an eight-and-half-by-eleven yellow pad from the agent at the desk with the promise he would return it that afternoon. It was a blank-sheet day for John Riley, his second in the same week, the first time that had happened in more years than he could remember.

With him as the only passenger, they had given him a six-seat LearJet, a fresh cup of coffee and the acute sensation of speed. Bad ass, raw power, was what, more than 7,000 pounds of thrust from the twin Pratt and Whitney engines that hurtled them skyward, into the air so quickly that John Riley caught his breath, holding his coffee in one hand and gripping the armrest with the other. Banking southeast, the Chesapeake was out the port window before he even knew where he was. Turning south down the Bay, the plane climbed to 30,000 feet with the Delmarva Peninsula passing beneath them as they made their way out over the Atlantic, tracking south along the coast.

Settling into the flight, his coffee resting on the tray before him, John Riley reflected on the meeting. 'Pay a man like Phil Hastings $100,000+ for maybe three days of his time and you're going to see some work done…' And as always after a business meeting with Brigit, he marveled at her presence and intelligence, even with a man like Hastings. At five six, trim, with quick, darting eyes, she had the ability to factor in what everyone else at the table wanted without ever losing sense of what she needed. What she had was purpose, a profound and abiding sense of purpose in all things she did.

Banking slightly to the right, a new course was set that put the sun more fully through the window on John Riley's left. Not wishing to pull down the shade, he shifted to the seat opposite, on the starboard side of the aircraft, taking his coffee with him. Looking across the aisle, he viewed the horizon through the three windows opposite, a brilliant, crystalline sky, the sun off the sea as he came to an ease, his mind wandering back to his drive-by yesterday of the building going up at 1st and I Streets, Northeast.

Peering over the railing, he had looked deep into the now-finished hole of the thing, near sixty feet down to its bottom. Dark and dank, the dirt there had not had sun on it for thousands upon thousands of years. And as always at the top of a hole or walking its bottom, he had breathed in deeply, holding the air, sensing it, knowing that this was where John Riley touched the earth in what he did - the mud and damp from which all life had came, thousands and millions of years ago, up from the swamp…

Awakened by the co-pilot on their approach to West Palm Beach Airport, John Riley ran his hands over his face, rubbing his eyes awake and clear, watching as Palm Beach Inlet passed on the right and settling back in his chair for the landing. One thing he was going to miss after

The Deal was the wonders of general aviation. They wake you up, smiling, the plane lands, you spend maybe 93 seconds taxiing to the terminal, you take maybe five steps down to the tarmac, go inside, clear security at street level and you're in your car, rolling out of the airport, maybe not even really sure what city you're in...yes, he could get used to this...in fact, he had.

And, as usual, Matt Malloy had guessed right. Hennessey Land Company had contracted for 250 hours of service with Execujet with just barely 200 used, 203 to be exact. The only usage likely from now on was next Tuesday's trip to Chicago. So, like Matt said, his ticket to West Palm was on the house.

Not so the car. Even being a nerd engineer was no excuse for John Riley not knowing that they didn't make convertibles any longer, certainly none for the Hertz fleet. Two hundred and twenty-three dollars plus taxes and gas for maybe four hours use of a Mercedes 500 SE convertible was a hard pill to swallow. Worse still, it was white with a coral interior. Too bad Bryan's not here, he thought as he signed the papers and retrieved his license and credit card. At least then he would have learned Gaelic for 'pimpmobile.'

Making his way to Route 1 from the airport and heading north on it, John Riley crossed Lake Worth over the Flagler Memorial Bridge, continuing east on palm-lined Royal Poinciana Way to its end, a broken evergreen hedge of perhaps six feet marking the western edge of the Breakers Hotel property. As instructed by Matt, he turned left here onto North County Road, leaving the restaurants and store fronts of Royal Poinciana Way for the lush green and cooling shade of a Friday noon in Palm Beach.

Initially concerned the white Mercedes convertible might draw the attention of those about, John Riley had already encountered several Rolls Royce convertibles, and maybe a Bentley, none of which seemed to have turned a head, except his own. Moreover, he had come to appreciate the ride of the thing, a quiet confidence, a sense of direct contact with the road matched by the certainty of power and acceleration should he need it. What most struck him, though, was the quiet and calm of the engine. With the top down, he could hear the sound of the tires rolling over the asphalt surface of the road beneath.

South Florida could be brutally hot in mid-September, mid-nineties with humidity to match. But not today. As forecast, it was a clear, dry day, bright with sun-warmed air moving about the open space of the convertible in easy flows and turns. John Riley found himself relaxing now, rolling along North County Road, catching glimpses of Palm Beach homes of varying shades of pink and blue, yellow and ochre, craning to see through driveway openings in boxwood hedges of differing heights, some seeming to tower maybe twenty feet above the surface of the road, and thick, too, six feet and more at the driveways.

'Just drive around, John…make a morning of it,' that's what Matt Malloy had advised and John Riley found himself doing just that, now coming to the hedge lining the southern edge of Palm Beach Country Club. Turning right here, he was shortly at ocean's edge, a brilliant blueness stretching out over the sea and into a celestial sky whose color eased his eyes as the roadway now took him north, along the beach, majestic residences lining the road to his left, open to sea and sky, two and three hundred foot fronts with pathways down to the beach and the quiet, calm surf that lined it.

Bahama Lane was now before him where he took a left and a quick right back to North County Road, again straining to see the houses that lined it left and right, some of the driveway breaks backed up by interior boxwood hedges and landscaping as he approached Onondaga Avenue, a brief detour before finding his way to the inlet.

Parking the car, John Riley walked the short width of a park area, crossing over a concrete path and now resting his arms on a galvanized pipe railing at the inlet's edge. A pilot boat was standing out, making its way to the sea, directing John Riley's eyes to the east and the ocean where an island freighter, a scratchy blue with a sand yellow superstructure, stood by for the pilot to guide it in.

'This is the end of the road, north, anyway...did I miss something?' And again, Matt's words "Relax, take some time..." He breathed a little deeper, purposefully dropping his shoulders wondering how a person can *purposefully* relax.

Turning, he fixed on a concrete and wooden slat bench, going to it now, sitting down, his eyes on the pilot boat as it made its way east. John Riley's mind went back to Brigit and how she was going to get out, how Hennessey Land could work without her... and again Eileen's eyes on her in the hospital room...

"Morning..."

John Riley turned to his left. A patrolman rolled toward him, his hands gripping the hand brake of his mountain bike. John Riley nodded back as the patrolman took in the inlet, surveying the area along the left and right of the park, now turning to the convertible.

"Now that's a classic..." He turned to John Riley. "Yours?"

John Riley looked toward the car, fixing on it for a moment, then on the patrolman. "Yep, for the next three hours, anyway."

A black man now made his way across the park from the road, carrying two fishing rods, a tackle box and a large bucket. Powerfully built, he seemed at middle age, his middle maybe carrying more weight than in years past. Leaning the rods against the railing, he rested the tackle box at his feet, now smiling at the patrolman, who nodded back, and now at John Riley, he doing the same.

At the railing, the man pulled a manila rope out of the bucket and dropped the bucket attached to the rope into the inlet, letting it fill before drawing it out, leaning into the railing to heft it up and over the rail before setting it by the tackle box. Looking up from the bucket, he looked at them, smiling. "Never do know, now…might even catch something…"

The policeman nodded his understanding, now turning to John Riley. "He's all right…the Froelich's man…been here for years, maybe even birthed here." Looking from John Riley to the convertible, he mounted his bike, speaking over his shoulder as he pedaled away. "You have yourself a good day, now, sir."

John Riley turned from the patrolman. Sitting up, he watched the man affix spinners to the ends of the monofilament line on each of his rods before taking some wax paper-wrapped bait and fixing it to one rig before stepping to the rail and casting into the inlet's ebbing waters.

Returning to his tackle box, he picked among his lures, settling on one that he affixed to the line of the other rod, the longer one. Rising now, he stepped to the rail, then taking a glance at John Riley, an easy nod and smile now before bringing the rod back and casting the lure far out into the inlet, watching it splash and then jigging it in…

John Riley sat back, the bench now coming into the shade of the midday sun, the cry of sea birds and the pure, open quiet of the place…all this now broken by the screech of a ship's whistle to his left. Turning to it, his eyes fixed on a tug making its way into the inlet, its tow short-hauled as it made its way from the power station on the mainland to sea. Rising, he stretched, nodding to the man fishing as he stepped into his convertible and started south on the inland side of Palm Beach Island, as instructed.

Making his way on Lake Terrace, he caught glimpses of Lake Worth through driveways and hedges, braking right at the Country Club and around its western edge, a quick view of a green and fairway, then past where Matt had said Pamela Harriman's place would be, on the lake. He had no remembrance of it from the night he dined there with Keith Pierson, one hedge now pretty much the same as any other until he came to the backs of the stores on the north side of Royal Poinciana Way.

Now stopped at the traffic light, John Riley was at a dead loss for the purpose of the trip. 'Drive north on North County Road to the inlet and then back to Royal Poinciana and tell me what you see.' Well, he thought, he hadn't seen much. The light turned green and John Riley crossed Royal Poinciana Way, turning left on its far side and east to its end, there turning right on South County Road.

John Riley had been to such places as this – Palm Springs, the Monterey Peninsula, Saratoga, the Greenbrier. Now crossing Worth Avenue, he noted the quiet of the place. It wasn't the season yet, of course, but they are all quiet places, no matter the season, anxiety simply not tolerated, even the hint of it.

He was south of the Everglades Club now, the island becoming narrower as he found his way to South Ocean Boulevard, the Atlantic on his left. To the right, his eyes were drawn to Mar-a-Lago, Margaret Merriweather Post's Palm Beach residence when she tired of Hillwood, overlooking Rock Creek Park in Washington, DC, and other such places.

His mind went back to the Brady Estate on Foxhall Road in Washington, the land Hennessey owned that Keith Pierson would not now have for his Washington residence. A deep breath taken, even a smile coming to his face as he approached a par-three golf course, open to the public.

Pulling into the parking lot, he stepped out of the car, stretching briefly before starting for the clubhouse, a modest Mediterranean style, two-story building with a terra cotta roof and a covered terrace restaurant on its second floor, overlooking the ocean. Seated at the ocean rail, he was in full shade, his eyes surveying north to south along the dunes, fairway green for most of what he could see, topped with dune grass moving easily in the ocean air.

Ordering a blackened mahi-mahi sandwich and iced tea, he sat back, eyes closing for a moment, the pureness of the place now moving over and around him, his mind going back to North County Road, up and then back and what he had *not* seen, what was so obvious and certain to Matt Malloy that he, John Riley, had missed entirely. "What would have so struck Matt Malloy's eyes that he would have sent me here"?

"Your sandwich, now…"

His thought broken, John Riley looked up, his ear cocked at the waiter's accent - Irish, and now the clear blue of his eyes, the red of his hair as he continued. "And will that be all, now? More tea, perhaps?"

John Riley shook his head, mouthing a 'no, thank you', the waiter's smile, open and warm, putting him in mind of Matt Malloy and an evening spent as his guest in 1978. It was the annual dinner of the Society of the Friendly Sons of St. Patrick at the Capital Hilton in Washington. Matt Malloy was the President that year and had brought John Riley in as a member. What he had remembered most of the evening, though, was the after-party, on the balcony of the Presidential Suite. They were at the south rail of it, looking out, the upper floor and roof of the White House in the city glow, several blocks off.

Standing away from the rail, his both hands on it, Matt Malloy began to speak, his eyes away.

"When I was introducing you for membership tonight, John, telling all assembled of the Rileys of Washington and Hennessey Construction and what you've done with it, and then of your dad serving in the Pacific..." He had paused here, looking quickly at John Riley and then away. "Well, I almost couldn't get it all out...my throat near closing...quite a man, your dad...Paddy...yes, he was that." There had been a pause here, a breath taken. "But that's not what near stopped me..."

Matt Malloy had turned now, facing into the Suite and the maybe seventy-five men assembled there, standing, drinks in hand, the revelry of the night continuing, all talking and laughing in their black ties and cummerbunds. "Look at them, now, John...just look at them...near everyone a winner, all claiming the green but hardly a one of them knowing of the trek that got them all here, what it took to get it all done...". Matt Malloy's eyes fixed on them for a moment, then turned to John Riley.

"Back in December 41 and for months after, I spent nearly all my time trying to get in the service, any service...a way to get in the fight...but they'd have none of it. I was forty-two and, by the grace of God and Jack Hennessey, a name lawyer in the labor field. We were needed elsewhere - to get the unions and Big Business pulling together to make the tanks and ships and airplanes that were going to be needed to win the war." He nodded here, a quick look away and then back.

"Really depressed me...and Paddy and two others I knew. They *did* get in...and then Paddy getting killed...that just made it all the worse...some dark days there." Matt Malloy's eyes closed for moment, his head down, now coming up and at John Riley.

"It wasn't until '46 that I came to terms with it all, not going...even came to being thankful for it." He turned, gripping John Riley's left forearm, holding it firmly. "In 46, you see, they were all back, the ones that were coming back, anyway...and they were *different*, John, changed by it all." His eyes went off now, past him and now back, direct, near tearing. "Yes, *changed*...

"The hesitancy, you see, in their eyes?" Matt Malloy's own eyes were now on him, clear and bright in the shadows of the balcony. "It was *gone*. The uncertainty of who they were, whether they belonged? That was *gone*. The looking to others for direction, the wondering if they were supposed to be in the room, talking square up with some banker or lawyer...whether this or that was alright in some deal or another...that was all *gone*...

"They weren't Irish any more, you see. No...they were *Americans* and they knew now there was no one better at being an American than they were ...yes, the war's when it happened, the war did it, I think, the two or three years out, the hell of it, the lost of it, the killing, then back, alive, of doing things they had no sense of even being possible and then doing them themselves, of coming to know a man could do just about anything he set his mind to do..." He paused here, his mind working, his head nodding.

"You see, John, I never would have seen that if I had gone over...never...and I never would have come to understand the why and the how of it all...When you near die for a place, when your father *does* die for a place, for what the place *is*, then you *own* it...yes, it was *over*...and it wasn't anything *given* us. No. It was because the ones that got back, the best of them, were nothing *but* American...that's *all* they were...by what they *did*..."

The drive back through town was quick, Worth Avenue coming up sooner than expected and the light at Royal Poinciana Way turning green as he approached it, crossing it and back on North County Road. Again, leaving the commercial area, he looked left and right, slowing to twenty miles per hour, the thought passing that, sometimes, the harder you look for something the less likely you are to see it.

A glance at his watch, past one pm, he came to the stop sign at Country Club Road. 'Already been here...'

Checking right, he looked left, then dead ahead, again, the twelve-foot-high hedge of Palm Beach Country Club, his eyes fixing on it, then quickly left and right, and around behind him, putting the car in park, and stepping into the roadway. Turning south, and for a far as he could see – *hedges* - left, right, and now back at the Country Club's hedge on... "Christ in heaven, that's it! The hedges! Of course."

Getting back in the car, he reached for the phone, ordering Matt Malloy's number as he did a U-turn, now heading south on North County Road. As he came to the stop sign at Tangier Road, Matt Malloy answered. "Yes...?"

"Matt!"

"John?"

"Yes. It's the hedges, right? That's what you wanted me see down here? The *hedges*?"

"Ha! Good on ya, boyo! Good on ya! Yes, the hedges, miles and miles of hedges... Hedges as far as the eye can see...and behind them, behind the hedges?"

"I don't know, now, do I? Can't see past them, through them...that's the whole idea, right?"

"Good on ya, lad. And yes, it's why I sent you...the 'extraterrestrials' is what I call them, the folks who live behind the hedges. Their gifts at making or inheriting money have so far outstripped their ability and instincts on its useful application, its true value and worth, that they become, literally and in fact, *separated* from mother earth. They don't know whether they've locked others out or themselves in, but they are no longer of this planet."

John Riley held the phone closer to his right ear, covering his left to hear better.

"They assume, have taken unto themselves an ability to control the *entirety* of their lives, denying themselves chance encounters with those not already known and screened. The very hint of surprise is totally abhorrent to them. It's the same day, every day, the same perfect, all day. No one out seeing in, no one in seeing out. Against all things natural, human and holy, nothing changes, absolutely *nothing.* They live in a never-ending, same *perfect…*"

Matt Malloy paused now, took a breath, clearing his throat, seeming to shift his body, maybe seeing John Riley in his mind, fixing on him, bearing in. "Fact is, John, it's not a perfect world…That's the whole idea…"

John Riley sat up, startled, looking quickly to his left, a man's hand on a bicycle handlebar, now up at his face, it smiling in a questioning manner.

"Everything alright here?" the eyes looking about the inside of the convertible.

John Riley nodded his head, his hand up for the patrolman to wait as he spoke into the phone. "Matt, I'll call you from the airport…got to go."

Putting the phone back into its cradle, he turned up to the patrolman whose eyes were focused behind the car. Turning to the rear-view mirror, John Riley could see there were at least three cars stopped behind him. He turned quickly to the patrolman. "Sorry about that, really sorry."

"No problem. Just wanted to be certain you were alright."

"I'm fine, sorry…" Looking right and left, John Riley made a quick smile and drove across Tangier Avenue heading for Royal Poinciana Way and the airport.

CHAPTER THIRTY-FIVE
The Numbers

J ohn Riley sat on the starboard side of the Learjet, anxious to get home. The call with Matt Malloy had been brief, John Riley closing with a request for George Cole's phone number. Matt Malloy had responded by saying that he was having lunch with George Cole at the Westchester the next day and that John Riley was welcome to join them, and one other, a special guest, one of John Riley's distant knowing.

As on the flight down, the Learjet was quick to the runway. Not even slowing as it turned east on the tarmac, John Riley knowing now to sit back in the seat. Even still, he was taken by the force and speed of the thing, seeming to be airborne in several hundred yards with a rate of climb that kept him against the seatback and his arms on the arm rests with little time to check the landmarks below.

Leaning forward against the acceleration of the climb, he reached for the yellow pad he had borrowed in Washington, laying it flat on the tray table from the seat back in front of him, his mechanical pencil in hand.

He started with the big number - $890 million - this written large at the top center of the pad. Working that number to the bottom of the page, he reduced it by 22 percent, this being the federal and state capital gains taxes that would have to be paid. This rounded to $196 million, reducing the $890 to $694 million.

This was the amount of after-tax cash that would be distributed to Mary, Mary Kate, Michael and himself should one of the insurance companies come through. With half of Hennessey Land's stock, Mary Riley would get $352 million. John Riley and his siblings would each get $116 million. He wrote the names down now, with the appropriate number next to each, and sat back, his eyes affixed to the numbers, most directly by his name and $116 million…

Shaking his head slightly, John Riley flipped the page, now writing across the top center of it the number $57 million followed by the letters HCC – Hennessey Construction Company. He had been approached by a large mid-west firm looking for an anchor in the mid-Atlantic region and that was the number, give or take. After-tax, that was about $45 million. With his stock options as CEO, he would get about $13 million of that with Mary getting $15 and Mary Kate and Michael each receiving $7 million. He wrote these numbers down as well, again next to each name, his eyes on $13 million…

He had, of course, told the others about the offer, but there was not the slightest interest, by him or any of the others. He flipped back to the first page, his eyes again falling on $116 million next to which he wrote $13 million – his life's work in dollars and cents. Now another number - $2.28 million. That was his salary and bonus, not counting stock for 1992. Not too shabby, and he banked nearly half of it. And thinking of Hennessey's book of business, he had no reason not to expect something on that order for the next three or four years, maybe more…

John Riley looked to his right, out the window of the Learjet, a broken cloud cover with the waters of the Atlantic beneath. Trust funds were the words that came next to mind, the grandchildren's education…and the pittance that would be against the corpus of a $116 million trust fund. *One-Hundred-and-Sixteen-Million-Dollars*…how does a person mark their life against such a thing as that, just dropped down on top of him?

Of his children, Annie, the youngest, struggled with Tom's teacher's income and hers as a social worker. But even now it was a struggle to get them to take money for things. They had chosen a path, a way of living, and there was no place in it for trust funds or anything of the sort. And the middle girl, Katherine, they were doing well, George climbing at McKenzie, making his way. He had gone to Virginia Tech on a half football scholarship. It would be impossible to even guess what John Riley being worth over $100 million would do to the life they're already abuilding, not to mention a ninety-one-year-old grandmother having three times that.

And Brigit? With bonus, she had been making more than he for the last several years and no time to spend any of it. And this isn't even counting her husband, Bertie Winslow, a Wall Street investment banker with Brown Brothers Harriman who started on top and just kept on going. John Riley suddenly having $117 million wouldn't affect their life together at all.

Mary Kate and Michael? He had by chance heard that Mary Kate had turned down more than $11 million for her firm two years previous, and as the sole owner would have gotten *all* of that. And this not even to mention Michael Rhinemann, MD, a New York City top neurosurgeon. How would $100+ million change their life?

Of all of them, Michael Riley had always seemed the least concerned about financial matters, his name in the top tier of donors in the charity function invitations John and Eileen Riley received, one or more a month. For most of the last thirty years, he had rented a two-bedroom apartment in Kalorama nearby Brigit's condominium, using the University Club for whatever entertaining he might wish to do.

When getting married, he had bought a large house in Cleveland Park, just up from Kalorama, an easy bike ride to his K Street office, weather and season permitting. 'Wrote the check,' Mary Riley had said, 'That's what he did, your fancy-pants, K Street lawyer of a brother. Aye, wrote the check like it was for a bag of groceries, sure... Ach! Where's his brains gone to, now, I'm asking, all married and now on a hill in Cleveland Park with the such and suches...'

'Ach,' John Riley mouthed silently in the cabin of the Learjet. 'Mary Coughlin Riley, *Jaysus,* what's she to be saying with this?' He looked back down at the pad, flipping back to page one, his eyes fixing on Mary's share, more than one-third of a *billion* dollars... '*Jesus Christ.*' He looked ahead at the forward bulkhead of the cabin, now laughing to himself, even out loud.

For the first time in his entire life, John Riley had come to a true appreciation of *irony*, that for which the Irish had so keen a sense, and that which his engineer's mind had never quite gotten right – until just *now*. And now he *really* laughed, near gagging for breath, so loud the co-pilot flipped the latch on the door to the flight deck, starting to come out with John Riley waving him back. "I'm fine...nothing at all, fine...nothing..."

Looking down at the pad again, he fixed on the number next to Mary Coughlin Riley's name - 352 *million* dollars. John Riley looked up from the pad, his head resting against the seatback, his mind, now, thinking in a brogue.

'Sure now, John Riley, this is how it all started, now, isn't it? Aye, with the lawyers telling that if Mary were to pass, good woman that she is, near all would be lost to a weak market and the tax collector, and sure now, when she sees *that* check, nine figures long, above a *third of a billion dollars*, aye, now, lad, she's a goner, sure, hand to chest, face down on the table, dead as a doornail!' And again, the laughter, as long and hard as John Riley could ever remember...

CHAPTER THIRTY-SIX
Mary's Song

F or most of his life, religious and spiritual things had not come easily to John Riley, though he greatly admired others to whom they did. All this had passed, now, in the time after he had begun walking his mother to Saturday mass. At eight o'clock each week, he would sit by her side, the rhythm of the service passing over and among those gathered.

To his initial discomfort, she would remain in the pew after the mass was done, sitting quietly and still, her eyes closed. No rosary beads fingered across her lap, no mantras spoken or inferred, though at times her lips would move, seeming to sputter slightly the bits and pieces of the otherwise silent coursing of the places, people and things of her mind.

In time, as he sat alone beside her, in the quiet nave of the church, his own mind came to a searching, a gradual sense of other layers of being, an awareness of purpose and the need for it, all in and through his memories of things done and people known. He had read once that the principal purpose of sleep was to allow the brain (or was it the mind?) to organize what it had taken in during the waking hours, and to get ready for the next day's onslaught of information.

And this is what Saturday morning mass with Mary had come to be to John Riley. A time for his mind to think and muse, to absorb a week and the people in it and the things that had happened, then coming to a sense of what they might *mean* and to where they might lead.

He was still uncomfortable when others spoke of Jesus Christ as a person, someone with whom they might have a personal encounter, even friendship. What he had come to was a sense, and a recurring and deepening one, of what he understood to be Godness, and it was this that drew him back each week, that and Mary.

She had been slower in her walk this morning, her arm holding him closer to her, her leaning into him more than usual. Going to bed Friday night, though, she had made a point of reminding him about mass this morning, 'Give my door a good knock, now, John, won't you? Be sure, now, that I'm up? Having to dress and all.'

The Mass now done, the lights of the church were dimmed and the place empty of its other worshipers. She had kneeled forward for a bit, blessing herself as she rested her arms on the pew-back in front of her, now blessing herself again as she sat back, her eyes closed for a moment and then at him. They had held their green, her eyes had, though their crispness was gone, the sharpness of the iris against the white of her eyes, this having gone from the milk of years past to now a cream.

"I was born in Ireland, you know." Mary Riley's eyes went just off him, away. "Oh-two being the year, the century had just begun and me with it. Aye, another land it was, so far away, now, poor Uncle Denny, and the rest of it near as dark. Then the ship over and to here…Aye, the times…wars and sunny days and meeting ya Dad, Paddy Riley himself, the glory and bluster of him, and hopes, too, the things he'd done and was to do…so grand a fella to behold, he was, your Da, running the pitch as he did, knocking lads over…Aye, come from the heavens of hell he did." Her eyes closed now, a lip bitten, then the green of her eyes back on him.

"Then the marrying of him…Aye, Paddy Riley, and the loving and you John Joseph Riley, you coming, and the world changing and growing and Jack Hennessey, such a man he was…and the losing of Dennis, dear lad that he was, and the coming of Mary Kate and my Michael as quick…and Kevin, too…dearest lad ever there was." Her hands went to her face now, a cry stifled, a breath taken, her eyes opening blank and away. "Then come the day my life ended…Paddy gone to a heathen's bullet on an ocean isle…dead, and me with him." She wiped her nose with a tissue from her purse, now looking at him.

"But I wasn't, now, was I? Dead, I mean?"

"No, Mom…" John Riley reached his right arm around her now, holding her, feeling her settle against him, more bone it seemed in just this week. "You were alive…you were *all* we had, all of us, each of us."

"Aye, true enough, true enough…and Joe Hara, too, he coming home from it all and we coming here…" She looked about the church, eyes stopping at a window or statue, then back on him. "It's so much of me, here, this place, it is, this church, so much of my life here, and before, even to Brookland by the Shrine." Her eyes fixed on the altar, her mind working some memory.

"I remember my First Communion…" She turned to him and quickly back ahead, on the main aisle where it met the altar rail. "They did it later then, twelve years maybe I was, no more than that. I remember being done in white with a short veil, me being last because I was the tallest…" She turned, fixing on him for a moment, her head nodding to affirm "I was *always* the tallest, you know, now… 'Mary Coughlin, she's the tall one, you know,' that's what they'd be saying."

Her mind was working again, deeper now, eyes closing a measure as she worked it through, then open and wider now, fixed ahead as she spoke - evenly, deliberate, as if reporting on something. "The most important thing we learn from those who raise us is 'right' from 'wrong,' the good from the bad, that, that's the most important thing." She nodded, almost as if she were agreeing with something that she had just heard someone else say, her eyes now to him. "That's true, now, John Riley, is it not?"

John Riley sat away, his arm now off her shoulder and at his side. "Yes, I guess it is…yes."

"Aye," Mary Riley nodded, her eyes again searching and reaching inside the high arched ceiling of the nave of the church above. "And this is where we learned it, most of it. This is where our people learned it, too. In church, sermons and gospels, parables and stories of Jesus…Aye, the stories…and of love."

Her eyes went ahead, now, as she rose, John Riley rising with her, stepping into the aisle, she taking his arm. Leading to the head of the aisle, she stopped them just short of it, looking about, as if to get her bearings, then at her son.

"It was just here, then, don't you know…" She looked down at the floor and to the left and right pews. "Yes, just here - I told Mary Kate's Patrick of it all yesterday. You walking Mary Kate to here and her Michael stepping from that pew, there, into the aisle. Joe Hara, now, a step closer for him, too, now looking at you and saying 'Who gives this woman in marriage?' and me rising, taking your place and saying 'I do, the Mother!'" She looked at him. "Do you remember that, now, John?"

"Yes…" John Riley fought the emotion rising in him, his throat near closed, fixing on his mother, as he had done that day. "And for all of it, Mom, Mary Kate beaming and Michael taking her hand, the look on his face, it was *your* eyes, the look in *your* eyes…yes, that's my clearest memory, that's what I'll *never* forget."

"Aye, lad! *Love* is what you saw, the purest love I have ever known, or ever hope to, and it lives in me still to this day, from that moment, from that day, and more."

She motioned him to the pew behind him and he stepped in, leaving room for her as she sat beside him, taking his hands in hers. "I had spent my life loving my own, don't you see, and coming to hate all that weren't…we lived lives, then, most of us, now, in the shadows of others, them that kept us out of this place or that, and them we'd be keeping away from us, cursing them all, each and every one of them."

She looked to her right, where she had risen to give her daughter in marriage to Michael Rhinemann, a Jew… "It ended there…that day, that's what you saw in my eyes, son." She turned back to him, gripping his hands firmer.

"But the ending didn't start there, John, don't you see? No. It started with Joe Hara telling me in Southwest of the wrong-headedness of what I would say or might be thinking, or me thinking on what Jack Hennessey thought or did and so many others…and then that day, seeing it in Mary Kate's eyes, and her Michael's, too…a newborn at sixty-six years…that's what I was…Aye, newborn and free of it…all of it…of it all."

Mary Riley sat back, looking about, her head shaking. "And all this," she said, her hands and arms up a measure at the altar before her and the arches above.

"This was where we came to understand it all, to know, that what they were doing to us was *wrong*. It wasn't just that they had more than we did, got more, that they kept us down, that we got less for the same work. No. It was more than that. We learned here that it was wrong, *wrong*, and a *sin*, too." Mary Riley looked at her son, a twinkle in her eye.

"Aye, now, a sin, a *sin,* and it was in this that we had the better of them…and together, in our faith, we had the power in us to make it *right*…not just to get what we had coming to us, but to help make it *right*, to *fix* it, don't you see…and we did." She looked to him, the silent, quick nod of the righteous, not quite a gloat, but close, her eyes away as quick, her face gone blank, she speaking now as if from another place altogether.

"It was love that did it, don't you know…sure, amongst ourselves and out from that, one Mick and one Paddy at a time, and the Brigits and Norahs, too, each to his and her own and it was done…gone…and it all come from here…" Her head was nodding slightly now, eyes still away.

"This was the *good* in us, the church was, His own words, now, coming to us…Aye, and *The Way*…tis where we was loved and loved one another, where we could each of us meet, as best we might, whatever it was life had in store for us." Back now at him, her eyes fixing on him.

"And we were taught, *taught* to love, don't you see, and we were taught it *here*, and in the schools we built, now, taught to *love* those about us, even our enemies…and those who would hold us down…it was them who *didn't* love, it was they who *failed* in this, *His* one Commandment…to love one another."

Mary Riley took a deep breath, it gone as quick, her shoulders down and relaxed, at ease, then a slight shrug, a lightness coming to her as she sat away, now turning back over her shoulder, down the nave, its full length, to the open front door and the brilliance of the September morning, it coming softly on her face now as she turned to him.

"Of what I *know* of love, John Riley, and for all the time it took me to learn it, I learned it here, in church, much of it this church. It's what *He* taught us, what we learned from *Him*…and for all the stuff of it, the rules and the fools of it, it's where we got of it what we have of it…the need of it, love, that is, to live a good life, a loving life, a life worthy of who we are."

Mary Riley reached for her bag, resting it and her hands now on her lap, her eyes away. "Aye, an old story told anew, Mother to child and on…" Her eyes came to him now, bright, even to beaming, her head shaking slightly.

"I've done now, John Riley, I have. Lived near a century, might even see its end, but no matter. However many years I have, God only knows, and I'll be taking whatever he sees fit to give me… I've had a life and more, I have, and for all of it, now, I thank Him, for all the tears and all the hugs, for all of it." She fixed on her son, her eyes warm and full.

"I'm so *proud* of you John Joseph Riley, and Mary Kate, too, and my Michael...the life each of you has built, the things each of you has done, the good lives you're all living." Mary Riley closed her eyes, breathing deeply, holding it for a moment, her eyes now ahead. "So glad I am for each breath I take...a gift, is what, a gift of God, each one..."

Mary Riley rose now, stepping into the aisle, gripping the pew-end as she curtsied and bowed in the direction of the altar, turning back down the aisle, her head up and shoulders square, her step so sure, and now the briefest wave of her hand for him to stay. Mary Coughlin Riley herself, now, aye, stepping for home, she was, and on her own time.

John Riley, his right arm over the back of his pew, fixed his eyes on her silhouette as she walked the full length of the aisle, his head back a measure, now, as she stepped into the full light of the morning sun, moving easily down the steps and then on to East Irving and to home.

Turning slowly ahead, John Riley's eyes found the altar, closing now, his hands coming to rest, spread and down, one each to a thigh, still. A quiet came to him, his breathing eased, his mind coursing the richness of his life, his time this morning with Mary, this moment alone with himself, of himself and the Godness he had come to know...and then to Paddy and his brother Kevin. Aye, now, and to Jack Hennessey, too...

CHAPTER THIRTY-SEVEN
Brigit and Hank

"So, Miss Brigit, how were the accommodations?"

"Pretty fancy word for a sub-par bed and breakfast with rotary phones." Brigit Winslow spoke through the open window of the front passenger door of Hank Johnson's four-door Toyota Corolla, now opening the back door and throwing in her overnight bag.

Hank Johnson reached for the door handle of the front passenger door, pushing it open. "You're fed, then?"

"Sort of..." Brigit got in the car, fastening her seat belt as she looked about the interior of the car, running her hand over the padded dashboard in front of her. "Nice car. Love the color. Battleship gray, I believe...?"

Hank Johnson checked the rear-view mirror, now pulling into the traffic lane of Grace Street on Chicago's North Side. "You wanted to disappear, right?"

"I thought..."

"You still want to disappear?"

"I guess..."

"Well, a twice-titled, nine-year-old, gray, four-door Corolla is about as invisible a vehicle you can get and still have any hope of killing a small dog should you happen to hit one with it."

Brigit Winslow stretched her legs in the foot well of the car, arching back, tensing her arms, shoulder and neck muscles, a quick shake of the head. She had been a ward of Atlantic Security for most of the last twenty-four hours.

On landing at Midway Friday morning, she had passed her cell phone to an Atlantic associate, her 'body double' as Hank had called her – same hair color and cut, height and weight, wearing the same outfit that Brigit had worn from Washington, the same sunglasses, same sunhat. The double had arrived with the cleaning crew that morning and, after changing, left in a waiting livery limousine for Moline, Illinois, due west almost two hundred miles, as soon as the exchange had taken place.

The double was to make random calls to Hennessey Land Company numbers en route to Moline where she would spend the day and night at a Holiday Inn, meeting with other Atlantic Security associates. 'Blue suits,' they were meant to be taken for executives from the real estate acquisition division of a regional insurance company headquartered there.

Brigit had worked through the afternoon with Phil Hastings in a windowless conference room in the Butler Aviation compound at Midway. When done, she had left in a cleaning crew uniform, to be deposited at the bed and breakfast, just past six pm. Like the Corolla, it was owned at two removes by Atlantic Security.

"A safe house of sorts," Hank Johnson had said. "No credit cards, no cable TV, no registration log or driver's license number recorded…invisible. The guy running it thinks it's owned by an estate in extended settlement. All properly licensed as a bed and breakfast, but everyone there is in one stage or another of 'disappearing' for a week or so. Subpoena dodging, spousal separation, whatever."

They had come to a red light at Addison. Hank Johnson's eyes were fixed ahead, a breath taken now. "You sure you know what you're doing here, Brigit? Spending a ton on all this, you know…" He turned to her. "Your daddy, my good friend John Riley? Doesn't know a thing about any of this, does he?"

She kept her eyes ahead, now fixing on the traffic light. "You've got a green…"

Hank Johnson sat up, accelerated west on Fullerton, his eyes catching the sign for "I-90 South, One Mile" on his left.

Sensing he was about to speak, Brigit gripped the hand strap above the door at her right. "It's called 'Lewis and Clark'..." She turned quickly to him, then back ahead. "It means you have an ocean to find, you know it's West, and you're absolutely certain it's there, but you have no idea what's between you and it, or how you're going to get across whatever it is, if it can even be gotten across."

"And your Daddy?"

"How was dinner last night? What'd you think?"

Hank Johnson looked quickly to her then ahead as he eased the car to the I-83 entry ramp and went up it, now accelerating into the traffic.

"Well, dinner was great. Pretty much what you'd expect in a private suite at the Drake Hotel twenty-plus floors above Lake Michigan with a beautiful young lady...conversation was a bit stilted, though..."

"Really...how so?"

"Well, that's what you'd expect when you don't know the person's last name and she's not allowed to speak about any part of her life after college...and she wouldn't call me by my given name... 'Mr. Johnson' this, 'Mr. Johnson' that, all through dinner. Wait-staff just had to assume she was a call girl."

Brigit Winslow sat up, looking across at him, trying to imagine Hank Johnson having dinner with a call girl, or any woman, for that matter in anything that even smacked of a romantic interlude...Just wouldn't compute, her mind not able to get past the default Hank Johnson, anchor to others and never once in her memory having been wrong about anything he might care to speak about..."Sorry, hadn't thought of that."

Hank Johnson moved into the center lane, between two tractor-trailers. "Well, you wouldn't I guess."

"And?'

"And what?"

"And what about her, what's your cut on her…I need to know what you thought about her…"

Hank Johnson sat back in his seat, clearing his throat before speaking, his eyes on the road ahead. "Pretty solid…been around the block…certainly nothing lacking in confidence. My bet is she's real bright." A quick look at her and back to the road. "And I mean now *really* intelligent – super smart. Seems her father was in the Army Air Corps, B-17s over Germany, and all, waist gunner…not for the faint of heart, I'll tell you that." He checked his side view mirror, looking back at it twice.

"There was something, though…not quite sure what she said or how I got it, but something there saying it wasn't all cake and ice cream growing up. He was in the oil field, her father. She didn't offer it, now, and I didn't want to pry, but my sense is that he's gone and there something more to it than just passing away." Hank Johnson's eyes stayed on the road ahead, his mind seeming to be working on what he had just said, now a quick shake of the head.

"Anyway, seemed like the mother ran the outfit…there are two younger brothers, one played at OU, linebacker…They've both stayed to home…the linebacker has a small trucking outfit and the other's in farming…She's the only one that got out, you know, off the plains.

Brigit Winslow marked each word Hank Johnson spoke. Fixing ahead, she thought of how good some people are at sizing up others, that Hank Johnson was spot-on…so far. "Would you trust her?"

A quick glance over, then back ahead. "Trust her? With what?"

Brigit Winslow sat up. 'Yes, with what? With what? There's a lot at play here,' she thought. "Good question…" She looked away to her right. From the raised roadway of I-83, the land ran west and flat from Chicago as far as Moline and beyond, across the Dakota Badlands, all the way to the Rockies.

Hank Johnson cleared his throat. "This address you gave me for this morning. Any idea what it is?"

"Yes…A BMW dealership."

Hank Johnson's head began to nod. "Taking a trip, are we?"

"I am…" Brigit Winslow sat up another measure, her head turning to Hank Johnson, her eyes fixing on him. "Tulsa, Oklahoma."

Hank Johnson's head kept nodding, its rhythm unaffected by what she had said. A quick check of the left side view mirror.

"Now how did I know that, that you were going to say that? That you were planning to get in a car and drive the six hundred and ninety-seven miles from Arlington Heights, Illinois, to Tulsa, Oklahoma today?" A quick look at her, her eyes back at him as he turned ahead, continuing.

"Actually, it's a little less than the whole six hundred and ninety-seven miles because her mother lives about twenty-seven miles north and east of Tulsa, just off I-44. Nine hours or less, I'm making it in her 730i. Maybe eight hours if she really knows how to handle that thing. Now, how did I know that?"

Brigit Winslow fixed on Hank Johnson, leaning away from him.

"You think I don't know *who* she is? Really? You really think I can make a person like you *disappear* to anyone who wants to find you and *not* know where you're going? What you're up to? Do you?"

Brigit Winslow's eyes went dead ahead as her shoulders squared up and back. "No…I guess not."

"Well you got to know that you're in a league now where not knowing what's obvious to the other guy can cost you *big time!*"

Hank Johnson checked the rear-view mirror, pulling into the left lane to pass the tractor-trailer they'd been following. "Our play in Moline is good until tomorrow morning. That's about as far as you can stretch something like that out. You want time on the road to Tulsa and, what, maybe an overnight? Get to meet the family?"

He turned to her, nodding quickly then back ahead.

"Something like that..."

"Well, that's what I figured...makes sense..." Hank Johnson moved to the right, back into the traffic lane, again between two tractor-trailers.

"Now let me tell you how this is going to happen. She's going to meet us at a Holiday Inn, eight-point-seven-six miles south of Exit 23 on I-90. That's all been set up. She got the memo at 7:38 this am and is confirmed to go. Your gear and my gear go in the trunk of her Beamer, then you sit shotgun up front, I get in the back..."

Brigit Winslow turned sharply at him, forming something to say that he cut off at the pass.

"*One word,*" he said, his right hand shooting up now, a fist made save the index finger, it dug into the material lining of the roof of the car, "One word, *just one*, just the *slightest* hint, a passing inflection by you to me at *any time* in *any location,* anything indicating in the slightest manner or way that you are not under my complete and absolute protection, I *blow* this caper to your Daddy and you and me are on the first available Execujet for National Airport."

He fixed on her, his eyes burning in, piercing, even scaring her, then ahead. *"Do you understand EVERYTHING I just said to you? Do you?"*

"Yes...everything."

"Good...done." Hank Johnson shifted in his seat, his shoulders back a measure. "So, I'll be in the car with you on the way down. You'll forget I'm even there in ten minutes, trust me. I can make myself disappear, too." He checked the rear-view mirror. "And from now on, and until we get back to DC, we will never be more than fifty feet apart, n-e-v-e-r. Are you good with that?"

"Yes."

Yes, Brigit Winslow was good with this, surprised, now, to find herself at great ease, her body relaxing as her mind focused on the drive to Oklahoma with Melanie Ingram.

Melanie Ingram was Brigit Winslow's way out, but Brigit had to be sure. They had spoken five times over the last four days, each call a little deeper, a little better. The money was the easy part. That was done from the start. Seeing her as CEO of Hennessey Land, though, was another matter - the next level up.

They had done a total of seven trips together working on The Deal, one top-tier MBA, thirty-something to another, but never together long enough to be certain she wasn't 'on,' playing a part expected. It was, after all, business. They were meeting to get from each other information on real estate and how it was being operated and how it was performing, the parry and thrust of two players, each wanting the best part of the same deal.

There was one slip, though, an off-hand comment that had stuck in Brigit's mind. 'It's our mamas, you know, who make us...' Could have been just a play, some Oklahoma corn-pone to put Brigit Winslow of the Chevy Chase Rileys married up to the Plymouth, Massachusetts Winslows, off guard. Either way, Brigit needed to meet the woman who made Melanie Ingram 'who she is' before she brought her on as CEO of Hennessey Land.

Settling in the front seat of the Corolla, she remembered now something her father had once told her.

'How a person drives a car can tell you a lot about them.' Well eight or so hours riding shotgun followed by dinner, an overnight, and breakfast with the woman who made Melanie Ingram who she is, should tell Brigit Winslow just about all she's ever going to need to know about the woman.

CHAPTER THIRTY-EIGHT
The Squires

A fter returning from Mass, John Riley had breakfast with Eileen and Mary Kate, learning here that Michael Riley would be discharged from the hospital Sunday morning. Incredible. Tuesday on the precipice of death, to Thursday complaining of tubes and bedpans, to Sunday home for lunch with the family. Truly incredible. What most weighed on John Riley's mind this morning, though, was Brigit. She had not returned his call of Friday afternoon, nor that of Friday evening. It was now more than a full day since they had parted at National Airport. He needed to be outside.

Explaining that he had left papers at the office for his lunch with Matt Malloy, John Riley had excused himself, now heading south on Connecticut Avenue with no particular place to go. Having taken a left at Tilden Street, the tree cover of its greenway eased his mind as the Explorer swept down and to the right, past Peirce Mill. Turning right on Beach Drive, he coasted through Rock Creek Park, the clear September air swirling through the open windows of the Explorer.

Soon at the Kennedy Center, he continued onto Independence Avenue, turning off it for Maine Avenue, the Southwest waterfront and then to Water Street and its restaurants and marinas. Continuing to the traffic circle at its east end, John Riley slowed to a stop, his eyes on the Thomas Law House on Sixth Street. It was pretty much a twin across Sixth Street from the house Jack Hennessey had lived in for the last forty years of his life, which had been gifted in his will to St. Dominick's parish as a home for boys.

Actually, he thought, there was something at the office he may have need of – his briefing book from the Hennessey Trust meeting on Wednesday morning. George Cole had reported on his proposal for a capital campaign for the Trust, building it out to include scholarships as well as loans. John Riley remembered now that Matt Malloy had showed great interest in the idea, noting that a friend was due in from California who may want to hear about it. They had set up the Saturday lunch then.

Picking up his briefing book at the office, John Riley took the opportunity to clear his in-box from his day in Palm Beach, this all putting him at the portico of Matt Malloy's building at the Westchester ten minutes before noon. The weather having held despite predictions of rain by midday, John Riley took the opportunity to walk about 'Sunken Forest.'

This was the name Matt Malloy used to describe the center of the circle around which the Westchester complex had been built. Perhaps eighty feet across and terraced down to a pond at its center, it was something of a local landmark with its seasonal plantings and the shape and care of its landscaping. Stepping down one of its paths to the pond, his eyes came upon a man sitting on a bench on the opposite side, perhaps in his mid-seventies.

Looking up, the man's eyes fixed on him, a smile coming to his face. "Would you be John Riley?"

Surprised, John Riley stopped, standing more erect as he studied the man's face, though not recognizing him. "Yes…I am."

The man rose, starting toward him, an easy gait to his step as he came around the pond, perhaps not yet seventy, after all. "Matt said you might be coming and I'm so glad you have."

Stepping toward him, John Riley extended his hand, studying the man's face as he straightened, cocking his head.

"You were the last Squire, right?" He felt a smile come to his face, a sense of wonder. "You were with us the day Paddy caught that monster bull rock...am I right?"

"Yes, you are." The man smiled. "I'm Michael Byrnes..."

"Of course, yes..." Reaching for his hand, they shook again.

"Well, I see you've all met..." Matt Malloy approached from the main building, leading a bus boy pushing a service trolley along the drive about the circle. "Welcome, welcome..."

They all shook hands with Matt Malloy nodding in the direction of the portico of his building, each in turn opening and holding doors for one another and the bus boy, too, he being discharged on the setting of the table - a tray of sandwiches with salad dishes placed, and iced tea poured around. Motioning to the living room, Matt Malloy led them through the foyer to a sun bright room looking west and, through a small solarium, to the south.

Taking the compliments of his guests on his accommodations, Matt Malloy was nodding each to a chair as a knock came to the door. Excusing himself, he returned with George Cole, his six-foot-plus height and set centering the room as hands were shaken and smiles exchanged.

"Something of a reunion, we have here, gentlemen. Yes, a reunion, indeed." Smiling they looked at him, George Cole fixing on him more closely than the others.

"Fifty-seven years ago this May, we were each of us, in one manner or another, at Jack Hennessey's place." Nodding to Michael Byrnes and John Riley, he continued, his eyes going to George Cole. "It was to be Jack Hennessey's last fish roast, George. Michael and John, here, were there, Michael being Jack's last Squire and John catching himself a 38-pound rock that afternoon, with me taking the picture of the fishing party that hangs in John's office."

Matt Malloy now turned to Michael Byrnes. "George Cole was not there in person, you see, but he was in 'provenance'…" Michael Byrnes' smile betrayed an uncertainty as to Matt Malloy's meaning. "Yes, you see, Michael, George Cole is the grandson of Charles Ramsey, Jack Henne…"

"Charles Ramsey?" Michael Byrnes' eyes went quickly to George Cole, turning to him, a bright smile coming to his face. "I knew Charles Ramsey…"

He stepped to George Cole, his hand again extended, his eyes up and fixing on him. "I knew your grandfather, worked with him around Jack Hennessey's place. A wonderful man…Always teaching me things…about everything."

Michael Byrnes turned to Matt Malloy. "The Sunday before Jack died, he had me drive down to Port Tobacco." He turned now to George Cole. "Am I right?"

George Cole nodded, smiling.

"I picked up your grandfather there and drove him to Jack's house. Mrs. Kennedy came in special to prepare lunch for them, Jack and your grandfather, just the two of them…on the veranda." He held George Cole's hand in both of his, his head nodding slightly.

"In my time with Jack Hennessey, there was no man he held in higher regard…" A quick look to Matt Malloy and then back to George Cole. "Whenever I think of my year with Jack Hennessey, I think of him, your grandfather… Amazing…I'm so happy to meet you."

George Cole nodded, his left hand now covering their two hands joined. "Thank you. He spoke highly of you as well." George Cole's eyes went to Matt Malloy. "Of all the Squires…"

Matt Malloy looked away, clearing his throat. "Yes…well, now that we knowing who we all are, how about lunch?"

Taking Matt Malloy's lead and direction, they stepped to the dining room, George Cole to Matt Malloy's left, John Riley on his right and Michael Byrnes opposite.

John Riley caught Michael Byrnes' eye as he shifted in his chair, bringing it closer to the table. "So, Michael, fifty-seven years…a long time…may I ask where you've been?"

Reaching for a sandwich as he sat down, Michael Byrnes smiled at Matt Malloy. "How much time we have?"

The others laughed quietly as Matt Malloy sat back. "Well, let's see now, George has to leave at one. Now, I'm not certain about John, here, but I'll be in my nap by 1:15, whether at this table or on the couch." He nodded toward the living room. More polite laughter.

"Now, knowing that modest men such as yourself, Dr. Byrnes, find it difficult to talk about themselves in other than extended apologies for bragging, why don't I fill in John and George, here, and get to why I've asked you all here today?"

Michael Byrnes nodded. "Well you're certainly the *oldest*, so why don't you just go on ahead…" More laughter.

Smiling as he took his napkin to his lips after a taste of iced tea, Matt Malloy sat back. "Michael here was not only the last Squire, he was the first Hennessey Scholar, that's what we called the beneficiaries of the Trust.

"He used it to go to Georgetown pre-med and medical school. With war and all coming, his course work was accelerated, and he graduated in late 1942 and went directly into the Navy where he served with distinction…and bravery. He was one of the first Americans on ground zero in Nagasaki in the months after the war." Here Matt Malloy raised his glass, as did the others.

"Michael's parents passed away during the war, his father in '42, and his mother in 1944, when he was in the Pacific, on the hospital ship *Hope*. With no siblings to hold him here, he stayed in the Navy, retiring as a Rear Admiral in 1977. In the Pacific Fleet for most of his service, he settled in San Diego and later Los Angeles. There he rose to the regional director of the U. S. Public Health Service.

"And it was here that he began his work with Loyola High School, mentoring seniors considering a career in medicine. On his second retirement, ten years ago, he raised some local money and started what can only be described as Hennessey Scholars, West."

Matt Malloy closed by turning to Michael Byrnes, nodding slightly. "How's that?"

"Admirably succinct."

Matt Malloy looked at the others. "It's always about rank with Michael Byrnes, always!"

They all laughed and laughed well, maybe John Riley the hardest, pointing at Matt Malloy and then Michael Byrnes, feeling the warmth of the moment.

Sipping his iced tea, George Cole turned to Michael Byrnes. "Matt tells me most of your work in Los Angeles is with Latino boys..."

Michael Byrnes shrugged, wiping his mouth with his napkin. "We go to the need, and in Los Angeles, that's where the need is...young men in an ocean and swirl of celebrity and want, too few places to go up and their fathers all trying to figure out what's happened to them, where their lives went." He turned to Matt Malloy. "Our forebears had the drink, Devil Whiskey...theirs have the drugs, and it's worse."

John Riley sat forward, fixing on Michael Byrnes, who sat forward in turn, his hands flat on the surface of the table as he continued.

"It's worse because it's how a lot of the men with the big cars and fancy clothes make their money…the drug trade is the biggest business in their neighborhoods, and it's destroying its own customers…insidious."

Matt Malloy nodded, looking at Michael Byrnes, and then off to George Cole and John Riley, his right hand on the surface of the table, his index finger tapping.

"It's even worse than that, much worse…more fundamental…" He sat up, his arms resting on the arms of his chair, his head back for a moment as if collecting and arranging thoughts and data and how to put them all together.

"As you all know," he began, "I've had the good fortune in years allowed to me and people known, to have learned a good deal about how the world we live in works." There was a collective nodding of heads as Matt Malloy sat forward against the table.

"Now, someone asked me, just the other day, 'On what, Mr. Malloy, do you consider yourself to be an *authority*?'" He looked at each of his guests, letting the question settle, his own head nodding, still in reflection. "It was a good question, and there's nothing I admire and appreciate more than a good question." He smiled. "Know what I told him?"

Three heads now nodding, wanting to know.

"Told him I'd get back to him."

A good, quick round of laughter.

Matt Malloy looked at Michael Byrnes. "Your call, Michael, about your work and being in DC this week, it came two days after that question was asked." He looked at George Cole.

"George, your call about building out the Hennessey Trust came three or four days after that." Now at John Riley. "Couple of days after that, you came by trying to figure out what you were going to do with Keith Pierson, prince of a fella that he is, and the Hennessey Land

Company." Matt Malloy shrugged, his hands open and out.

"How all this pointed me to the answer, I can't tell you exactly. But I did come to it." He paused, sitting back in his chair. "Here sits before you, gentlemen, perhaps as steeped an authority as there may be in this city on human capital and its application to the good and betterment of the commonwealth."

They all sat back in their chairs, reflecting for a moment on what Matt Malloy had just said, then, looking at each other, nodding to a shared awareness that this was exactly what Matt Malloy is and had been for some years. Their eyes now turning to him, each sat forward to the table, their arms finding its surface and their eyes on him to learn where this was to take them.

"At the end of the day, gentlemen, human capital is *all* we have. Ourselves, what we *can* do, what we *do* do. It's what the Hennessey Trust has been investing in since 1936, and it's what Michael Byrnes' program in Los Angeles has been investing in for ten years. Human capital. What people are *able* to do." He looked at George Cole and John Riley.

"Michael's program takes smart kids out of bad homes and gives them the care and discipline they need to use and improve their minds, and build their *character* - twelve hours a day of it, six on Saturdays. They're getting high school degrees of real value – history, math, science, English. And they compete athletically, test and push one another.

"Then they put them into *community* colleges, nearby where they live. There's a dorm of sorts, for those who have no housing. And, most important, they're interned to a business, something that's making money and under the wing of a successful businessperson, one-on-one..." Matt Malloy fixed on Michael Byrnes, nodding. "Took that right out of Jack Hennessey's playbook...".

John Riley sat back away from the table, his eyes now going to George Cole whose eyes were already on him, both now nodding.

Matt Malloy sat away from the table as well, his napkin coiled in his lap. "Time was, back in the day, the foreign-born and impoverished had something the folks in charge needed...the thick of their backs and the sweat of their brows." He nodded to George Cole.

"Those in charge needed it so much, they kept the immigration doors open so there'd be an inexhaustible supply of them...men scrapping for subsistence wages. It wasn't pretty, now, a lot of it, most of it, maybe...but for all the screaming and yelling, it worked." Matt Malloy sat forward, fixing on George Cole first, then John Riley.

"They got structured in, you see, had some money to save, the smarter ones, the better ones, they formed unions, put their kids through schools. Hell, the Catholics built their own schools...And they went through two world wars, with an intergalactic-grade depression between them, and *Bingo*! We got the 1950s and 60s...the American Way!" He paused here, letting what he had just said settle in.

"Well, that model's not working any more. There are too many things to hang a difference on – color and language and religion...and now our world's gone technical. Used to be a man with a back that could heft a twelve-pound shovel full of coal could get work on one of Mr. Carnegie's new open-hearth steel furnaces, the high-tech achievement of the age.

"Yes, sir. They'd get a front-row, bottom-rung seat on how the whole thing worked." Matt Malloy paused, looking at each of them. "Not now, no sirree, Bob... today, a high school graduate needs six months minimum of tech training just to get a sniff of what's going on, to have any hope of a place on the bottom rung, getting structured in..."

Matt Malloy reached for his iced tea, sipping it before patting his lips with his napkin. "We're spending hundreds of millions of dollars on programs to get kids out and up…well, a lot of that can just be social workers creating jobs for more social workers." A pause, another sip taken, another pat.

"That's not what we need." Matt Malloy's eyes went to George Cole on his left and John Riley to his right. "What we need are people who want to build things, to do business, get others to do things with them…*Leaders.*"

Matt Malloy fixed hard on George Cole. "We looked at civil rights mostly as a moral issue, something was wrong and it needed to be fixed, for everyone…just plain *wrong.*" Matt Malloy's head nodded. "But it was an economic thing, too." He shook his head, eyes away.

"The talents lost and wasted…kept down…" His eyes came back, again on George Cole, now shifting to Michael Byrnes. "The same for the folks Michael's working with." Matt Malloy's head now shook side to side, his eyes away. "Maybe together now a *quarter* of our population. Tens of millions of people, maybe a third of the whole outfit, and more than that into the next century."

George Cole fixed on Matt Malloy, his head nodding slightly.

"George wants to grow the Hennessey Trust, build it out, raise outside money, bring in inner city schools…recognize the heroes we already have, his grandfather for one." He nodded at George Cole. "I've supported him in this." Matt Malloy sat forward.

"But it's not enough, not near enough…" He sat back, looking at each of them, fixing on George Cole. "We need a national program, programs in fifty, no, a hundred cities across the country, programs like the one Michael started in Los Angeles…".

Michael Byrnes' eyes locked on Matt Malloy, his head cocked, now turning to John Riley and then George

Cole as he reached for his iced tea, sipping it quietly and returning it to the table, his hands on the table's edge.

"We need a leader, a man of impeccable character and reputation, a man whose appointment will be news in itself, a man who will attract others, their time and their support…a man who will give his full devotion and commitment for *five* years."

Matt Malloy's eyes had been on George Cole, fixed and bearing in. He now turned to John Riley.

"And to get such a man, we're going to need some money, some *real* money, enough money that there will be no doubt as to the commitment of those behind the enterprise and its inevitable success." Matt Malloy paused here, a breath taken, his hands resting easily on the table's edge, his eyes on them now with purpose and direction.

"Gentlemen, the resources needed to get started on such an enterprise sit at this table, here and now, right here, right now." Matt Malloy's hands reached out left and right, gripping the forearms of George Cole and John Riley. "This close."

There came to Matt Malloy's face an easy smile, his eyes going to each before him as he removed a piece of paper from a folder lying on the table to this left.

"I propose for your consideration this noon, gentlemen, the establishment of the Hennessey-Ramsey Trust. Its purpose will be to honor the lives lived by Jack Hennessey and Charles Ramsey and to continue their work." Adjusting his reading glasses, Matt Malloy's eyes went to the paper he held in his hands.

"Born into a world unfair, they made more than the most of it, they made the best of it. Each a man of honor and purpose, they marked their time and place on this earth by what they learned and by what they taught, through even to the close of their lives. And it is on us

who follow to continue and to grow their work, to give hope and venue to those who would follow still."

CHAPTER THIRTY-NINE
Cleveland Park

*H*ow many years ago was Tuesday morning in Chicago?

The question had been rolling over in John Riley's mind since he'd left George Cole's home on the Port Tobacco River in Charles County, Maryland. He had spent much of the morning there, some thirty miles south of the Capital, rehashing the lunch they had had Saturday at Matt Malloy's apartment, what they had each agreed to consider.

"At 65, John, five years is a long time...maybe as much as I have left at full bore. And that's what this would take, full bore for five years."

John Riley had nodded his agreement, not from any particular knowledge of such things but from his respect for George Cole's experience in them

"Then there's the money..." George Cole had looked away, his head shaking, now back at John Riley. "Matt's talking about $90 to 100 million." George Cole's eyes were now fixing on John Riley in a 'And what are *you* going to be doing about this' sort of way. "Well, Matt has a good heart and he means well, but I'm telling you, John, it'll be more than that, half again at least, maybe double, and that's for the first five years. What happens after that?"

John Riley had sat back at this point. Was George Cole laying down the reasons why he wouldn't do it? Or was he probing, challenging John Riley to come up with the money? Sitting forward, John Riley's elbows rested on his knees, his hands joined, his eyes at George Cole, moving him back a measure. "Supposing I could get you $150-175 million...are you in? Would you do it, full bore for five years?"

George Cole sat all the way back now, eyes wide open, his hands on his thighs. Rising up from his chair, he turned away from the coffee table, his eyes on the marsh abutting his property. Once, long ago, tobacco was packed and loaded here for England, as were slaves landed from Africa, in chains. Wrapping his arms around his chest, George Cole turned back to John Riley, looking down at him, their eyes locked. "Hennessey Construction, the Rileys…you folks have *that kind* of money? Micks out of Swampoodle? That kind of money? Sho'nuff?"

John Riley laughed now, a roaring laugh, taking him up out of his seat, turning away, clapping his hands, his eyes toward the marsh, then back, fixing on George Cole, catching his breath, his head nodding, his arms out. "Could be, could be…looks like it, really… probably going to happen…Tuesday, in Chicago…Big doings…"

John Riley saw now an appreciation in George Cole's eyes that something was happening, right now, on a wooden deck by a river gone to a marsh in rural Maryland. Squaring up, his face went serious out of respect for his friend, knowing how what he was about to say could affect his life.

"I expect that a substantial amount of money will be committed to the Hennessey Land Company on Tuesday, to be available in the week or two following. I spoke with Brigit on the way down here today. 'Done deal' was how she put it." He paused, his focus sharpening. "Now, as to whether I can swing a hundred and fifty million or so of it to Matt's project, I'll know that this afternoon."

John Riley could see in George Cole's eyes that he knew what was coming next, his head even starting to nod as John Riley spoke. "But that won't happen without you…the only way I'm putting this on the table is if *you're* in, if you, George Cole, will lead it, full bore."

"*Yes, how many years* …." John Riley heard himself say under his breath as he pointed the Explorer over the

Douglass Bridge on up South Capitol Street. The Southwest Freeway was ahead as he thought back to waiting on George Cole's deck for George to speak with his wife, Sylvia. It had been a full half hour before they both came out, arm in arm. "We're in," Sylvia Cole said. "If the Rileys have $150 million for it, we have the time."

Michael Riley had been released from Georgetown University Hospital at ten that morning and taken by ambulance to his house on Highland Place in Cleveland Park. Developed in the late nineteenth century, Cleveland Park began as a summer colony, Victorian homes, mostly, placed sparingly between Connecticut and Wisconsin Avenues. Comfortably above Washington City, its residents were spared the hot, fetid air of a Potomac River summer, reclaimed swamp and marshland, much of it, never entirely surrendered by the mosquitoes of its primordial origins.

John Riley felt an edge coming to him as he coursed the parkland along the Potomac, rounding the Lincoln Memorial and passing the Kennedy Center toward Rock Creek Park, climbing up out of it at Connecticut Avenue. Holding at a traffic light before turning right on Connecticut, he found himself taking a deep breath, holding it as the grip of his hands tightened on the steering wheel. "They have no idea of what's coming…not a clue…"

After checking with Michael Riley's doctor and his wife, Margaret, John Riley had set a lunch for one pm. They were all to be there - his wife Eileen, Mary Riley, Mary Kate Rhinemann with her husband Michael, down special from New York for the day. Matt Malloy would be there, as well.

John Riley had spoken to each of his siblings about the need to restructure Hennessey Land to lessen the impact of Mary's inevitable passing. But that was some time ago, more than a year now. He had not brought them up to date on the idea of selling Hennessey Land in its entirety. And for all the necessity and clear advantage of doing it, it hadn't occurred to him until this moment that one or more them, Mary most importantly, may not want to.

A horn sounded from behind. John Riley waved in acknowledgment, taking the right up Connecticut, the one mile to Newark Street. Waiting there for traffic to clear, he turned left and up Newark before going right on Highland Place, perhaps the highest point of Cleveland Park. Following its bend to the left, he parked behind Eileen's car, in front of Michael's house. Getting out of the Explorer, he caught sight of a hired car parked to his left, headed down the street, the driver in it reading the paper. Probably Matt Malloy's transportation.

"Looks like we're all here." He shook his head, eyes down. "Don't even know how to start..." A deep breath taken, John Riley held it for a count, releasing it as he mounted the brick steps up to the veranda wrapping the house across its front and around its right side. 'Should have brought Brigit in.' he thought as he reached the top of the stoop, stepping onto the gray wooden deck of the veranda.

"John!" Mary Kate rose from a dark, well-cushioned wicker chair to his right. Stepping toward him, her hands out to take his, she kissed him on the cheek. "Michael's here!" She turned back to Michael Rhinemann who now rose from his wicker chair to greet him, leaving Matt Malloy sitting at the near end of a couch, smiling, a brief wave of the hand.

"Good to see you, John."

Michael Rhinemann and John Riley shook hands, John smiling, a nod of his head. "Thanks for coming..."

"Yes, and what's this all about, anyway, John?"

Mary Kate stepped closer, her eyes fixing on her brother as she took her husband's arm, her head cocked at him then quickly going to Michael. "Did he tell you anything?"

"No, not a peep." Michael Rhinemann turned to John Riley, smiling, maybe baiting him. "Told me I was needed in Washington so it's to Washington I came." He kissed his wife on the cheek, John Riley taking the chance to slip past them to Matt Malloy, shaking his hand before turning back to Mary Kate and Michael. "All caught up with Matt, Mary Kate? When was the last time you were together?"

Mary Kate smiled coyly, turning toward John. "I'll tell you how long it's been since I last saw Matt Malloy if you'll you tell me what's going on..."

"So, you've come, have you, now, John Riley. Good on ya, lad..." Mary Riley held the screen door open, nodding to Matt Malloy. "A fine son I've raised, here, now." She turned to John Riley, eyes fixing on him like a mother ascolding. "Calls a lunch, he does, taking folks from their Sunday afternoon, and his brother not five days safe harbor from the Grim Reaper himself...tells not a soul of what's it all about, and then arrives late, he does, to his own meeting, a full quarter hour of it."

Mary Riley, full out on the veranda now, went to Michael Rhinemann, taking his right arm with Mary Kate on his left, the three of them lined up in front, all fixing on John Riley, Mary Kate clearing her throat, her head up and asking. "Well...?"

John Riley ran his eyes across the three arrayed before him and then down at Matt Malloy. "Yes, well, I guess we'd better get to it. Is Michael available?"

"Yes, he is..." Margaret Riley stepped onto the veranda, holding the screen door open. "He's at the table, John, as you asked...like to get him to his room, though."

"I'm fine right here. Been in a bed for five days and I'm sick of it." Michael Riley's raised voice carried clearly from the dining room through the foyer.

John Riley motioned them all in through the screen door, helping Matt Malloy up and following him in over the parquet wood floor of the foyer into the dining room, a large, wooden-paddle ceiling fan turning silently above, the air moving easily through the room.

"Here, Mom, sit next to me." John Riley motioned to his right, the others making way for Mary as she moved to the chair, John pulling it out and seating her before sitting himself to her left, taking the head of the table, the others seating themselves as they might.

Placing his hands flat on the surface of the heavy oak table, John Riley lowered his head for a count then looked up. "I want to bring you all up to date on what we've been doing with Hennessey Land Company...we need some decisions." A look around the table, a forced smile to reassure. "As I told you all a year or so ago, we need to take some steps, do some restructuring for tax purposes."

"*Inheritance* tax purposes, now, son." Mary Riley sat up, head back, her stare shifting from John Riley to the others and then back. "Say it clear, now, what you're meaning. 'Tis me *dying*, is what. We all know that..." Mary Riley sat back to the laughter of all. "Should have done years ago...So what are you bringing us, now?"

John Riley sat away from the table, his eyes on his mother, then to the rest. "Yes, well we had been thinking in terms of getting out of one area entirely, probably retail. That's the strongest part of what is a pretty weak market...we were looking at the proceeds from that to provide just about enough cash to pay what the IRS would be looking for."

"A lovely comfort, that is." Mary Riley sat forward, her eyes wide and bright. "A new turn, it is, I'm thinking, to 'dying for your country,' now, don't you think?" She looked about nodding, the others laughing, she now as well, all there happy for her spirit. She now turned to her son, her arms on the table, palms down "And...?"

John Riley sat up, his hands gripping the table's edge. "Well, over the last five or so months, three potential buyers have upped the game." He looked around the table, Matt Malloy at the far end, Eileen at his left, with Mary Kate and Michael next to her, Margaret and Michael opposite them, next to Mary. "They want the *whole thing*, the 'lock, stock and barrel' of it..."

"Jaysus!" Mary Riley sat back off the table, blessing herself. Michael Riley leaned forward, taking Margaret's hand, his eyes at John for a moment, but then past him. Mary Kate had caught her breath, turning to Michael Rhinemann, his eyes from her to John Riley as he sat forward, looking at the others as he started, then back to John. "You mean, then, a buy-out? Cash?"

John Riley nodded as he took a deep breath, fixing on the table surface before him. "And we are now down to two, both large insurance companies - one national, one regional." A swallow. "Each of these has its own valuation." A breath taken, now, all eyes on him, at him, not a sound to be heard. "The offers are 884 and 902 million dollars..."

"Jesus, Mary and Joseph..." Mary Kate sat off the table, her arms now limp, Michael Rhinemann's hand going to her near shoulder. Michael Riley turned to his wife, her eyes back at him, gripping his hands. "Are you alright, Michael?" she said before turning to John, her head shaking back and forth, distraught, seeming to say 'This is too much for a man just home from open-heart surgery.'

John Riley read Margaret's eyes, closing his own, now looking at Michael Riley who was waving him off, taking a breath.

"I'm fine, John, really...not to worry." Michael Riley sat off the table, his right hand going to his temple, the index finger going in tight, little circles. "It's the pain killers, you know...dulled me brain, they have...thought you said $900 *million* dollars..."

"He did, now, don't you know!" Mary came up from her chair, then down. "He did say $900 million!" She looked at her son, her left arm reaching for his forearm, grabbing it. "You did now, son, didn't you? You did say $900 *million?*"

"I did."

John Riley covered his mother's hand with his own, gripping it to reassure. "Brigit's been working with a firm in Chicago. A separate channel from what we'd been using. Spoke with her earlier today. 'Done deal' is what she said, if we want it."

John Riley viewed the table, waiting for what had taken him months to appreciate to sink in, the eyes of all away, their minds racing, coursing the ways of their living and how such a thing will impact them, their lives and the lives of those they love, and others beyond.

In time, he sensed a calm of sorts, their arms more relaxed at the table, their eyes now searching for others' eyes to see what they may be thinking, a peace coming now, an easing anyway.

Reaching for the water pitcher Margaret had set out, he poured Mary a glass, then one for Eileen, and now a third for himself. Sipping it, he placed the glass on the coaster in front of him, this catching the eyes of all, which now turned to him.

"Brigit, Bryan Canny and I have a meeting in Chicago Tuesday morning...it's to be a simple stock transaction. We each - Mom, Mary Kate, Michael and I - will sign over our shares in Hennessey Land. Four checks will be cut, one to each of us, with the capital gains taxes the only IRS money owed..."

"That simple?" Eileen's eyes were on her hands as they rested on the surface of the table. "And Brigit? Where's Brigit in all this?"

John Riley reached for his wife's hands, taking them both in his. "She's to get a cash settlement, a 'golden parachute' is what they call it. I had three comp firms work up estimates. Added them up, divided by three, and that's hers."

Eileen Riley's eyes turned to John's. "Then she's leaving the company?"

John Riley nodded. "Yes. There'll be a consulting arrangement. But it's up to her how much time she puts in." He squeezed her hand. "She's out, Eileen. Out, over...free of it."

Eileen Riley caught her breath, blessing herself as she looked across the table to Mary, nodding as she closed her eyes.

John Riley turned to the others, Michael Riley's eyes on him and the devil was in them, sure. "So, brother, give us the numbers, now, won't you? What we're each to be getting from it all?" His eyes were gleaming, his brogue pitch perfect, his words bringing the room to a dead stop as they all turned to John Riley.

A deep breath taken, John Riley held it for a count, and then, "Well, depending on how your accountants want to handle it..." He nodded to Michael Riley and Mary Kate. "But after capital gains it's on the order of $116 million...each."

Michael Riley's jaw dropped, his eyes going to Matt Malloy who nodded 'Yes' and then to Mary Kate. Mary Kate looked from him to her mother, then to John Riley and now silent and away. John Riley's mind went back to his return flight from Palm Beach, when it first struck him, the amount of money, the weight of it. His head nodding through this, John Riley now turned to his mother.

357

Mary Riley sat bolt upright, her arms extended, pushing her back in her seat, off the table, eyes fixed, locked on those of her son.

"Mom…" John Riley cleared his throat, his head down and then up. "Yours after taxes is about $350 million…"

Mary Riley closed her eyes, her arms easing as she came forward to the table, folding her arms now on it, her head resting on them, face down.

John Riley fixed on her, pausing for a moment, then reaching for her. As his hand touched her shoulder, Mary Riley shuddered, sitting up, now, away from her son, her eyes going to the others, coming to rest on Matt Malloy, he smiling at her, his head nodding, but only barely.

Looking now around the table, her head shaking slightly, Mary Riley's eyes came to rest on her hands, joined now at the table's edge. "There's something wrong here…something not right."

Looking up, she turned first to Mary Kate, then to Eileen, smiling now, this gone as she spoke to them all. "We've done well, the Rileys have. It's called Hennessey Construction, but it's the Rileys that made it what it is today, Paddy first, then me and now for more years than any, John." She looked at her son, another smile, and now to Mary Kate.

"And the lives you've all built…Mary Kate, my treasure, off to New York on a dark night and come up fighting and winning, finding your Michael, now, and a son…Aye, and what's there to say beyond how proud I am he's carrying my dear Patrick's name…so proud…" Her eyes went to Michael Rhinemann. "And you Michael Rhinemann, how happy you've made my Mary Kate."

A hand here to the corner of her right eye to wipe a tear as she turned to Michael Riley. "'Tis a terror you were, Michael Francis Riley, but you come up straight, taking Captain Kane's lead and others, too. Aye, my fine fancy-pants, New York lawyer, married to a wonder of a woman and a son, now, too!" Mary Riley sat back, her arms out at the room and house they were in. "And here you live, atop Cleveland Park in as fine a house as any would ever have need of, ever!"

She sat back in her chair, looking at them all and settling on her son John.

"Of the days of my life, John Joseph Riley, I count maybe twenty above all the rest. One such was being with you at church yesterday morning…" Her hand reached for John Riley's forearm, gripping it full and sure. Turning across the table, she fixed on Mary Kate. "And then there was being in the same church with your Patrick on Friday morning, too."

She closed her eyes, her lips moving ever so slightly, perhaps in prayer, a moment taken, sitting up now and back, her eyes coming open and bright, looking about the table.

"When you were all growing up, now, you'd know the Hennessey sites abuilding and the ones done, too…you were all part of it, don't you see. We did well because we built well and lived well, too, lived good lives, did what we said we'd do and did it right, kept our word. Yes, we did. Got known for it…" She paused here, eyes away, a quick sign of the cross made.

"I, Mary Coughlin Riley, me, I *own* forty-one percent of Hennessey Construction and God help any man looking to take a dime in value of it from me. I live well on the dividends from that company, a company that would not exist if I had not done what I did. You can each say the same of your own lives, each one of you, now…You've earned your way…tis what makes you *free*…tis why we come." She turned to John Riley.

"And for Hennessey Land, what can I say but good on ya, lad, and your Brigit, too, for what she's done. It blinds the eye, it does, aye, the value of it, but it weighs the mind, now, too… three hundred and fifty million dollars…Aye, now there's a sum."

John Riley pushed away from the table, his hands resting on its edge, the others, too, their eyes on him, and then on those about, and all now back to Mary.

"As I was telling you yesterday, John Riley, in the quiet, after Mass…I've done, is what…Lived my life, the most of it, anyway. Every breath taken now a gift, every minute lived from here on a blessing." She pushed off the table here, turning to Matt Malloy and now the rest.

"And anyone thinking I'll be wasting one full second of it worrying about three hundred and fifty *million* dollars is daft." Another nod here to Matt Malloy before turning to John Riley. "So, like I said, good on ya, boyo, but I'll be taking none of it…"

It was as if each of them had taken an electric jolt, sitting them each straight up in their chairs, then back in them, eyes moving about and then away, their heads shaking, their lips moving, though no words spoken, all but Matt Malloy. Sitting at his ease, he alone seemed to have some sense of what was happening.

Eileen Riley was the first to speak, clearing her throat, her eyes up and down the table, now leaning forward. "But Mary, what about your grandchildren? And their children, too? It seems…"

"Aye, the grandchildren, my five treasures, and my three here, too." Mary Riley sat forward, her elbows on the table, again at John Riley. "Son, that offer you got for Hennessey Construction, a few years back?"

John Riley sat up, his head back, nodding.

"Didn't you tell me, now, it put my shares at some $20 million in value?"

John Riley nodded a 'yes' back.

Mary Riley fixed on Eileen. "So, then, Eileen, there we start. Twenty million among five grand children. Aye, now, that's a sum, and still more now I'm thinking with our book of business and the recovery…" A nod of the head here and a wink of the eye.

"Then there's the dividends I've been getting. Ach! I spend a tenth of them, if that, give another quarter away, with the rest going to trusts I've already set up for them, the grandchildren, that is." She sat back. "Heavens to Christ, they could spend each of their entire lives getting educated and never know the want of a meal or a dry place to sleep!" Her head was shaking at her own words, a mind in wonder, her eyes now up and at them.

"Then they'll all know what you'll be leaving them, from your own doings, and Hennessey Construction to boot…she looked about the table. "The word awes me still, but there it is, *millions,* that's the word, millions to go around, now, I reckon. They may already be in line for more than any one of them can get out from under and still have a life of their own to claim…"

The room was silent, Mary's words coursing their minds, a sense of it seeming to come to them, what she was saying. Mary Kate was the first to stir, sitting forward, her eyes on her mother, now shifting to John Riley. "So, where…?"

"I don't know…"

John Riley looked down the table. No one was looking back, no one but Matt Malloy, a smile coming to his face. "Matt?"

Mary Riley sat forward. "Excuse me, Matt, before you say anything, now, I want to be making myself clear here…" Her eyes coursed the table. "Not only do I have no interest in it, the money, but I'll be taking no *responsibility* for it neither." She fixed on Matt Malloy. "Tell me, lawyer Malloy, if I were to die now, the federal government would be getting how much of it, my share that is?"

"Fifty-five percent." Matt Malloy appeared to have anticipated her question.

"I see." Mary Riley turned back to her son John, nodding. "Near 200 million, then, gone to the bureaucrats and their musings." She looked about the table. "Well, now, we can do better than that, by God!" She turned back to Matt Malloy.

"I am not going to go to sleep this day until I have executed a document that will pass ownership of my shares in Hennessey Land to something that can do some good with it. Period, full stop."

John Riley sat back, his eyes on his mother, now coming to the fullness of her intention. She not only didn't want it, she *needed* to be *rid* of it, today, this afternoon. A smile came to his face as he recalled the lunch at Matt Malloy's apartment the day before, his meeting with George Cole this morning, his eyes now going to the table's end and Matt Malloy. He was smiling now, as well, his eyes bright, a sense of anticipation in them, the slightest nod of the head. "Then what's to be done with it?"

Mary Riley's eyes had followed her son's to Matt Malloy. "The Hennessey Trust! Aye, that's what!" Her hands out, her eyes up and about, bright and glorying in the thought of it, her hands coming down full on the table surface. "And where better? Tis Jack's own land, now, isn't it? Collected it all, didn't he?" She fixed on Matt Malloy.

"Can you do that, Matt? Today? Get someone in and work up a piece of paper for me to sign, and a notary, too…get it all signed and done?"

The smile on Matt Malloy's face faded. The prospect, the truth, perhaps, of the Hennessey Trust coming into $350 million sat him back in his chair, the weight of it all now seeming to fall on him. Nodding, he sat forward.

"Yes. This can be done…" He studied Mary's eyes. They had not wavered, barely blinked. "You are certain in this, then, Mary? *Absolutely* certain?"

"Are you daft, man? Daft? I've done ninety-one years. All of them. Couldn't spend $350 million if I had another ninety-one! Now, will you be helping me here, Matt, or won't you?"

Matt Malloy checked his watch. "It's 1:48…should be able to get something here by 4 pm."

"Good. See to it, then." Mary Riley looked at Margaret Riley. "Looks like you have me till four. Is that alright?"

Margaret Riley managed to close her mouth and form words, first a weak "Yes" and then a stronger "…of course."

Matt Malloy rose. "Michael, where would be the nearest phone?"

Margaret Riley stood, motioning to the kitchen, starting in that direction to get the door for him.

"Wait, Matt." Mary Kate looked around the table, her arms and hands open, questioning. "What in heaven or hell is the Hennessey Trust going to do with $350 million?"

Matt Malloy paused, reaching for the back of an empty chair, sitting back down, his arms folded on the table, his eye on Mary Kate. "Fair question." He looked about the table, his mind churning. "But actually, it'd be more than that…closer to $450 million."

Mary Kate rocked back, now looking at her mother, then Michael Rhinemann.

"Matt's right." Michael Riley turned to Mary Kate, then Mary. "It'd be a gift, Mom, to a charitable organization. There'd be no taxes on any of it, federal or state…"

Mary sat up, her head shaking and fixing on Matt Malloy. "Now, there, Matt Malloy, all the more…I'm asking you again, now, will you be helping me, here, or won't you?"

"Yes, Mary. Of course…" He rose, pushing himself back from the table and up as he followed Margaret into the kitchen.

Those in the room all fixed on the swinging kitchen door, John Riley speaking as it came to a stop. Avoiding his mother's eyes, he turned to Michael Riley. "It's even more than that, really. The valuation we've been using is current market. Hennessey Land's holdings were over $1.2 billion in 1988, before the S&L mess. Three or so years from now, they'll likely be worth even more than that...certainly in five years."

"Christ, that's more than half a billion dollars, way more..." Michael Riley fixed on his mother, his head shaking.

"Aye," said Mary Riley, "if I *live* that long, but we're all here because I may not, now, aren't we? And where'd we be then?" No one answered. "I'll tell you where...with me worrying for all of it, and about the money, money that I had nothing to do with its making and even less interest in its having." She looked at the kitchen door, her head back. "Matthew Aloysius Malloy! Have you done now, man, got it started?!"

The kitchen door opened, Margaret sticking her right hand out, its thumb up for all to see.

Mary Riley nodded, sitting back in her seat. "Well, that's something anyway." She folded her arms across her chest, eyes ahead and still.

John Riley studied his mother's profile, now turning to the rest.

Mary Kate sat forward, speaking quietly, carefully. "So, again, what's the Hennessey Trust going to do with whatever the amount?"

"Anything it wants." There was quiet laughter as Matt Malloy came through the kitchen door, retaking his seat. "There's a lot it can do, there's a lot to be done." He sat forward. "George Cole's just in as Chair and he has ideas about growing it, doing a capital campaign."

"Well looks like Mary's got that covered." Michael Rhinemann looked at the group, they all responding with quiet laughter and the nodding of heads, all save Mary Riley, arms still folded and still.

John Riley sat forward. "We spent some time talking about it yesterday...Matt has a friend, the last Hennessey Squire – Michael Byrnes. He's running a program in Los Angeles. They're pulling bright kids, kids with real stuff, out of bad homes, putting some positive structure in their lives. Some are in dorms, the highest risk ones... and getting them discipline. They point them to college, but community colleges. The idea isn't to get smart kids out of bad places, but to educate and train smart kids who'll stay in their neighborhoods, make business there, lead. Made a lot sense as he spoke about it...looking to start a national effort..."

Michael Rhinemann fixed on John Riley. "This George Cole, is he *the* George Cole?"

John Riley nodded as Michael Riley sat forward, speaking. "The same. Just stepped down as Chair of the DNC Platform Committee."

"And he's looking for something to do..." Matt Malloy fixed briefly on John Riley who nodded back. "My bet is, with this kind of money, he'll take on the Trust full time...I can all but guarantee it."

Michael Rhinemann nodded, sitting back, looking at Mary Kate whose eyes went to Matt Malloy. "What else can the Trust do with the money?"

"Like I said, anything it wants, pretty much." He sat forward. "And with this sort of funding, we'll be looking for ideas...a bigger board, too...That's for sure."

Mary Kate Riley Rhinemann sat upright, her eyes fixing on Matt Malloy. "Is that an invitation?'

"Absolutely." Matt Malloy sat forward, his eyes on her. "It's a four-*man* Board, all sixty-seven or older." He looked at John Riley and then back. "Can't imagine George not going with anything that makes sense."

"In New York?" She looked at Michael Rhinemann, their eyes engaged as she continued. "There are some things I've been thinking about..." She turned to Matt Malloy. "Same sort of things John's talking about, as I think about it, getting young people engaged..." She turned now to John Riley. "I really like the idea about them staying in their neighborhood."

"So does George." Matt Malloy turned toward Mary, speaking to her. "He's Charles Ramsey's grandson, you know, Mary."

Mary Riley's eyes shifted, came alert, her mind working. "Charles Ramsey?" She turned to Matt Malloy. "Jack Hennessey's Charles Ramsey?"

Matt Malloy nodded a 'yes.'

Mary sat up. "I remember Charles Ramsey...worked the yard and things for us, after Paddy went to war...Aye, a good man, he was, and all of that...worked for us right till we moved out." Her eyes fixed on Matt Malloy, her head nodding. "His grandson, then, Charles Ramsey, he'd be running the Trust, would he?"

"Yes..."

"Aye, and what's to say more than that, now? Charles Ramsey's grandson running Jack Hennessey's Trust, the near half *billion* of it...now there's a thought to hold...Aye, a thought to hold, indeed..."

CHAPTER FORTY
The New Deal

$\mathbf{M}$att Malloy was laughing as he poured himself a cup of coffee at the sidebar in Hennessey Construction's headquarters. "Something else, I'll tell you that." He mixed in some cream and sugar as he turned to the table and sat down.

"First in was Mary Kate. That was about 5:00. Said she's in with her shares..." He shook his head, sipping his coffee. "She wondered if all the others were in, the whole company, could you just put Hennessey Land into the Hennessey Trust? *In toto*." He looked at the others in the room - John Riley, Brigit Winslow, Hardin Brooks, Bryan Canny and Hank Johnson.

"Her thinking is that it was going take a year or two before the Trust was re-purposed and built out, anyway, and why not capture that value in Hennessey Land's holdings?" He turned to John Riley. "Anyway, John here was next...that was about 5:15."

Brigit Winslow turned quickly to her father, her head back, hands on the table.

John Riley smiled at her nodding, as he sat forward. "Yes...and I like the idea of the Trust holding Hennessey Land intact for a while." He looked at Matt Malloy. "The IRS has rules on this?"

"Of course. They have rules on everything. But on this, there's no real effect." He looked at them all, his arms extended and hands open. "Then, just as Tom Kite lipped out at Shinnecock Hills, Michael calls in...he's in, as well." Matt Malloy looked around the table. "Didn't know whether I was at home watching the golf or at a scripting session for *Mr. Deeds Goes to Town*. Near a billion dollars offered up and given away in an afternoon!"

There was great laughter now, body-shaking, lung-cleansing, mind-blowing laughter. It was a vaulting to a new place, a new normal that cleared their path to getting done what no one of them could ever have even imagined only a week ago. Brigit Winslow was the first to speak.

"Well, one thing for sure, we still have to go to Chicago tomorrow. Can't leave Phil Hastings twisting in the wind, trying to explain how he got a $80 billion insurance company all excited about buying Hennessey Land and them ending up with none of it, not one square foot." She looked across the conference table to John Riley, waiting for his assurance, which came by way of a nod of the head.

"Yes, we have one last trip to Chicago. Pay our respects to our friends at Mid-America, if nothing else."

Brigit Winslow sat up, fixing on her father, her head at an angle, questioning.

"Hank and Bryan are down to take care of that." John Riley turned to Hank Johnson. "You all set there, ready to go?"

"Oh yeah, we're ready…"

"It's going to be special, alright." Bryan Canny rose from the table, stepping to the coffee service, pouring himself a fresh cup. "Trying to figure a way get it on tape." He sipped his coffee and looked up at the rest. "It's going to be that good…"

"Wish I could be there for it…" John Riley rose, going to the window overlooking McPherson Square.

Matt Malloy looked at Hank Johnson. "What do you have planned?"

Hank Johnson laughed to himself. "Thought we'd start with a private reading of the National Historic Trust's gracious acceptance of the Hay Adams Hotel, to be held by it in perpetuity, a gift of the Riley family."

"Oh, he's going to love that." Brigit laughed as she rose, now pacing the table opposite the windows. "But we have to get serious, here. Everything Phil Hastings has asked for from Great Basin, and I mean *everything*, they gave him. His reputation's on the line here...ours too." She surveyed the rest, all eyes on her. "They have to come away with *something*..."

"Agreed..." John Riley turned back from the window, his eyes on Matt Malloy as he stepped to the head of the table, his hands on the back of a chair. "Matt, suppose the Trust were to offer them – in consideration of their good faith and efforts – a ten-year right of first refusal on any property currently held by Hennessey Land?"

Matt Malloy sat back in his chair, his mind working John Riley's words, now nodding. "I like that, John. I like that a lot." He looked at the others, fixing on Brigit Winslow. "Gives them strong prospects of a foothold in the market, in the exact properties they're ready to write a check for right now, but costs them nothing."

"Nor the Trust..." Bryan Canny sat forward. "First digs at market price...a phone call is all." He looked at Matt Malloy.

"That's about it, really..." Matt Malloy turned to Brigit who had stopped pacing, her arms folded, eyes away, her mind seemingly still running. "And I think we can sweeten it a bit further."

Brigit Winslow's eyes went to Matt Malloy as she sat down at the table, opposite from John Riley. "In what way?"

Matt Malloy sat forward. "I took the liberty this morning of speaking with George Cole..." Heads moved, eyes about the table, the sense of a collective awareness, perhaps, that it was 'out,' what they had done, beyond the family, the moment when real time on it all starts - the point of no return had been passed.

John Riley felt the eyes of the others shift to him as he fixed on Matt Malloy. "So..." John Riley looked quickly at the others then back to Matt Malloy. "So, what'd he say, what was his reaction?"

Matt Malloy's head nodded slightly. "Hard to say, really, other than utter silence. It was on the phone." He looked around the table. "Not every day a man has near a billion dollars fall in this lap, his mind racing as quick to how he's going to save the world with it..." Matt Malloy surveyed the table, coming back to John Riley.

"First thing, John, is, he wants to meet with you. You good for lunch with him today?"

John Riley nodded. "Certainly. Can you join us?'

"Be assured," Matt Malloy replied, turning to Brigit. "He closed the call reiterating that he's all in, five years, more if needed, 24/7, full bore." Matt Malloy smiled now. "George Cole is the 'sweetener'." He turned to John Riley.

"I suggest that you take George Cole to Chicago tomorrow. As Chairman of The Hennessey Trust, now sole owner of the Hennessey Land Company, he can explain the extraordinary developments of recent days, how it all happened, closing with his personal assurance that the right of first refusal will be honored."

John Riley nodded to Matt Malloy and turned to Brigit Winslow. "How's that? Good enough?"

Brigit Winslow held her father's eyes for a moment then turned to Matt Malloy. "That's fine, Matt. George Cole? That's about as good as it gets."

CHAPTER FORTY-ONE
Homeward Bound

John Riley checked his watch – 2:16 Central, 3:16 Eastern. A week to the hour of rushing home, of not knowing whether he would ever see his brother Michael again. There'd been the dread he felt for his own loss of him, then the crushing blow it would be to his mother. "She deserves better…" he remembered thinking to himself.

Looking left and down from his seat forward of the G-IV's port-side wing, the southern edge of Lake Erie filled the window. Cleveland was to the right, a river wandering through it to the water, jetties arching out into the water's expanse. For an engineer with his full knowledge of the principles of motion, airfoils and barometric pressure, he still marveled at the whole idea of human flight. Here he sat, 36,000 feet in a crystal-clear sky, hurtling forward at 500 miles per hour and hardly a sound or other sense of it heard or seen save the slow passage of the earth below. Incredible.

The others sat aft, a settee on the port side behind him facing two seats on the starboard side. The talk continued of the day's doings, stories retold, new details added, embellishments as well.

Bryan Canny was now telling of the meeting at Mid-America Holdings, opening with being ushered into the board room. On seeing that is was only the two of them, Bryan Canny and Hank Johnson, Keith Pierson turned quickly to Townsend, his lawyer, his eyes bearing down on him as if expecting Townsend to conjure up John Riley and his daughter from beneath the sidebar.

"'Fraid we'll have to do, Mr. Pierson, just me and Hank, here." Bryan Canny was in full voice. 'Here, Hank, have a seat, now.' So, Hank sits himself down, all proper, hands folded on the table's edge. 'Looks snappy in his pinstripes, don't you think, Mr. Pierson?' And here's me, fumbling with the briefcase, finding the National Trust for Historic Preservation's press release. "Here it is!"

"Pierson and the lawyer are sitting now, knowing the whole thing is stinking up and right in front of them, too. Front row seats for it all. I give a copy to Hank, and two across the table to them, one each. 'John wanted to be certain you had an advance copy, knowing how special the place is to you."

"'The 'place'? What *place* is this?' Pierson reached for the release, face all gone to wrinkles and lumps, and pores, too.

"'The Hay-Adams, you know. In Washington...'"

"He grabs the paper off the table, starts to read. I'm reading too, now, aloud, his hand waving me off. 'What the hell is this?' A look to Townsend, who, God's word, has *shrunk*! Sure as I'm sitting here, the man's got smaller, trying to get under the table, sure, now, wishing he was.

"Now the eyes are on me, Pierson's eyes and they're a pair, I'll tell you. Christ's Blood, if there wasn't six feet of conference table between us, and Hank beside me, I'd have been pissing my pants."

"'Where the hell's Riley! Thinks he can give *my* hotel away! To some pissant historic trust! Where is that son-of-a-bitch!'

"Well, he's up now, Pierson is, and Hank is as quick, standing by me side." A nod to Hank Johnson on the settee of the G-IV.

"Pierson starts coming 'round the table...and the lawyer? He has *disappeared*, gone for heaven or hell but no longer in sight. Hank eases me back and squares up, this stopping Pierson in his tracks. Something about Hank Johnson here, standing full up, hands joined at his front, well, it'll give a man pause and never mind the pinstripes! And Pierson? Well, he's at the end of the table, breathing deep now, thinking maybe if there's a gun about.

"This is when Hank opens the bag and pulls out the oar paddle, pitching onto the surface of his fine mahogany table."

"'Now what in the hell is that!'

"'Your boys left it in the Potomac...Thursday last...morning they ran down John Riley on his row...' Hank then pulls out the invoice, puts it on the table.

"'And that?"

"That's the invoice for a new set of oars. They're not cheap, you know, and they come only in pairs, the good ones. There's an address inside...you know...where the check's to be sent.

"Pierson's steaming now, just put on another boiler by the look of him. Hank takes my arm, easing me to the door, taking the side between me and Pierson. The last sound we heard was the paddle hitting the door just as Hank closed it!"

John Riley laughed again, a few deep breaths and now his mind wandering back to the meeting in Hastings' office – Great Basin's CEO, two of their lawyers, another executive, then Phil Hastings, Brigit, himself and, mostly, George Cole.

They had spent a lot of time together over the years, he and George Cole, the best of these fishing the *Stormy Petrel* out of Deale. And while he had seen George Cole on *Meet the Press* and the like, this was the first time he had ever been in the room, had felt his presence, the strength of the man, the force of his being and competence, the true meaning of commitment to the good, to making things better.

John Riley had had no doubt of the rightness of what they had done with Hennessey Land, but it wasn't until he heard George Cole speak of it, explain what had happened and what the Trust would be doing that he came to an full understanding of the wonder of such a thing. It was not the gifting of it, what he and his family had done. No. It was what it would mean to others, what it could get done, the value and worth, the *weight* of it, applied to a cause. "Yes," he remembered thinking to himself, sitting next to George Cole, just "Yes."

Then there was Charlie Olmstead.

The business on Hennessey Land had closed, the *right of first refusal* passed about and signed. A good day, something done they could all be proud of. And as they were leaving the conference room, Phil Hastings had pulled him aside. "There's someone here who would like to speak with you, John." Phil Hastings spoke closer to John Riley's ear. "It's Charlie Olmstead. He's across the way, in my office. He'd like a word."

John Riley froze where he stood, not knowing how to respond, all parts of him at dead stop.

Phil Hastings leaned close again. "It's important to him." Hastings stood straight, now, his eyes on John Riley, somber, his lips mouthing the words "He's dying…cancer."

John Riley took a half-step back, his head up now, nodding as Phil Hastings led him out of the conference room and to his office, opening the door and letting John Riley in before closing it behind him.

"John…"

John Riley turned to his left. Charlie Olmstead sat at the end of a couch, sitting back, a forced smile, his right hand on the arm of the couch, seeming to grip it.

John Riley went to the leather chair by the end of the couch. Clear that it would be difficult for Charlie Olmstead to rise, he offered his hand, shaking and releasing Charlie's as he sat down on the front edge of the chair seat. "Charlie…good to see you."

"Good of you to take the time, John…"

"Of course."

His hands now resting on this thighs, Charlie's face grimaced. "I haven't much time, John...hardly any at all." He motioned to the door. "Phil Hastings is my best friend. Went to law school together. He was visiting over the weekend and in passing asked if I knew the Rileys from Washington." Charlie Olmstead's jaw closed, now gritting. "This was how I learned you were to be here today. I asked a favor, and, well, here we are..."

"I'm glad of it. It was the right thing." John Riley sat closer. "Is there anything I can do?"

Charlie Olmstead's eyes closed briefly, opening now, fixing on him. "Yes, there is...in fact, you're the only person in the world that I would trust with this." He sat up a measure, holding John Riley's eyes. "As you can see, I'm dying. Maybe a couple of days, maybe tonight." His eyes closed as he began to speak.

"When you face the end, John, the *dead* end, all the things done, all the mistakes, all the wrongs, they rise as out of some cavern, deep and dark and frightening...but what can be the greatest fear is of ignorance, your own and that of others, what they may not know...what you might be taking with you...forever." He opened his eyes, turning to John Riley.

"I have come to know love, John, in all its parts and pieces. I love your sister, Mary Kate. She was the first woman I ever did love and I love her still...in a distant, but wonderful way. In my darkest hours, though, a fear has grown in me that she would learn of my passing...and wonder...was *I* happy?" His eyes closed with this, now opening and at him, his head nodding. "I understand from friends in New York who know her, you see, that she is happy...but how is she to know that *I* am happy?"

He leaned toward John Riley. "I need to leave with you, John, that I have lived a wonderful life, that I have found happiness and true love in it, and it is my greatest

375

hope that she has as well. That she knows that I was thinking of her at the end, and that I wanted her to know that I was happy, truly happy." Charlie Olmstead's eyes closed slowly, his head nodding forward.

John Riley reached for his hand, taking it gently in his own as he sat forward, speaking in a near whisper. "Yes, Charlie. I can do that...I *will* do that...I will tell her."

Charlie Olmstead's eyes opened, his head back, a smile to his face, the first since John Riley had come into the room. "Thank you, John, that's very good of you..." He sat back, his eyes closed. "Now, if you can ask Phil to come in? Ellen's waiting out front...I need to get home...rest."

"Certainly," John Riley had said as he rose, covering Charlie Olmstead's hand with his own. "I will pray for you Charlie. God be with you."

"Thank you..." Charlie Olmstead rested his head back, his eyes closed...

In the now quiet of the plane, John Riley thought back to his last look at Charlie Olmstead, the ravages of the chemo showing clearly at the edge of his baseball cap, his eyes closed, head back, his lips, thin and without color, parted...has he just gone? John Riley had thought to himself.

"So, John Riley, penny for your thoughts."

John Riley sat bolt upright, startled at first but quickly happy for the interruption.

George Cole sat across the aisle, filling the seat. "Not every week a man passes on a hundred million dollars."

John Riley stretched his legs under the seat in front of him, flexing his arms as he turned now to George Cole. "I guess..." He smiled, felt the devil in his own eyes as he spoke his words. "Might sound a little crazy, George, but the way I see it, that hundred million is *your* problem now."

George Cole put his head back and roared, laughed so loud and full that those behind them all turned forward.

"What's so funny up there?" Hank Johnson called out.

Regaining control of himself, George Cole spoke over his shoulder. "You'd never believe it, Hank, not in a million years…not in a *hundred* million years…" He looked back to John Riley, still chuckling, his head shaking.

John Riley shrugged. "All I want, George, is to get back to building things…that's what I do best, like best. This Hennessey Land thing has been a millstone around my neck for over a year and I'm glad to be done with it." He looked back over his shoulder. Melanie Ingram was sitting next to Hank Johnson on the couch, listening to Bryan Canny. "So, what do you think of Melanie?"

George Cole looked over his shoulder, fixed on her for a moment, then back on John Riley. "She's smart. No doubt of that. Stanford doesn't hand out MBAs to dummies. We had a nice chat in the car on the way to the airport. Pleasant enough…"

"Yes…" John Riley nodded. "Smart and pleasant, and can be tough." He took a quick look toward the back of the plane. "She quit Mid-America just a week ago. Walked out. Left a bundle on the table there so she could go anywhere she wanted." John Riley turned to George Cole.

"She and Brigit spent a lot of time together on The Deal. Looking at properties. When Brigit heard she'd left Pierson, she called her up." John Riley fixed on George Cole, sensing he knew something was coming.

"Brigit spent the weekend with her. They drove out to her mother's place in Oklahoma. Hank went along for the ride. He's pretty high on her, too." John Riley looked forward. "Brigit had her flown up to Chicago this morning…signed her on as Hennessey Land's new CEO."

George Cole turned again over his shoulder then back at John Riley. "Really?" Another look toward the back of the plane then to John Riley. "She good on the numbers…finance, taxes?"

"Not too sure about *all* of that. She spoke a good line in the meetings I've been to with her. Her real strength is running real estate, especially retail…and don't be worrying about the numbers. You'll have Brigit as interim CFO…when she gets back…get it all worked out."

"Gets back? When will that be?"

John Riley sat back, settling in his seat, his head back, eyes closed. "Like I said, George, that's *your* problem now."

George Cole laughed out loud, gripping John Riley's shoulder as he rose and returned to the others.

There are times when, in the blink of an eye, the parts and turns of a life can join, even fuse, finding a renewed purpose, a burst of energy and light of such wonder and joy as to escape the bounds of time itself.

John Riley's mind went back now to the terminal as they were about to board the G-IV for home. Standing next to Brigit, her eyes were on him, she not moving with the others to the plane, her hand going to his arm, holding him back.

"That's your plane, Ms. Winslow!" An agent approached them, calling over the whine of a Learjet's engines, it taxiing to a full stop nearby, its door falling open to the tarmac, its engines still running.

"Thank you!" Brigit shouted back, a brief nod of thanks, now handing him her overnight bag. She turned back to John Riley, eyes brilliant, radiant, at him, her entire face alive, brand spanking new, the whole of it.

John Riley turned toward the Learjet, watching as the agent put her bag in the plane's cargo bay and started back for the terminal.

Standing full up, now, his head back, John Riley turned to Brigit, unsure, motioning to the Learjet. "So... where...?"

"San Francisco!" she shouted. "...and Bertie!"

"Bertie!" John Riley caught his breath, his eyes wide on her. "Yes! Wonderful! Just, wonderful!" He reached for her hands, taking them, thrilling in her presence. "When do you get back?"

"Back? Get back?" She laughed here, shaking her head. "No idea!"

Her eyes on him now, Brigit Riley Winslow stepped to him, into his embrace, holding him as never before, then breaking to the plane and, over her shoulder, above the engines...

"I love you, Daddy..!"

EPILOGUE

J ohn Riley drove himself from the airport to his office, quickly changing out of his business suit into a pair of freshly-done khakis, work shoes and a Hennessey Construction Company shirt, long-sleeved, his mechanical pencil in the breast pocket behind the company logo.

Grace Parker came in, the day's mail and inter-office files in hand, laying them in his in-box. "There's a note there on top. From Mr. Malloy. He wanted to be certain you saw it today."

John Riley looked at the stack of papers and envelopes and folders, taking a breath as he reached for the note. Picking it up, he looked at it, his name across the front in Matt Malloy's tight script. Tapping his left hand with it, he looked at Grace Parker, a smile coming to his face.

"You know what, Grace?"

"No, Mr. Riley, I don't know 'what'…"

"I need to be down in a hole, deep down in a hole."

"Yes, sir, Mr. John Riley, I do believe you do…"

It was just past five by the time John Riley parked his Explorer beneath the elevated site office on First Street at the corner of I Street, NE. The site was closed for the day, several of the crew still about, those recognizing him nodding as they went about their business. Going to the barrier at the edge, John Riley looked down into the hole, dark and deep, once packed with more than 63,000 cubic yards of earth. Looking to the northwest corner of it, he was happy to see the wooden stairway down had not yet been removed.

Stepping to it, his left hand running across the barrier fence as he walked, he breathed in the air of the thing, sixty feet down, the wood and steel structure lining its inside, the scent of it all, the smell of work and things getting done. Coming to the northwest corner, he loosened the wire latch of the gate and stepped onto the top level of the stair. Looking over its edge, he fixed on where the sun struck the inside of the hole, the angle of its light showing the depth of it as he started down.

It was cool once below, the heat of the mid-September afternoon gone to the earth and damp of the bottom. And quiet, too, barely a sound to be heard, the movement of cars and trucks and buses above traveling up and away.

Looking across the floor of the hole, he could see in the far corner two front-end loaders, parked beside each other. They were to come out by crane first thing as the site was made ready for a layer of concrete, the future daily home of ninety-three cars of those working above - lawyers, accountants, lobbyists, whatever.

Removing his helmet, he sat down on the second step, his arms now to his knees, his mind coming to an ease he had not known in some months. The weight of things foreign to him, these had been lifted. He was now, and forever would be, free of them. John Riley was again where he wanted to be, where he knew what he was doing, his place. Sitting back, he felt the envelope of Matt Malloy's note in his breast pocket. Taking it out, he opened it, the script done evenly across the paper.

Dear John,

I cannot let the happenings of the last several days pass without comment.

In all my years, I do not remember ever being in the presence of such clarity of thought, such generosity of spirit, and such plain ol' Yankee common sense as I had the distinct pleasure and great honor to witness among the counsel of your family. It was a tonic to my aging soul that will count among the most cherished memories of my entire life.

I know that Jack Hennessey would have been proud, proud beyond words. And that is where I am, without words to express the wonder of what I witnessed...all save one. And this one word, I do not know the full reason behind it, why it comes to me, but I share it with you now in the hope that you will receive it with my deepest respect and most sincere regards.

Welcome, John Riley, welcome, welcome, welcome.

Your friend,

Matt Malloy

THE TRILOGY

Swampoodle

It's May 1936 and Jack Hennessey's life is closing. An infant refugee of the Great Hunger, he is 88 years old. Diagnosed with terminal cancer, Jack is determined to see Hennessey Construction, his life's work, survive for those he leaves behind. As each of his final days unfolds, he comes to a deeper sense and understanding of life's meaning. His is a triumph of love over blood ties and life over loss, a life lived to the full as the Capitol City goes through boom and bust from the Civil War to the Great Depression. You'll want to share the story of this remarkable character with all those you cherish.

St. Patrick's Day

Told in the vibrant voices of this Irish-American family, *St Patrick's Day* is the story of the Riley's of Washington, D.C, making their way up from poverty to the well-to-do suburb of Chevy Chase, Maryland. Left to Paddy Riley by Jack Hennessey and now run by Paddy's widow, Mary, Hennessey Construction is in trouble with land needing to be sold to save it. Built around Mary's estrangement from her daughter Mary Kate, the book explores the many faces of love as the family overcomes discrimination and loss to find success and fulfillment, all nudged along by a bitter-sweet miracle over the St. Patrick's Day weekend of 1968.

Mount Olivet

The Riley's have prospered with Mary's son John succeeding her as CEO of Hennessey Construction. Mary Kate's advertising agency has thrived in New York and their brother Michael is a lawyer in the power canyons of Washington, DC. As the story opens, Michael has emergency by-pass surgery with Mary Kate returning home to be with him, doubly troubled by the imminent departure of her only son for military service in Israel. It is September 1993 with the story unfolding around John Riley's coming to understand the life values he and the others have taken from their heritage, most especially from Mary whose counsel draws on her appreciation of love as a life force and the faith that brought her to it.

www.pdstclaire.com